CROSS-OVER
PHENOMENA

TRANSATLANTIC SERIES IN LINGUISTICS

Under the general editorship of
Samuel R. Levin
Graduate Center
The City University
of New York

ANALYTIC SYNTAX

OTTO JESPERSEN

THE STUDY OF SYNTAX

The Generative-Transformational Approach
to the Structure of American English

D. TERENCE LANGENDOEN

INTRODUCTION TO TAGMEMIC ANALYSIS

WALTER A. COOK, S.J.

IRREGULARITY IN SYNTAX

GEORGE LAKOFF

CROSS-OVER PHENOMENA

RX15A

PAUL M. POSTAL

Thomas J. Watson Research Center, IBM

HOLT, RINEHART AND WINSTON, INC.

New York   Chicago San Francisco   Atlanta
Dallas   Montreal   Toronto   London   Sydney

Library of Congress Catalog Card Number: 76-133047

SBN: 03-085230-7

Printed in the United States of America

1 2 3 4   40   9 8 7 6 5 4 3 2 1

Foreword

The present work was written in the late winter and early spring of 1968. It appeared in July 1968 as a United States Air Force report, under Contract No. AF 19(628)-5127, in *Specification and Utilization of a Transformational Grammar*, Scientific Report No. 3, IBM Thomas J. Watson Research Center, Yorktown Heights, New York.

Naturally, the framework of investigation and the assumptions underlying it correspond to the period of writing. In a field like the theory of grammar, where our knowledge of facts is rapidly expanding and our understanding of them slowly deepening, it is inevitable that publication delays such as that involved in the present edition must find certain aspects of a work out of phase with the latest theoretical ideas. This is certainly true in the present case. However, while a number of new facts bearing on the subject of this study have come to light since July 1968, and a variety of new proposals about linguistic theory have been developed that would radically alter the approach to these questions today, it has not as yet proved possible to integrate these aspects into a newer and more adequate treatment of the subject matter dealt with.

I have decided therefore to publish the present work in essentially its original form, taking it as illustrative of a certain definite stage in the development of the transformational approach to the grammar of coreference and pronominalization. At the same time, it may serve as an introduction to the study of a variety of detailed topics in this area that have, as far as I know, not previously been publicly discussed in print.

P.M.P.

Preface

Given sufficient funds, one could amass a library of hundreds, possibly thousands, of works on English grammar. These would contain a good deal of the knowledge about this aspect of English gathered over several hundred years by many hundreds of students and researchers. I am confident, however, that in none of these works would it be observed that sentences like the following have the properties they do:

(1) *a* Charley placed a snake near Louise.
   b Louise, Charley placed a snake near.
   c Near Louise, Charley placed a snake.

(2) *a* Charley placed a snake near him.
   b Him, Charley placed a snake near.
   c Near him, Charley placed a snake.

The key facts are that all of (1)*a*–(1)*c* are well formed and essentially equivalent in the propositions they express. (2)*a* is ambiguous, the contrast being whether the forms *Charley* and *him* designate the same individual. (2)*c* embodies exactly the same ambiguity. (2)*b* does not, however. In the dialect of the present writer, it is clear that the *him* of (2)*b* must refer to an individual distinct from that referred to by *Charley*.

Given some knowledge of traditional grammar, one might immediately try to explain this in terms of a grammatical law:

(3) A pronoun can never *precede* its antecedent.

This explanation assumes not implausibly that *him* is a pronoun and *Charley* its antecedent. However, (2)*c* shows that this hypothetical grammatical principle is false, even for English, since (2)*c* has a reading under which *Charley* is the antecedent of *him*.

There are, I think, two conclusions to be drawn from this. First, despite the massive literature on English grammar, there is an almost endless domain of grammatical facts about English sentences yet to be even registered. Secondly, and more importantly, when hitherto unknown facts about English are observed, there are in general no traditional (or modern, for that matter) principles of grammar which explain them. If one grants that these conclusions do indeed follow, that is, that examples like (1) and (2) are not unique but truly representative of a massive unseen iceberg of grammatical data, we are safe in inferring that the principles of English sentence formation and interpretation (grammar) remain essentially unknown.

The present work is an investigation of some of the kinds of subtle, hitherto largely hidden, facts about English grammar illustrated by (1) and (2). We examine a mass of restrictions partially similar to those illustrated by the absence of one "expected" interpretation of (2) *b*. Ultimately, we arrive at the partial specification of a principle of grammar which explains such restrictions, considering along the way its connections with many aspects of English grammar and its relations to universal grammar.

P.M.P.

Yorktown Heights, New York
September 1970

Contents

PART I
THE CONTEXT OF INQUIRY

1 INTRODUCTION

A. BACKGROUND

The present work is a study in English grammar and, more importantly, in grammatical theory. In the most general sense, I take *grammar* to cover the whole domain of how semantic interpretations are associated with phonetic representations. More narrowly, since phonology is not our concern here, I will take grammar to cover the question of how semantic interpretations are associated with what have been referred to in transformational studies as *surface structures.*

Our investigation lies within the overall framework of transformational studies initiated by Noam Chomsky more than a dozen years ago and progressively developed and modified by many others in the ensuing period. However, I would not wish the reader to assume that I necessarily accept any particular assumptions made within this framework other than those particularly discussed and accepted in the text. Many views stated in this framework, even by me in past writings, no longer seem valid or as valid as they once might have, and many new assumptions and ideas not yet given a public airing must be considered. Hence nothing could be more misleading than to regard transformational theory as a fixed body of doctrines that is being applied below to a new body of data.

My position is that serious grammatical investigation at the moment is rather like traveling in quicksand. There are no firm supports. Every step is uncertain. Every move is questionable. There are no well-worked-out, unshakable analyses of particular portions of individual languages from which general principles of grammar can be inferred. There are few well-supported, substantively detailed general principles of grammar that can serve as a guide in the analysis of particular cases. The linguist interested in providing a principled account of a significant range of actual factual details must thus stumble around trying to formulate a general principle here or there that can constrain the description of particular facts and trying to find firm analyses of factual fragments that will constrain the formulation of universal linguistic principles. Ill-considered boasts to the contrary,[1] we are, in short, really almost at the beginning of the study of the incredibly complex and still largely unknown domain of natural language grammar.

The grammar of English, which would generally be taken to be well studied, is hardly less mysterious. As will become clear as we progress, most of the facts discussed below are new and have never been publicly dealt with before despite a history of grammatical studies in English that might be traced back to the sixteenth century.[2] The principles which, in part, may explain these data are, needless to say, even less well known. And the fragment of English dealt with in this study is hardly unique in this respect. It is all very well and comforting, therefore, for the layman or literary figure to believe that English grammar is a well-understood and already described body of doctrine, perfectly grasped by the authorities. But it is sheer delusion and imagination of the most harmful sort for linguists to accept this view, which cannot stand sixty seconds' confrontation with the facts.

B. FUNDAMENTALS OF COREFERENCE

One of the most important and interesting properties that a grammar must assign to sentences correctly is one I shall refer to here vaguely and inadequately as *coreferentiality* (*coreference*).[3] Two elements are coreferential if they refer to the same object, event, relation, state, and so on. We can discuss coreferentiality perfectly well, even though it must be admitted that the notion of reference as such remains quite obscure. The possibility for such discussion depends on the fact that there are clear instances of the relation in sentences. Roughly speaking, coreference is manifested in the fact that the correspondence between *nominals* and *entities* is many-to-one, rather than one-to-one.

For instance, examples of coreferentiality are found in such expressions as:

1.(1)   Drummond disgraced himself.
1.(2)   Mary Lu thought she would faint.
1.(3)   A girl who I know fell down in the snow.

---

[1] Many writers attempt to give the impression of a well-worked-out system of grammar by terminological fence building. Grammar is defined, often progressively, in a very narrow way such that more and more facts are left to other domains, "semantics," "pragmatics," and so on, that are, in general, not studied. Since a priori we do not know the bounds of grammar, this is, to say the least, a rather dangerous course of action.

[2] Thorne (1966) refers to Bullokar (1586). This is the earliest reference to a work of English grammar known to me.

[3] A somewhat more precise discussion is found in Chapter 19, where several subtypes of coreference manifestation are distinguished.

In 1.(1) it is recognized that the nominals *Drummond* and *himself* refer to the same object; that is, there are two nominals related to a single entity. In 1.(2) we know that on one reading *Mary Lu* and *she* designate the same female entity. And in 1.(3) it is clear that *a girl* and *who* denote the same person.

Coreferentiality shows up for nominals in that semantically one understands one element to be entering into more than one "logical grammatical relation." Thus in 1.(1) one understands a being named Drummond to have been both agent and patient of some action of disgracing;[4] in 1.(2) a being named Mary Lu is understood to be related to both an act of thinking and the activity of fainting; in 1.(3) some girl is both the patient of an instance of knowing and the agent of an action of falling.

An important task for any serious grammar is the correct assignment of coreferentiality relations to nominals. Thus observe that the very forms (italicized) that are related this way in 1.(1)–1.(3) are *not* so related in 1.(4)–1.(6):

1.(4) *Drummond* thought his father disgraced *himself.*
1.(5) *Mary Lu*, who *she* criticized harshly, was still kind to Barbara.
1.(6) *A girl* saw a boy *who* I know.

The grammar must indicate for each pair of surface structure nominals whether they are coreferential. Even this does not suffice, however, since in many cases the structure of a sentence involves coreferentiality between elements one or more of which is *not actually present* in the surface structure. Hence there is coreferentiality in such examples as:

1.(7) Wash yourself.
1.(8) Gort wants to levitate.
1.(9) By working rapidly, Loomis finished early.

This shows up in several ways, but again chiefly in our recognition of one element's entering into more than one "logical" relation. Hence in 1.(7) one individual is understood as both agent and patient of *wash*; in 1.(8) it is known that the individual who wants something is identical to the one who is agent of *levitate*; in 1.(9) we know that an individual named Loomis both worked rapidly and finished early. In this respect, these forms that do not contain *n*-ads of actual surface structure nominals with identical reference are nonetheless in contrast, with respect to coreference, with examples like, respectively:

1.(10) Jim washed the baby.
1.(11) Gort wants his master to levitate.
1.(12) Because Bill worked rapidly, Loomis finished early.

---

[4] Actually, this is too superficial since 1.(1) is probably a *causative* structure. It might be more accurate to identify *Drummond* as the agent of a causative predicate and the "subject" of a predicate representable as 'is disgraced'. The whole is then roughly equivalent to: "Drummond$_i$ caused Drummond$_i$ be disgraced." See Lakoff (1965: IV-16,IX-1).

Coreference is by its very nature fundamental to the nature of language. This in itself makes it of the utmost importance for linguistic theory. But this property of sentences becomes even more significant as a testing ground for linguistic principles and theories when it is realized that coreferential elements involve a host of special restrictions and properties. Furthermore, the facts are in general clear and the explanatory tasks hence relatively fixed. This makes it seem very odd how little attention is given to the topic of coreference in traditional grammar,[5] and even in contemporary approaches other than transformational grammar.[6]

The present study is concerned with a really minor aspect of the problem of coreferentiality, namely, the fact that the distribution of coreferential nominals in the surface structure of English sentences is far more restricted than is accounted for by any previously given linguistic rules or principles. This problem is explored within the general framework of transformational grammar and, in particular, in terms of a crucial property of this theory. Within this framework, but in almost no other, it makes sense to speak of a linguistic element *moving*, or changing its position. This is a definable idea in the transformational approach because syntactic structure is bifurcated into two different domains, *deep structure* and *surface structure*, and because the elements of these two different domains are not fully disjoint, that is, the same element may occur in both deep and surface structures. Hence, given a deep and surface structure for the same sentence, we may speak of an element's having moved in a perfectly precise way in terms of a comparison of its position in the two structures. In fact, many of the rules in a transformational grammar have just the function of altering the position of elements.

It is argued that the observed constraints on the distribution of coreferent nominals are directly related to the movement of nominals by transformational rules. That is, it is claimed that the restrictions are a function of restrictions on the operation of transformational rules which move nominals. It is shown that a large class of cases where coreferentiality is expected but not found reduce to a single type. Principles are suggested which explain these facts about English and

---

[5] The chief contributions here might be the notions of *pronominal reference* and *antecedent*. But it was seldom if ever observed that these are quite vague on the one hand and fail to uniquely characterize coreference on the other. For instance, in an example like:

   (i) A big *gorilla* was kissing a small *one*.

the italicized nominals would have been said to be related by pronominal reference and the initial instance would have been called the antecedent. While this description might seem correct as far as it goes, observe that the example involves no coreference.

[6] Even the transformational framework has by no means given the topic the attention it deserves. But the amount of work done in this framework, especially very recently, outdistances that in all others combined by an enormous margin. For only a small sample of this work, see Bach (1968); Chomsky (1965); Gross (1967); Karttunen (1967); Lakoff (1968, to appear); Langacker (1969); Lees and Klima (1963); McCawley (1967, 1968, to appear); Postal (1966a, 1966b, 1968, 1969, to appear); Ross (1967a, 1967b).

it is proposed that these are not special features of English syntax but rather aspects of universal grammar.

The maze of unsolved issues and the incredible complexity of facts which are encountered in the investigation of this minor feature of what is only one major aspect of grammar should serve to support the initial suggestion that grammar is truly an unknown area. If the present investigation does this, it may have served a purpose greater than whatever clarification it provides on the topic of coreference and grammatical rules themselves.

C. THE PROBLEM

It has been observed by Lees and Klima (1963:21) that English passive sentences do not have reflexive subtypes (or, equivalently, that English reflexive sentences do not have passive subtypes):

1.(13)   I saw O'Leary.

1.(14) a *I saw $\left\{ \begin{array}{c} I \\ me \end{array} \right\}$ $\Longrightarrow$

    b I saw myself.

1.(15)   O'Leary was seen by me.

1.(16) a *I was seen by $\left\{ \begin{array}{c} I \\ me \end{array} \right\}$ $\Longrightarrow$

    b * I was seen by myself.[7]

Even more clearly, forms like:

1.(17)   *Myself was seen by $\left\{ \begin{array}{c} I \\ me \end{array} \right\}$

are impossible.

Within a transformational grammar, the impossibility of structures like 1.(17) is easily accounted for by ordering the passive transformation before the reflexive transformation, as Lees and Klima (1963:21) suggest, and as is required on independent grounds [see Chapter 2]. The ungrammaticality of 1.(16) b may, at first, also seem trivially representable. As Lees and Klima advocated, it is only necessary to constrain the passive rule *not to operate with identical noun*

---

[7] 1.(16) b has, of course, a perfectly well-formed reading under which *by myself* means 'alone'. It is the passive interpretation which is impossible and this is what the asterisk prefix notation on an example means here, and often below. That is, this often is used to indicate not that the string in question is ill formed on all readings, but only that it lacks an expected interpretation, the nature of which is contextually made clear.

phrases [henceforth NP].[8] Within the framework of transformational theory as of the early 1960s, this appeared to present no difficulties.

However, as of the present moment, there is a body of evidence which suggests that deviations of the type illustrated by 1.(16)*b* cannot be rightly accounted for by special restrictions on the rule that forms passive sentences. This consists of data which show that the passive-reflexive incompatibility is not an isolated, *ad hoc* phenomenon[9] but rather an instance of what, I shall suggest, is a previously unnoticed principle of language.

Before turning to this body of evidence, it would be well to make a few remarks about forms like 1.(16)*b* above, which we have claimed are not well formed. Many people are unclear about judgments of such sentences and this is understandable on several grounds. First of all, the deviance of these cases is subtle and not at all of the overwhelmingly obvious sort exhibited, say, by 1.(17) type sentences. Secondly, sentences like 1.(16)*b* are perfectly under-

---

[8] *Identical* here means *referentially identical*, that is, coreferential, of course. We do not seriously consider in this study the question, which turns out to be immensely complicated, of how coreferentiality is to be represented formally in underlying structures. I know of four different proposals, three within the framework of transformational grammar. In the earliest transformational studies, no indication was given in underlying structures of this property, so that both of the sentences:

   (i)   John cut himself.
   (ii) John cut John.

would have had identical underlying forms containing lexically and constituent identical NP. Coreferentiality was then represented by application of an *optional* rule of pronominalization. This approach was very inadequate. A later suggestion by Chomsky (1965:145–147) proposed to index lexical nouns with numerical subscripts, identity of index then indicating coreferentiality. That is, the structure of (i) and (ii) would now be:

   (iii) $John_{23}$ cut $John_{23}$.
   (iv) $John_4$ cut $John_{67}$.

Pronominalization rules are then regarded as obligatory in cases of identical indexes. At one time I accepted this view [Postal (1966a)], which is certainly an improvement over the previous one. I believe it can, however, be thoroughly disconfirmed. A third proposal in roughly transformational terms is that underlying primitive NP are purely indexical and that identity of these indexes alone is relevant. This view is taken now by Bach (1968) and McCawley (1967). Within the framework called *stratificational grammar* a distinct proposal has been made that involves multiple connection of one clump of semantic properties, "semons," to more than one element (such as "agent," "patient," and so on, where the connections represent "logical grammatical relations." [See Gleason, (1964), Hockett (1966), and Lamb (1966).] This proposal can also be definitely disconfirmed.

   In the present paper we adopt the notational device of representing coreferentiality between NP by having identical lexical items with identical subscripts. This *looks* like the system proposed by Chomsky (1965), but we treat it merely as a tool of presentation and explicitly deny that it is the proper system for representing the actual formal linguistic structure of these relations.

[9] This view is accepted by Langacker (1969).

standable semantically. They have unique interpretations and involve no semantic violations at all. Let us compare examples of this type with ones like:

1.(18) *a* Harry was sitting next to Mary.
  b *Harry was sitting next to himself.

1.(19) *a* Lois was near Tom.
  b *Lois was near herself.

1.(20) *a* Joan resembles Barbara.
  b *Joan resembles herself.

In the *b* forms of 1.(18) - 1.(20) there are violations involving coreferentiality. But the contrast with 1.(16) *b* is clear. These new examples all involve semantic anomalies.[10] None of them have natural, literal interpretations. This reveals that there are at least two different kinds of restrictions involving coreferential nominals. One class involves deviance from well-formedness without semantic anomaly; the other, deviance including semantic violation. Our chief aim in this study is the investigation of deviances of the former variety, of which 1.(16) *b* is an example.

Thirdly, and possibly most importantly, stress is relevant.[11] The examples like 1.(16) *b* are supposed to be forms with ordinary (in fact weak) stress on the reflexive form. If, however, these examples are provided with contrastive stress, then the sequences are well formed. This is especially true if such particles as *even* are added:

1.(21) I was even seen by my*self.*

Here the italics indicate the extra strong contrastive stress. It is the well-formedness of the strongly stressed versions that perhaps contributes most to confusion about the word-for-word identical unstressed variants. Careful consideration of the unstressed forms will, I think, convince most speakers of their syntactic deviance. It must be emphasized too that since these are perfectly all right semantically, any sense of deviance or oddness in them must have a syntactic origin. It should be clear that these comments about stress are designed

---

[10]Notice that types like 1.(18) and 1.(19) would be described by logicians as instances of *irreflexive relations.* They would not, however, attribute this feature to *resemble* and a logical reconstruction of this property would take it as one that does not exclude reflexivity. This provides no basis for the anomaly of examples like 1.(20) *b*. I think, however, that the logician is partly right here. The anomaly in 1.(20) *b* though undeniable, is rather different from that in 1.(18) *b* and 1.(19) *b*. Neither the logician nor the linguist, as far as I know, has any accepted concepts or terminology for dealing with the former type.

[11]Hockett (1966:279) gives a diagram of the structure of a sentence "the man was shot by himself" with no indication of the stress of the reflexive form. I would assume that his assumption of grammaticality here is based on the well-formedness of the sentence with strong stress on the final word's final syllable.

to cover not just the passive cases given earlier but all those "independent evidence" cases to be given below. There also, the differences between ungrammatical ordinarily stressed sentences and grammatical ones with contrastively stressed pronominal forms must be carefully drawn. Toward the end of this study, in Chapter 19, we will suggest grounds for this difference, giving an explanation of why the principles that exclude the weakly stressed cases are apparently not operative in the contrastively accented versions.

2 REFLEXIVIZATION, PRONOMINALIZATION, AND THEIR ORDERING

A. REFLEXIVIZATION

We shall have constant need throughout to refer to two transformational rules of English which determine which of a set of coreferential nominals will take on pronominal form. *Reflexivization* is the rule involved in such sentences as:

2.(1) *a* Harry stabbed himself.
  b I am displeased with myself.
  c Barbara believes herself to be clever.
  d I talked to Jones about himself.

The exact formulation of reflexivization will not concern us. Indeed it would be hard even to raise this question since we are not dealing with the nature of the underlying formal structure of coreferent nominals (see footnote 8 of Chapter 1).

  I shall assume, however, that the function of the rule is to assign a certain feature analysis to those NP which are marked by it [Postal (1966a)]. In particular, the NP marked by reflexivization is, I assume, assigned the features [+Pro (nominal)], [+Anaphoric], [+Reflexive]. The first of these accounts for similarities in behavior with other pronouns, both of referential and nonreferential varieties.[1] The second distinguishes pronouns derived by rules of pronominalization (reflexivization, pronominalization, and others) from those

---

[1] Examples of nonreferential pronouns include such italicized forms as:

  (i) I was looking for an elephant but I couldn't find *one*.
  (ii) *Something* struck John on the head.

  Relations between referential and nonreferential pronominal elements are partially explicated in Postal (1966a). A more adequate treatment is certainly required, however.

which are not.[2] The third feature is more or less self-explanatory.[3] However, it should be noted that one cannot assume uncritically that *all* instances of reflexive forms are generated by reflexivization. Emphatic reflexives, reflexive prefixes,[4] and reflexives inside of "picture noun" nominalizations[5] among others are all yet to be shown to be derived by the same rule as operates for ordinary reflexives like those in 2.(1). That is, it is by no means clear that reflexivization is behind such examples as:

2.(2) *a*   Harry himself offered her a chair.
    b   Self-criticism is rare among politicians.
    c   Harry purchased a picture of himself.

Of course, one would like to show that only one rule for reflexive forms suffices, but the wish for generality and the demonstration of its possibility are different matters.[6]

---

[2] One property that both reflexive and nonreflexive referential pronouns have in common is an inability to occur with most types of appositive clauses. Hence observe that just as (i) is ill formed, (ii) is unambiguously interpreted as involving no coreference:

    (i)   *Charley cut himself, who is careful.
    (ii)   Charley said that he, who is careful, would not cut himself.

The natural sentences corresponding to these are of course:

    (iii) Charley, who is careful, cut himself.
    (iv) Charley, who is careful, said that he would not cut himself.

And observe that (iv) is ambiguous with respect to whether *he* is a coreferent of *Charley*. The claim is then that the restriction exemplified by (i) and (ii) is to be at least partially stated in terms of the specification [+Anaphoric].

[3] It is also probably inadequate and should probably be divided into two features corresponding to the *upward bounded-downward bounded* bifurcation of Ross (1967a: Chapter 5, especially 335–338).

[4] Such prefixes are discussed extensively in Chapin (1967), who argues for a transformational description of many of them which is compatible with a derivation by way of reflexivization.

[5] For discussion of some of the peculiarities of such nominalizations see Ross (1967a:148–157) and references therein. Many interesting facts about them are also noted in Jackendoff (1968) in a theoretical framework which, however, I find less than helpful.

[6] Thus it is a confusion for Jackendoff (1968) to assume implicitly that examples of reflexivization in picture noun nominalizations, which do not follow the principles for ordinary reflexives, are to be regarded automatically as counterexamples to the clause mate formulation of reflexivization. This assumes without any argument or justification that the proposal of reflexivization involves the claim that every reflexive form is derived by its operation. In fact, the rule simply says that NP meeting its conditions undergo it. Moreover, in several places below, including Chapter 17, Section D, we uncover significant evidence that many instances of reflexivization within picture noun nominalizations must be attributed to rules distinct from the reflexivization rule, demonstrated by their different ordering relations. Hence Jackendoff's assumption that all instances of reflexive forms follow from a unitary operation is not only logically unsound but factually incorrect.

It should be observed that I am assuming that the process of reflexivization involves not only the rule *reflexivization* but also some rule determining the agreement of the reflexive form with its antecedent. It is not clear to me whether this latter rule is the same one that operates to determine agreement for nonreflexive pronominals. On the basis of past assumptions about pronouns and syntax in general, it might be assumed that the pronominal agreement rule is essentially trivial. However, there is, I believe, now evidence that this rule involves linguistic structure of the most abstract and poorly understood sort, structure that includes *the system of time representation* for sentences. Consequently, this rule is far from being well understood.[7]

The chief points to be made about reflexivization here are that it determines reflexive form for the *rightmost* of two coreferent nominals—that is, the rule operates left-to-right[8]—and that it operates only for nominals which are, at that point in derivations, within the same simple clause. This restriction, first noticed by Lees and Klima (1963:19), is more precisely stated as follows. Two nominals may undergo reflexivization if they share all clause memberships, that is, one is contained within every clause that contains the other. I shall refer to nominals meeting this condition as *clause mates*. The constraint is then that reflexivization applies only to coreferents that are clause mates. It does not follow, however, that reflexivization applies to *any* pair of coreferents that are clause mates. This condition is necessary but not necessarily sufficient.[9]

---

[7]Evidence of the role of time relations in pronominal agreement is provided by such sentences as:

    (i)*a* The one who recently became male hurt himself.
      b The one who recently became male hurt herself.

The fact is that these two contrast semantically. If we represent the time point of the inchoative verb *become* as T_O, then (i)*a* refers to an event of injury after T_O, (i)*b* to such an event before T_O.

[8]It might be claimed that there is some evidence for right-to-left application in at least some contexts on the basis of examples like:

    (i) *a* Himself, Harry never indulges.
      b Myself, I will never understand.

However, as discussed in Chapter 16, there is the strongest evidence that these must be derived by reflexivization operating left-to-right, with subsequent movement of the reflexive word forward.

    An even more superficial argument for right-to-left reflexivization might be based on sentences such as:

    (ii) Finding himself bankrupt drove Harry to suicide.

But of course it is easy to show that in these the reflexivization is a function not of the object of *drove*, but rather of the deleted subject of *finding*, this deletion following the application of reflexivization.

[9]The possible relevance of other conditions of reflexivization is discussed somewhat inconclusively in Chapter 17.

Evidence of its necessity is given by the impossibility of application in such cases as:

2.(3) *a*   *Charley said that himself was beautiful.
      b   *I expect that you will agree with myself tomorrow.
      c   *Charley spoke to the girl who laughed at himself.
      d. *I smiled at the girl, who immediately grinned at myself.

It is important to emphasize that the clause mate constraint on reflexivization is applicable at neither the deep structure nor surface structure levels but rather at some point in between, this being defined by exactly that class of transformational rules which can apply in derivations before reflexivization. That the constraint is not relevant at the level of deep structure is shown by such examples as:

2.(4) *a*   I believe myself to be correct about that.
      b   Margaret found herself unable to move.

These surely must have deep structures fundamentally similar if not wholly identical to sentences like respectively:

2.(5) *a*   I believe that I am correct about that.
      b   Margaret found that she was unable to move.

But in these the coreferents are in different clauses. That the clause mate condition is inapplicable to surface structures is trivially shown by a variety of examples like:

2.(6) *a*   Wash yourself.
      b   Who do you think Mary saw praising himself?

In the surface structure of 2.(6) *a* there is only one NP, so that the notion of clause mate is inapplicable entirely. In 2.(6) *b* *who* and *himself* are coreferents but not clause mates since there is a clause boundary before *Mary* [and also in front of *do*, but the latter is more controversial]. But it is easily shown that at some earlier stage 2.(6) *a* has a subject NP which meets the clause mate constraint with the object and that 2.(6) *b* has an ancestor structure in which the element *who* is a clause mate of the ancestor of *himself*.

In fact, the number of rules that operate on deep structures before reflexivization applies is rather large, as is the number that operate after this rule. Hence the clause mate constraint actually becomes applicable somewhere in the "middle" of derivations, if we may use this imprecise terminology.

Let us now turn to questions of the relative ordering of reflexivization. Consider in particular the ordering of reflexivization and the passive rule (henceforth: *passive*). It is not difficult to see that this must be such that within any clause reflexivization applies *after* passive, that is, the ordering must be:

2.(7) Passive
       Reflexivization

This follows from considerations of the following sort. First, in simple sentences where there is no basis for positing any movement of nominals by transformation, reflexivization operates left-to-right:

2.(8) *a* Charley stabbed himself.
      b Lois groomed herself.
      c *Himself stabbed Charley.
      d *Herself groomed Lois.

This means that the *general* statement of reflexivization will have it operate left-to-right. We have observed that reflexive passives with ordinary stress are ill formed:

2.(9) *a* *Charley was stabbed by himself.
      b *Lois was groomed by herself.

Observe, however, that the derivations in 2.(9) presuppose the ordering of 2.(7). Suppose this ordering is reversed, so that reflexivization applies before passive in the general, left-to-right fashion. The results would be:

2.(10) *a* *Himself was stabbed by Charley.
       b *Herself was groomed by Lois.

Like 2.(9), the examples in 2.(10) are ill formed. What then is the argument for the ordering of 2.(7) since either order of application of the two rules seems to yield ill-constructed sequences? The argument is the great difference in degree of syntactic deviance between 2.(9) and 2.(10). While the sentences of 2.(9) are only subtly deviant, those of 2.(10) are crashingly unacceptable. Our explanation of this difference is that, while *both* of the examples involve some violation of a principle which excludes joint application of passive and reflexivization to the same clause, 2.(10) involves, in addition, a violation of ordering. It is this extra violation that explains why the sentences of 2.(10) type are so much further from well-formedness than those of the type 2.(9). Alternatively, we might say simply that ordering violations are much worse and yield more severe types of deviance than the types of violation illustrated by 2.(9). But either of these explanations requires the ordering of 2.(7).

The argument just given to show that passive precedes reflexivization can be matched for a number of other rules of a certain class[10] which reorder nominals.

---

[10]This class is later referred to indexically as the set of *A-movements*, still later characterized more substantively in terms of the properties of its members, and then renamed *constant movements*.

For these, which will be discussed below, the argument also shows that the particular nominal reordering must precede reflexivization.

B. PRONOMINALIZATION

Pronominalization is the rule involved in the derivation of the pronominal forms in such examples as:

> 2.(11) *a*   Harry said he would go.
>   *b*   Harry understood that Mary didn't like him.
>   *c*   The fact that Mary lost was tragic for her.

on the reading where these have coreferent interpretations. I shall assume that this rule assigns to the NP it marks the feature specifications [+Pro], [+Anaphoric], [-Reflexive] [Postal (1966a)].

The domains of pronominalization and reflexivization are essentially complementary, the latter operating on coreferents which are clause mates, the former on coreferents not meeting this condition. This complementarity might lead to regarding the two rules as essentially one.[11] However, there is strong evidence now that they are distinct rules. This evidence is of two sorts. First, it can be shown that their ordering relations with respect to certain other rules are distinct. This will be argued in Chapters 10 and 16 with respect to the rules called *WH-Rel*-movement, *WH-Q*-movement, and *Y*-movement. Secondly, it can be argued that reflexivization is a cyclical rule, while pronominalization is not cyclical and indeed must not apply cyclically.[12]

---

[11] I made exactly this mistaken assumption in both Postal (1968) and (1969). Fortunately, this error has little to do with the main line of argument in either of these two works. On the other hand, the rules are properly kept distinct in Postal (1966a).

[12] That pronominalization should be cyclical was first argued by Ross (1967b) on the basis of some brilliant observations of examples like:

(i)   Discovering that *he* had no liver worried *Harry*.
(ii) Discovering *Harry* had no liver worried *him*.

What was particularly relevant was that the italicized nominals cannot be understood coreferentially in (ii). Ross was able to explain such apparently unique and mysterious facts by assuming that pronominalization was cyclical and by taking the structure of (i) to be:

(iii) Harry$_i$'s discovering that Harry$_i$ had no liver worried Harry$_i$.

This argument is closely analyzed by Lakoff (to appear), who shows it cannot stand. He provides a full discussion of all previous arguments for the cyclical character of pronominalization and much evidence independent of that in this text that this is incorrect. He argues further that there is no known rule of English that has been shown to follow pronominalization in the ordering.

The notion of cylical application of transformational rules was first proposed by Chomsky (1965). It will be discussed in greater detail in Chapter 16 below. Here it is sufficient to say that this principle means the transformational rules[13] are applied to most deeply embedded sentences first, then to the next most, next most, and so forth until finally they are applied to the whole sentence. This entails that one runs through the entire set of cyclical rules on each level of embedding.

I will not give here the arguments for the variant natures of reflexivization and pronominalization with respect to cyclical application. One argument that pronominalization is *not* cyclical is given in Section D of Chapter 10. An argument depending on the assumption that reflexivization is cyclical appears in Chapter 16, Section C. Its independent basis is reviewed in Chapter 16, Section F. Here I wish to present an argument which shows that pronominalization must follow passive and by extension to the appropriate examples, must apparently follow every other transformational rule in English which effects the reordering of nominal constituents.

The argument depends on the phenomenon of backwards[14] or right-to-left pronominalization. Typically,[15] pronominalization is forwards, that is, the NP on the left takes the full lexical form while the coreferent on the right ends up in pronominal shape. But there are contexts in English in which the opposite situation obtains:

2.(12) *a*   After *he* won the race, *Harry* celebrated.
       b   Because Lucille liked *him, Jack* gave her a boat.

Faced with such examples, plus the usual restriction to forwards pronominalization, one's first tendency is to seek an explanation that preserves left-to-right as

---

[13] Chomsky (1965:134⁻135) is written in such a way as to claim that all transformations are applied cyclically. It is not clear that this claim was intended. At any rate, it is now known that the claim is false, in fact, radically so. There are many transformations which are not cyclical; probably cyclical rules are distinctly in the minority. See Chapter 10, Section B, for arguments showing that *WH-Q*-movement is not cyclical.

Chomsky, in the course of work on phonology, also proposed the idea of *last cyclical rules*. These are rules that can only apply on the last cycle of a particular derivation. The difference between such and post cyclical rules is that a last cyclical rule may be followed in the ordering by a fully cyclical one, that is, one which applies on all cycles. The question of the existence of last cyclical rules in English syntax has been extensively studied by Lakoff (1967), with interesting, if inconclusive, results.

[14] This term as well as its opposite are due to Ross (1967b).

[15] The "typicality" here is both internal to English and cross-linguistic. There are some languages, like Russian, which do not permit backwards pronominalization in most of the contexts where English allows it, while all languages seem to permit forwards pronominalization in these contexts.

the only direction of pronominalization.[16] In this case, one might seek to order a proposed rule of "subordinate clause movement" with pronominalization such that derivations are produced as follows:

Pronominalization

2.(13) *a*   Harry$_i$ celebrated after Harry$_i$ won the race $\Longrightarrow$

Clause movement[17]

b   Harry$_i$ celebrated after he$_i$ won the race $\Longrightarrow$

c   After he$_i$ won the race, Harry$_i$ celebrated

This causes some immediate problems. In particular pronominalization must then be made optional in these cases, although it is typically obligatory in others. This follows since forwards pronominalization is possible out of subordinate clauses too:

2.(14)   After Harry$_i$ won the race, he$_i$ celebrated.

In order to derive both 2.(13) and 2.(14) by means of exclusively forwards pronominalization, one must constrain pronominalization to apply before *clause movement* in derivations like 2.(13) to get 2.(13)*c*, but after clause movement in derivations like 2.(14). This is a unique kind of ordering.[18]

---

[16]An analysis of this sort is suggested in Harris (1968:81), where it is claimed that in all cases the antecedent is unchanged and forces alteration of a following coreferent:

The replacing of a noun by a pronoun (rather than by zero) is required if a noun of $\emptyset_S$ is repeated (referring to the same individual) in the operand of $\emptyset_S$, or if in $S_1 C S_2$ a noun in a later occurrence or in S_2 repeats one in the other sentence. For the $S_1 C S_2$ case we therefore have, from *John will come if John can:*
John will come if he can.
If he can John will come.
If John can he will come.
$\not\exists$ *He will come if John can.*

For the 0_S case, from *John thought that John is safe* (which $\not\exists$ when John is the same person, since pronouning is required), we have:
John thought that he was safe.
$\not\exists$ *He thought that John was safe.*
He was safe, John thought.
$\not\exists$ *John was safe, he thought.*

[17]There can be little doubt that a rule like the hypothetical *clause movement* mentioned here does exist. This would be, no doubt, a special case of the rule referred to as *adverb preposing* in Chapter 18, Section C.

[18]That is, unique in view of the fact that pronominalization cannot be cyclical. Cyclical application can produce just such situations in which rule ordering is apparently changed from derivation to derivation.

Even more seriously, although in cases like 2.(12) there is a plausible rule available to order with pronominalization, understood as working only left-to-right, in many other cases there is not. For instance:

2.(15) *a*   The boy who hated her$_i$ threw a rock at Mary$_i$.
    b   The boy who hated Mary$_i$ threw a rock at her$_i$.
    c   The fact that Bill$_i$ got 12 on the exam worried him$_i$.
    d   The fact that he$_i$ got 12 on the exam worried Bill$_i$.

It follows that one must accept that in some contexts pronominalization does work right-to-left in English. It is then necessary to specify the class of contexts where this is possible, since it is not free:

2.(16)   *He$_i$ celebrated after Harry$_i$ won the race.

That is, a sentence like:

2.(17)   He celebrated after Harry won the race.

can only be interpreted in such a way that *he* and *Harry* refer to different individuals.

The essential condition characterizing most contexts permitting backwards pronominalization[19] was apparently discovered independently in the fall of

---

[19] A brief history of the study of backwards pronominalization might be in order. Although it must have been noted somewhere, I am unaware of any references in the work of the standard traditional grammarians. The possibility of a pronoun preceding its antecedent is, however, briefly mentioned by Pence and Emery (1947:234) in a work written in a totally traditional framework. A special instance of backwards pronominalization, namely, that for subordinate clauses, was noted by Harris (1957:314), whose examples were:

(i) *a*   Bill will do it, if he can.
    b   If Bill can, he'll do it.
    c   If he can, Bill will do it.
    d   *He will do it if Bill can.

Lees (1960:103) also noticed a special case, namely, that in extraposed versus unextraposed subject *that*-clauses. His examples were:

(ii) *a*   *That John flunked disappointed John. $\Longrightarrow$
    b   That he flunked disappointed John.
    c   That John flunked disappointed him.
    d   It disappointed John that he flunked.
    e   *It disappointed him that John flunked.

where in all cases the relevant NP are understood as coreferential. The fact that what goes on in all the examples of (i) and (ii) is general and basically a function of the backwards condition was then, as far as is known to me, not realized until the fall of 1966 in the course of work in part referred to in the following footnote.

1966 by Ronald Langacker, John R. Ross, and the present writer.[20] The condition is roughly that, given two coreferential NP, NP_{left} and NP_{right}, the latter may pronominalize the former if NP_{left} is contained in an embedded sentence S_i, and S_i is contained in a larger sentence which contains NP_{right}, and NP_{right} is not in S_i. Hence, roughly, the one on the left must not be in a higher level of embedding than the one on the right.[21] Let us refer to this condition as the *backwards condition*.

Observe how the backwards condition explains the difference between such examples as:

2.(18) *a* The man who investigated him$_i$ hates Charley$_i$.
     b *He$_i$ hates the man who investigated Charley$_i$.
     c The man who investigated him$_i$ was hated by Charley$_i$.
     d *He$_i$ was hated by the man who investigated Charley$_i$.

---

[20] Langacker (1969) gives an extensive discussion of this constraint, which he attempts to define precisely in terms of the very interesting general notion of *command*. But Ross (1967a:359⁻363) observes, quite rightly, that the constraint can be stated in terms of command only by a distorted representation of the structure of subordinate clauses [such as those beginning with *because, if, when*, and so on]. Ross (1967b) discussed it against the background of the notion of transformational cycle which, he argued (wrongly, see footnote 11 and Chapter 10, Section D), is strongly supported by the backwards condition. Ross defines the backwards condition somewhat differently in terms of the notion *subordinate clause*. But he is unable to supply a general account of this notion.

[21] This is formulated in terms of "not in a higher level of embedding" because right-to-left pronominalization is possible if the NP on the left is embedded equally far down as the one on the right. If, for instance, both are in simple relative clauses on NP of the main clause as in:

(i)   The car which Charley$_i$ bought impoverished the man who supported him$_i$.
(ii)   The car which he$_i$ bought impoverished the man who supported Charley$_i$.

In addition, observe that neither formulation is precise enough. One must, for instance, guarantee that the left and right NP *are not separated by coordination*. Thus backwards pronominalization is not possible in such examples as:

(iii) *The boy who hated him$_i$ lost and John$_i$ likes fish.

Langacker (1969) states this as a general prohibition on backwards pronominalization out of a coordinate structure to an NP not in that structure. I think he is essentially correct here. But if so, one must distinguish between true coordination, where the conjuncts are, for instance, reversible without change of meaning, and *pseudo* conjunction which must have another origin. For observe that sentences like:

(iv)   The boy who hated him$_i$ lost and $\left\{\begin{array}{l}\text{immediately thereafter}\\ \text{so}\\ \text{then}\\ \text{consequently}\\ \text{therefore}\\ \text{as a result}\\ \text{because of that}\end{array}\right\}$ John$_i$ smiled.

This naturally suggests that sentences like (iv) have a *noncoordinate underlying structure*, a fact consistent with the irreversibility of conjuncts and the restrictions between the clauses (tenses, time adverbs, and so on). The proper formulation of the backwards condition will, I think, refer to subordinate clause, as in Ross (1967b).

In 2.(18) *a* and *c* the backwards pronoun is inside of a relative clause sentence and hence more deeply embedded than its coreferent on the right. In the ill-formed 2.(18) *b* and *d*, the backwards pronoun is in the main clause and hence less deeply embedded than its coreferent on the right, which is in the relative clause. This then violates the backwards condition.[22]

Given this condition, however, we are now in a position to argue for the point of real concern, namely, that passive and almost every other rule of constituent reordering must *precede* pronominalization. Let us show this by assuming the contrary. A structure like the following would then first be input to pronominalization and only then to passive:

2.(19)   The company that $Charley_i$ works for investigated $Charley_i$.

Application of pronominalization yields

2.(20) *a*   The company that $Charley_i$ works for investigated him_i.
       b   The company that he_i works for investigated $Charley_i$.

in case the rule is applied forwards and backwards, respectively. The latter is possible since 2.(19) meets the backwards condition as the leftmost occurrence of $Charley_i$ is more deeply embedded. Application of passive to the structures in 2.(20) *a* and *b* yields, respectively:

2.(21) *a*   *He_i was investigated by the company that $Charley_i$ works for.
       b $Charley_i$ was investigated by the company he_i works for.

But *a* here is wrong. The sentence it yields does not have the interpretation under which *he* refers to the same individual as *Charley*. If, however, the rules are applied to 2.(19) in the order passive-pronominalization, the first yields:

2.(22) $Charley_i$ was investigated by the company that $Charley_i$ works for.

and then the second can apply only left-to-right. That is, 2.(22) does not meet the backwards condition since it is the rightmost occurrence of $Charley_i$ which is more deeply embedded. The fact is, then, that *in the passive of* 2.(19) only forwards pronominalization is allowed, predicted by the order passive-pronominalization. Only the active form of 2.(19) permits both forwards and backwards pronominalization, again predicted by the order of rules with pronominalization later.

Consider also the "converse" case:

2.(23) $Charley_i$ investigated the company that $Charley_i$ works for.

---

[22] It is now clear in a number of ways that the backwards condition, first arrived at in 1966, is only the grossest outline of the conditions needed to predict fully the distribution of the phenomenon of backwards pronominalization in English. See Section C. of this chapter below

With the order pronominalization-passive, 2.(23) first yields only:

2.(24)   Charley$_i$ investigated the company he$_i$ works for.

since the conditions for right-to-left pronominalization are not met. Application of passive to 2.(24) yields:

2.(25)   The company he$_i$ works for was investigated by Charley$_i$.

2.(25) is correct and has the interpretation provided by 2.(23). The trouble here is that this order of rules does not yield the alternative passive representative of 2.(23), namely:

2.(26)   The company Charley$_i$ works for was investigated by him$_i$.

That is, this order of rules wrongly predicts that backwards pronominalization is obligatory in the passives of structures like 2.(23). On the other hand, the order passive-pronominalization applied to 2.(23) yields correct results. Passive yields:

2.(27)   The company that Charley$_i$ works for was investigated by Charley$_i$.

And this may now undergo either forwards or backwards pronominalization yielding both 2.(25) and 2.(26) as the passives of 2.(23).

This argument thus shows conclusively that the order of rules is passive-pronominalization, and analogous arguments can be used to show the corresponding ordering for a large set of other rules that move NP in ways similar to passive. When considering such rules below, we shall not give the argument in detail, but shall simply refer to the left-right argument, leaving it to the reader to check the details if he wishes.

C. LIMITATIONS OF THE BACKWARDS CONDITION

As indicated in footnote 22, the backwards condition is by no means fully adequate in itself to predict the distribution of backwards pronominalization in English. Primarily, as observed first, I believe, by S. Y. Kuroda, backwards pronominalization is in general banned *for indefinite NP:*

2.(28) *a*   If he$_i$ comes arrest that man$_i$.
     b   *If he$_i$ comes arrest a man$_i$.
     c   If a man$_i$ comes arrest him$_i$.

2.(29) *a*   The fact that he$_i$ lost disturbed the jockey$_i$.
     b   *The fact that he$_i$ lost disturbed a jockey$_i$.
     c   The fact that a jockey$_i$ lost disturbed him$_i$.

Secondly, there are relatively unique contexts in which the predictions of the backwards condition are just wrong. Backwards pronominalization is banned in such contexts as:

2.(30) *a*   What annoyed Bill$_i$ was my punching him$_i$.
     b   *What annoyed him$_i$ was my punching Bill$_i$.
     c   The thing that annoyed Bill$_i$ was my punching him$_i$.
     d   *The thing that annoyed him$_i$ was my punching Bill$_i$.

although predicted here by the general condition. This is especially peculiar since backwards pronominalization *is* possible as predicted in contexts like:

2.(31)   It was my punching him$_i$ that annoyed Bill$_i$.

And one would certainly wish to take structures like 2.(31) to be transformationally related to both of those types in 2.(30). Hence it would seem that what is needed is a special constraint of the form:

2.(32)   Backwards pronominalization is banned *across* a copular verb of referential identity.

Reference to the referential properties is necessary because of examples like:

2.(33) *a*   The man who wrote to her$_i$ was a friend of Mary's$_i$.
     b   The fact that the elephant likes him$_i$ is one of the things that puzzles Harry$_i$.

In these, the copula functions not as a predicate of referential identity but rather as a predicate of set inclusion.

Thirdly, Lakoff (to appear) has shown there is a large class of cases in which backwards pronominalization is possible, though banned by the backwards condition. Moreover, in some of these, only this type of pronominalization is possible. For instance, Lakoff observes that backwards pronominalization from a subordinate to a main clause is possible if the derived pronominal form *is not a subject:*

2.(34) *a*   I calmed him$_i$ before Harry$_i$ did something rash.
     b   *He$_i$ calmed me before Harry$_i$ did something rash.

Although 2.(34) *a* may not be totally acceptable, it is far superior to the completely impossible 2.(34) *b*. The subject constraint is discussed at length by Lakoff, who shows its relation to stress level and length of nominal.

Fourthly, and probably most fundamentally of all, the backwards condition is really only relevant for predicting pronominalization between coreferents that fulfill the conditions for being *peers*, as defined in Chapter 17 below. Roughly, the term *peer* refers to NP that are not embedded inside other clauseless NP. Hence the NP *Harry's* in an expression such as:

    2.(35) Harry's liver

is not a peer of any NP outside of this expression. The backwards condition has little to say directly about backwards pronominalization in such cases. Observe for instance that facts like:

    2.(36) *a* ?His$_i$ father hates John$_i$.
        b *He$_i$ hates John$_i$'s father.
        c I spoke to his$_i$ mother about Harry$_i$.

are not characterized significantly by this condition alone.

Finally, the backwards condition, originally taken to be a constraint on *coreferential pronominalization*, is actually seen to function more widely for anaphoric processes:

    2.(37) *a* John will run if he can.
        b If he can, John will run.
        c If he can run, John will.
        d *John will if he can run.

    2.(38) *a* John will buy an orangutan if he can find one.
        b If he can find one, John will buy an orangutan.
        c If he can find an orangutan, John will buy one.
        d *John will buy one if he can find an orangutan.

In 2.(38) *d, one* does not refer to a member of the class orangutan. Hence, evidently, the right formulation of the backwards condition will refer not to the rules of pronominalization but to anaphoric processes in general, or at least to a wide class of such.

Summing up then, it turns out that the backwards condition is both more general than originally realized when it was first proposed as a constraint for predicting only backwards coreferential pronominalization and yet less general in its applicability to the backwards pronominalization phenomenon, which is clearly controlled by a number of other at least partially independent principles of an unclear character.

PART II
THE GENERALITY OF
THE PHENOMENON

3 TOUGH-MOVEMENT

We now turn to materials showing that the passive-reflexivization incompatibility is not really a peculiarity of passive sentences proper, but only an instance of a more widespread phenomenon.

There is a class of adjectives in English, *hard, tough, easy, difficult, impossible, simple*, which have played a prominent role in discussions and justifications of the need for a transformational grammar of English and of natural languages generally [Chomsky (1964:61–65)]. The contrast between sentences like:

    3.(1) *a*   Throneberry is easy to please.
          b   Throneberry is eager to please.

is by now well known. It is not my intention to discuss this class in any detail. Like most others, the behavior of its members seems to involve a myriad of complex and mysterious factors as yet little explored.

It seems, however, that there is a special rule defined for this class [see Rosenbaum (1967:107)] which involves the movement of an NP out of the predicate of the complement sentence. Let us refer to this rule as *tough-movement*. A rough formulation is that this rule takes a nonsubject NP out of an extraposed complement of this class of forms and substitutes it for the initial pronominal subject of the sentence as a whole. Hence, very roughly, the rule of *extraposition*[1] maps structures like 3.(2) *a* into ones like 3.(2) *b:*

    3.(2) *a*   [It [for Tony to hit Jack]]   was difficult.
             NP S   S NP
         b   It was difficult for Tony to hit Jack.

---

[1] This rule was first worked out and formulated by P.S. Rosenbaum in his M.I.T. doctoral thesis, published as Rosenbaum (1967).

It is then *tough*-movement that derives sentences like:

3.(3)   Jack was difficult for Tony to hit.

by replacing the initial *it* constituent in 3.(2) *b* by the final NP from the predicate of the extraposed sentential complement *for Tony to hit Jack.*

Precise formulation of this rule must await a good deal of research into several factors. Firstly, the rule also strangely operates for a class of morphologically nominal forms including *snap, breeze, bitch,* and a number of more obscene expressions.[2]

3.(4) *a*   To clean this house is a breeze.[3]
     b   It is a breeze to clean this house.
     c   This house is a breeze to clean.

Many peculiar restrictions are manifested here: restriction to indefinite articles, limited class of prenominal modifiers (*real breeze* but **interesting breeze*), impossibility of plurals, and so on.

Secondly, there is the question of which predicate NP in the complement sentence can undergo *tough*-movement.

3.(5) *a*   Mary is easy for Bill to visit.
     b   ?Mary is difficult for Bill to take a picture of.
     c   ?Mary is difficult for Jack to get disgusted with.
     d   *Mary is difficult for John to give the book.
     e   Mary is difficult for John to give the book to.
     f   *The handsome doctor was difficult for Mary to become well known to.

---

[2] In my dialect these include a subset of the nontechnical, colloquial terms for male and female genitalia.

[3] For some speakers, 3.(4) *a* may *require* gerundive forms, which are, I believe, *possible* for all speakers. But these are not tolerable in the 3.(4) *b* or *c* forms:

    (i)   *It is a breeze cleaning this house.
    (ii)   *This house is a breeze (Bill's) cleaning.

The difference between ill-formed examples like (i) and (ii), and ones like:

    (iii) Cleaning this house is a breeze.

is an interesting evidence of the correctness of the extraposition analysis of *tough* constructions since (i) and (ii) require application of extraposition. But this is uniquely in general impossible for gerundives:

    (iv) Bill's winning the race disrupted our plans.
    (v)   *It disrupted our plans Bill's winning the race.

Note that (v) must be read with no intonation break before *Bill's*. With the break, such sentences are all right, but not a function of extraposition. Rather, they then devolve on the rule, whatever it is, behind examples like:

    (vi) It was a Chevrolet, the car that ran over Harry.

See the discussion of *right dislocation* in Chapter 15, Section F.

Thirdly, there are unquestionably constraints on the verbal/adjectival form that can occur as the head of the predicate out of which an NP is moved. Additionally, the definiteness of the NP which is a candidate for movement is relevant with, in general, true indefinites not undergoing the rule:

3.(6) *a*   *A car which I gave Bill is difficult for him to drive slowly.
    b   The car which I gave Bill is difficult for him to drive slowly.
    c   *Sm cheese is tough for Jack to eat slowly.
    d   Some cheese is tough for Jack to eat slowly.

Here *sm* refers to the weakly stressed ordinary mass noun indefinite article, that is, the variant of the count *a/an*. That in 3.(6) *d*, written *some*, is (one of) the strong stressed forms, in this case referring to types of cheese. Note that indefinite-looking forms are all right when they are generic, which is congruent with other scraps of evidence indicating that generics are structurally definite in some sense even with superficially indefinite forms [Postal (1966a)].

3.(7) *a*   Cars are tough to park in Manhattan.
    b   A fox is very easy to lure into a box.

Next, one must observe that the whole construction involves a subtle structural ambiguity of a not understood type. A string like:

3.(8)   It was difficult for Tony to rob the store.

has two different surface structures:

3.(9) *a*   It was difficult for Tony (to rob the store).
    b   It was difficult (for Tony to rob the store).

The difference in meaning is real though subtle. The first seems to associate the difficulty directly with Tony personally. The second allows for a more generic attribution of difficulty. The difference shows up clearly in two variant pronunciations.

Finally, as observed by Klima (1964:315), a subset of the relevant class of adjectives reveals properties typically associated with negatives:

3.(10) *a*   It was easy to find something.
     b   *It was easy to find anything.
     c   *It was difficult to find something.
     d   It was difficult to find anything.

3.(11) *a*   It is simple to find him sometimes in Chicago.
     b   *It is simple to ever find him in Chicago.
     c   *It is hard to find him sometimes in Chicago.
     d   It is hard to ever find him in Chicago.

That is, *difficult, hard, tough*, act like negatives. As in other cases of negative verbal forms (*doubt, deny*), it is difficult to know whether such facts should be taken to indicate some deeper negative analysis of the verbal forms or special cases for the rule which marks elements in post negative position.

These and other open points about *tough*-movement and the construction underlying it show that we are a long way from any possibility of stating it precisely. However, they do not, I believe, indicate that such a rule does not exist nor do they threaten the conclusion that the rule involves movement of an NP out of the complement predicate and into the grammatical subject position of the sentence as a whole. The key fact for present purposes is that *tough*-movement, like passive, does not derive the full set of expected coreferential NP-containing sentences. Hence, while both:

3.(12) *a*   For me to shave myself was difficult.
       b   It was difficult for me to shave myself.

are well formed as are:

3.(13) *a*   For me to shave Luke was difficult.
       b   It was difficult for me to shave Luke.

only the latter type provides a basis for *tough*-movement operation.

3.(14) *a*   *I was difficult for me to shave.
       b   *Myself was difficult for me to shave.
       c   Luke was difficult for me to shave.

It might be thought that again, as in the case of 1.(17), the ungrammaticality of 3.(14) *b* is explained by ordering *tough*-movement before reflexivization. This would leave the ill-formedness of 3.(14) *a* mysterious, just as no ordering can explain the passive-reflexive incompatibility revealed by nonsentences such as 1.(16) *b*. But actually these examples with *tough*-movement are not completely parallel in this way with the cases under passive. This lack of parallelism is due not to any difference in rule ordering—*tough*-movement must precede reflexivization—but rather to the phenomenon of cyclical application of transformational rules.

This principle requires that one run through the entire set of cyclical rules on each level of embedding. But, importantly, passive is a rule that applies on a single clause: *tough*-movement, a rule that moves an NP out of an embedded sentence into the main sentence in which the former is embedded. Therefore, all the cyclic rules, in particular reflexivization, will be applied to the embedded sentence in *tough* constructions before *tough*-movement can apply, since the latter rule can only apply on the cycle of the main sentence, whereas reflexivization applies on all cycles if the relevant sentences contain coreferential NP. Therefore, given a structure like:

3.(15)   [It was tough [for Harry$_i$ to shave Harry$_i$]].
          S   S   S S

Reflexivization will apply on the inner, embedded sentence, yielding:

   3.(16)   It was tough for Harry to shave himself.

And only then can *tough*-movement possibly apply on the outer cycle. Hence the grammar predicts in this case that 3.(14) *b* should be well formed and the mystery is why it is not. 3.(14) *a* is excluded by the fact that its derivation would require *tough*-movement to apply at a point where reflexivization has not yet operated on the embedding. But this is blocked by the cyclical principle.

   This lack of parallelism between *tough*-movement and passive notwithstanding, it is still the case that structures under *tough*-movement involve an unexplained gap in cases of coreferential NP. Following the lines of the original Lees and Klima proposal, it would now be necessary to say that both the passive and *tough*-movement rules must have particular referential identity conditions on them, conditions that exclude their operation in certain cases where particular configurations of coreferential NP occur. What seemed at first a peculiarity of passives is thus already seen to be more general.

4 *IT*-REPLACEMENT

There is a class of verbal forms, of which *seem* and *appear* are probably most notable, that define the environment of another rule which moves NP in English. Extraposition, the rule which moves a sentential complement to the end of the next most inclusive sentence, operates obligatorily with these verbs and they take both *that*—clause and infinitival complements. Hence from structures like:

> 4.(1) *a* [It [that Toby was a dummy]] seemed to me.
>   NP S   S NP
>   *b* [It [for Jerry to love Lucille]] seemed to me.
>   NP S   S NP

Extraposition yields:

> 4.(2) *a* It seemed to me that Toby was a dummy.
>   *b* *It seemed to me for Jerry to love Lucille.

The latter is of course not well formed. There exist, however, sentences like:

> 4.(3) Jerry seemed to me to love Lucille.

and following the insightful analysis first proposed by Rosenbaum (1967), these are naturally derived from the intermediate structures like 4.(2) *b* by a rule, called here *it-replacement*.[1] This operation substitutes the subject NP of the complement sentence for the initial pronoun. Deletion of the *for* then automatically devolves on other independently required operations in the

---

[1] Rosenbaum's term was *pronoun replacement*.

grammar.[2] Again there are many open questions about *it*-replacement, some of which are touched on below.

The important fact about *it*-replacement for present concerns is that it does not yield the full class of expected coreferential NP-containing sentences. Hence, although one finds:

4.(4) *a*   It seems to me that Schwarz is clever.
      b   It seems to me that I am clever.

of the expected infinitival variants, only one is well formed:

4.(5) *a*   Schwarz seems to me to be clever $\Rightarrow$ Schwarz seems clever to me.
      b   *Myself seems to me to be clever $\Rightarrow$ *Myself seems clever to me.
      c   *I seem to myself to be clever $\Rightarrow$ *I seem clever to myself.

Again there are unexplained gaps in the set of sentences derived by a rule at just those points where coreferential NP are involved.

It is worth pointing out some relations between the three kinds of cases considered so far, passive cases, *tough*-movement cases, and *it*-replacement cases, since these are not entirely parallel, especially with respect to their relations to cyclical application of rules. Recall that passive must precede reflexivization, which explains why there are no sentences like:

4.(6)   *Himself was stabbed by Harry.

---

[2] It is in general the case in standard English that when an NP is deleted, its preceding preposition, if any, also disappears. On the other hand, if the NP is moved, its preposition may be left behind. In other words, in English at least, prepositions may be stranded by transformations which reorder constituents but not normally by those which delete them:

(i) *a*   Harriet was attacked by the gorilla.
    b   Harriet was attacked.
    c   *Harriet was attacked by.
(ii) *a*   Bill is amusing to everyone.
     b   Bill is amusing.
     c   *Bill is amusing to.
(iii) *a*   The committee agreed on that.
      b   That was agreed on by the committee.
      c   *That was agreed by the committee.

This fact provides an argument for taking the *for* which occurs with the subject of infinitives to be a preposition, rather than part of some complex complementizer, as in Rosenbaum (1967). That is, under the preposition assumption, the deletion of the *for* when its NP is deleted follows from the deeper generalization about English, regardless of how this is to be stated. Unfortunately, the argument is weakened by the fact that certain exceptions to the regularity of preposition deletion correlating with NP deletion exist, for instance:

(iv) *a*   Harry bought a gun to shoot the bear with.
     b   Harry needs a car to keep his tools in.
     c   Harry got a shelf to put his boots under.

Why this construction should permit such apparent violations is unclear to me.

The ordering alone predicts that sentences like:

4.(7)   *Harry was stabbed by himself.

are well formed. It is the falseness of this prediction that is under study. In the case of *tough*-movement, however, we have a rule which is not, like passive, clause internal. Rather, *tough*-movement moves an NP from a subordinate clause into the next higher clause. Therefore, given the cyclical principle, *tough*-movement cannot apply until the cycle of this more inclusive clause. This means that reflexivization necessarily has already applied on the previous cycle to any coreferent NP contained within the complement clause. Therefore it is this cyclical ordering which predicts that:

4.(8)   *I am tough for me to stab.

is impossible. The ordering predicts, however, that we should derive:

4.(9)   *Myself is tough for me to stab.

and it is the failure of this prediction that reveals the existence of further factors involving coreferential NP. What needs to be stressed is the lack of parallelism between the two cases. In passive contexts the ordering predicts that sequences of reflexive pronoun followed by full NP coreferents are impossible. In *tough*-movement contexts the ordering does not predict this. In each case the ordering predicts one class of occurrent deviances but not another. But the predicted classes are opposite in the domains of the two rules as a function of the cyclical principle and the fact that *tough*-movement moves an NP out of its clause of origin.

In this regard, *it*-replacement is more like passive, even though it is like *tough*-movement in moving an NP out of its clause of origin. The reason for the difference is the fact that *it*-replacement moves the subject of its complement while *tough*-movement moves an NP from the predicate. Hence, given structures like 4.(10) *a* and *b*, different things happen on the complement cycle:

4.(10) *a*   It is difficult (for I to stab I).
     b   It seems to me (for I to be clever).

In the former, reflexivization will apply on the complement cycle because there are coreferent clause mates. But in 4.(10) *b* it will not. In each case the movement rule, *tough*-movement in the first, *it*-replacement in the second, will operate only on the next or whole sentence cycle. Each substitutes an NP for an initial pronominal *it*. However, the former rule takes a predicate NP, which was in fact reflexivized. The latter takes a subject NP, untouched by reflexivization at that point (this assumes of course that *it*-replacement precedes reflexivization, a point to be justified momentarily). Therefore the results of applying the two movement rules to the results of applying reflexivization on the complement cycle to 4.(10) are, respectively:

4.(11) *a*   Myself is difficult for I to stab.
  b   I seem to me for to be clever.

Nothing more of relevance happens to 4.(11) *a*. But reflexivization can apply to 4.(11) *b* on the whole sentence cycle. The results are then:

4.(12) *a*   Myself is difficult for me to stab.
  b   *I seem to myself to be clever $\Longrightarrow$ *I seem clever to myself.

Each is ill formed, a fact as yet unexplained. But the lack of parallelism is clear.

It was pointed out that the discussion assumed the ordering *it*-replacement-reflexivization. The justification for this is parallel to that for the passive-reflexivization ordering. Namely, although 4.(12) *b* sentences are ill formed, they are far superior to those of:

4.(13)   *Myself seems to me to be clever $\Longrightarrow$ *Myself seems clever to me.

which are predicted by the opposite ordering.

It follows that in all three cases, passive, *tough*-movement, *it*-replacement, there are unexplained gaps in the set of sentences where coreferent NP would appear. But the cases are not entirely parallel, the *tough*-movement cases being unique in that in these it is the nonexistence of preceding reflexive forms which is unexplained. This is explained in the other cases by rule ordering.

As with passive and *tough*-movement, it is then apparently necessary to constrain *it*-replacement in some way with a restriction of referential non-identity. Where *tough*-movement does not apply to a predicate NP of a sentential complement if that NP is coreferential with the grammatical subject of the predicate, *it*-replacement evidently does not apply to the grammatical subject of a complement sentence if this is coreferential to the object of the *to* prepositional phrase of the main clause. There are thus apparently at least three rules of English that contain restrictions of referential nonidentity on the NP in structures to which they apply.

5 *ABOUT*-MOVEMENT

Constructions of the form *about* + NP (or alternates with *of, over*, or *concerning*), with the interpretation that the whole is descriptive of what might be called "content," provide many interesting problems for the student of English grammar. Most relevant for present concerns is the existence of alternative word orders for otherwise apparently cognitively equivalent sentential expressions:

> 5.(1) *a* I talked to Mary about Louise.
>   *b* I talked about Louise to Mary.
>
> 5.(2) *a* I fought with Tony about that proposal.
>   *b* I fought about that proposal with Tony.

Let us assume that these alternative orders are derived by a rule, *about-movement*, which, schematically described, operates on *a* structures to yield the *b* type. It seems, intuitively, that the *a* order is more basic, and this is supported by some other evidence, unfortunately not of a type fully independent of the claims we wish to support later [see Chapter 18]. As with the three rules previously considered, there are gaps in the set of sentences derived by *about*-movement in cases of coreferential NP.

> 5.(3) *a* I talked to Thmug about himself.
>   *b* *I talked about himself to Thmug.
>   *c* *I talked about Thmug to himself.

The ill-formedness of 5.(3) *b* is explicable on the basis of an ordering that places *about*-movement before reflexivization. This ordering is required by the fact that 5.(3) *b* is much more deviant than 5.(3) *c*. At the same time, the latter is not completely well formed and this is the unexplained gap. *About*-movement cases are thus parallel to those with passive and *it*-replacement, not to *tough*-movement. This is not surprising since *about*-movement is a rule that operates within clauses; it does not move NP out of the clauses where they stand at the point it applies.

The gaps involving coreferent NP show up in *about* constructions in another way. Observe that in sentences like:

5.(4) *a* Schwarz talked to Harry about himself.
    b Mary spoke to Louise about herself.

there are ambiguities. In 5.(4) *a, himself* may be coreferential to either *Schwarz* or *Harry*; in 5.(4) *b, herself* may refer back to either *Mary* or *Louise*. Consider, however, the apparently parallel structures in which the *about*-phrase precedes the *to*-phrase:

5.(5) *a* Schwarz talked about Harry to himself.
    b Mary spoke about Louise to herself.

Surprisingly, these are unambiguous. *Himself* can only refer to *Schwarz, herself* only to *Mary*. This "ambiguity gap" is as unexplained as the ill-formedness of the examples like 5.(3) *c.*

We have been speaking of restrictions of the sort illustrated by 5.(3) *c* as constraints on the distribution of coreferential NP. It might be objected that a more accurate description would take them as constraints on the word order possibilities of morphological pronominal forms. But *about*-movement provides relevant evidence that this reformulation is inappropriate. For observe the following examples, which in terms of morphology and word order are not naturally distinguishable from 5.(3) *c.*

5.(6) *a* Joe talked about Lucille to himself.
    b Thomas wrote about your mother to himself.

These sentences are perfectly well formed in spite of the fact that an *about*-phrase with a nonpronominal head precedes a reflexive *to*-phrase as in the ill-formed 5.(3) *c.* These facts show that the initial formulation in terms of coreference was correct since the difference between 5.(3) *c* and 5.(6) is that in the latter the NP of the *about*-phrases and *to*-phrases are not coreferents.

It might seem then that *about*-movement must contain a restriction that the NP in the *about* phrase not be referentially identical to that in the *to* phrase. Actually, however, this is not quite true, despite 5.(3) *c.* Consider:

5.(7) *a* I talked to myself about myself.
    b I talked about myself to myself.

5.(8) *a* Carl whispered to himself about himself.
    b Carl whispered about himself to himself.

The well-formedness of the *b* forms in 5.(7) and 5.(8) is an apparent anomaly which requires special discussion [see Chapter 16]. It is an anomaly in the sense that it is an unexplained subset of cases where coreference *is* allowed, within the wider set of cases where coreference is for some thus far inexplicable reason banned.

Ignoring this special matter, we can conclude that *about*-movement is the fourth case found of an English rule which involves constraints that NP which undergo it cannot be coreferential to certain other NP in the phrase marker which the rule application deforms.

6 *PSYCH*-MOVEMENT

A. PERCEPTION PREDICATES

There is a very large class of verbal and adjectival forms in English which, I claim, involve the operation of a hitherto largely unrecognized rule referred to here as *psych-movement*. This rule is formally rather similar to passive in that it moves an NP from grammatical subject position into the predicate and causes it to be supplied with a preposition, usually *to* but occasionally *for* and maybe once in a while *from*. At the same time, the rule moves an NP from the predicate into grammatical subject position. The name chosen for this rule depends on the fact that almost all members of the class of verbal/adjectival forms under discussion designate psychological states, processes, or attributes.

If one considers sentences like:

6.(1) *a*   I tasted the meat.
     b   I tasted the dirt.
     c   *The meat tasted me.
     d   *The dirt tasted me.

6.(2) *a*   I smelled the soup.
     b   I smelled the rock.
     c   *The soup smelled me.
     d   *The rock smelled me.

it can be observed that there is a restriction of *active* verbs of perception in such sentences to animate grammatical subjects. Correspondingly, one notices a restriction with largely the same verbs to animate postprepositional NP in *stative (nonactive)* sentences like:

6.(3) *a*   The meat tastes funny to me.[1]
    b   *The meat tastes funny to the rock.

6.(4) *a*   The piano sounds funny to O'Leary.
    b   *The piano sounds funny to the table.

6.(5) *a*   The rug feels rough to me.
    b   *The rug feels rough to the vacuum cleaner.

6.(6) *a*   The house looks old to me.
    b   *The house looks old to the garden.

This suggests regarding *listen/sound* as suppletive variants and assuming that sentences like those in 6.(3)-6.(6) are derived by a sequence of rules, one of which is *psych*-movement. In the terminology which speaks of *logical grammatical relations*, this means taking the NP after the preposition *to* to be the logical subject in such cases, just as the sentence initial NP is the logical subject in sentences like 6.(1) and 6.(2). This implies that the preposition *to*, or rather a large class of occurrences of this form, are surface structure markers of underlying logical subjects that have been stuffed into predicates by *psych*-movement.

It should be emphasized that the proposals just made do not involve any claim that sentence pairs like:

6.(7) *a*   I tasted the soup.
    b   The soup tasted funny to me.

are in any way directly related transformationally. There are obvious gross differences. The verbs in the former type are active, those in the latter stative; the adjective is required in the latter and impossible in the former; and so on. The claim is only that there is an essential similarity in the relation between *taste*

---

[1] These constructions of course involve many puzzles. Part of the difficulty is the fact that the adjectives here are, I think, actually irregular forms of *ly* adverbials, a point suggested by their correspondence with *how* questions, typically associated with such adverbials:

   (i)   How does that meat taste (to you)?

In other words, it is wrong to set up these forms as a subset of "copulative verbs" analogous to *be*, which take adjective predicates, as in Lees (1960:12⁻13) and Chomsky (1965:107).
The perception examples in the text are related to nominal versions like:

   (ii)   This meat has a funny taste.

and to sentences with explicit embedded clause structure:

   (iii)   This meat tastes to me as if it were rotten.

and *the soup* in such sentence pairs, a relation which is to be reconstructed in part by deriving the *b* forms from more remote structures like:

6.(8) I tasted the soup funny.

by way of *psych*-movement. At the least, this permits a more uniform treatment of the common animacy selectional restrictions of such pairs.

B. PSYCHOLOGICAL PREDICATES

Other indications of similar relations involving *to* as a surface structure marker of underlying logical subjects are not hard to uncover. There is a class of verbal/adjectival stems containing several hundred members that refer to psychological features of animate beings. These stems occur in various adjectival and verbal forms. Examples include: *amuse, amaze, bore, confuse, disgust, excite, frighten, gratify, horrify, irritate, nauseate, puzzle, rile, surprise, terrify, threaten,* and *worry.* Among their adjectival variants, the members of this class have in general two contrasting series. One involves adjectival endings in *-ing* (occasionally *-some,* or *-ive*) and postadjectival prepositional phrases with *to.* The other involves endings in *-ed* and postadjectival prepositional phrases in *with, at, of, about,* or *by,* the choice among these being lexically determined. Examples:

6.(9) *a* I am amused with (at) (by) Harry.
     b Harry is amusing to me.

6.(10) *a* I am bored with Harry.
     b Harry is boring to me.

6.(11) *a* I am confused about that.
     b That is confusing to me.

6.(12) *a* I am disgusted with Lucille.
     b Lucille is disgusting to me.

6.(13) *a* I am excited about that.
     b That is exciting to me.

6.(14) *a* I am frightened of (by) that.
     b That is frightening to me.

6.(15) *a* I am gratified at that.
     b That is gratifying to me.

6.(16) *a* I was horrified at what he did.
     b What he did was horrifying to me.

6.(17) *a* I am irritated at Billy.
     b Billy is irritating to me.

6.(18) *a* I am mystified at what John did.
     b What John did is mystifying to me.

6.(19) *a*   I am nauseated at what he said.
      b   What he said is nauseating to me.

6.(20) *a*   I am puzzled about (at) (by) that.
      b   That is puzzling to me.

6.(21) *a*   I was riled at that.
      b   That was riling to me.

6.(22) *a*   I was surprised at that.
      b   That was surprising to me.

6.(23) *a*   ?I was threatened by that.
      b   That was threatening to me.

6.(24) *a*   I was worried about (by) that.
      b   That was worrisome to me.

I wish to argue that in all cases here the *b* forms are derived by rules that include *psych*-movement, while this rule plays no role in the derivation of the *a* forms. Let me emphasize that I am *not* claiming that the paired *a* and *b* forms are synonymous; in general they are not, although there is a close meaning relation. Nor am I claiming that the *b* forms are derived from the *a* forms or that they have identical deep structures. I only claim that the underlying nominal-verbal relations are the same. Hence in the *b* forms it is the post-*to* NP which is the logical subject, a function filled by the initial NP in the *a* forms. Evidence for this lies in the fact that while in the *a* forms it is the *pre*adjectival NP which must meet a condition of animacy [and, with some of the forms, humanity as well], in the *b* cases this is true of the *post*adjectival NP.

In addition, the behavior of the curious adverb *personally* supports the claim of *psych*-movement operation in the derivation of the *b* cases. That is, under this assumption, *personally* may be said to accompany the logical subject. Otherwise its occurrence must be given disjunctively in some manner. Observe:

6.(25) *a*   I personally am annoyed with Jack.
      b   *Jack is annoyed with me personally.
      c   Jack is annoying to me personally.
      d   *I personally am annoying to Jack.

The same argument supports the postulation of *psych*-movement relevance in cases like 6.(3) *a* above:

6.(26) *a*   I personally smelled the gorilla.
      b   *The gorilla smelled me personally.
      c   The gorilla smelled funny to me personally.
      d   *I personally smelled funny to the gorilla.

One important error to avoid with respect to paired adjectival forms like those in 6.(9)–6.(24) is a confusion of the *a* forms with passives.[2] It has sometimes been suggested that these simply are passive sentences with lexically determined prepositions distinct from the usual passive *by*. This is totally wrong, however. First of all, many of these forms have contrasting sentences that are the real passives, for instance:

> 6.(27) *a* I was surprised at that.
>   *b* I was surprised by that.

Here *b* is a true passive. Notice that it is not a paraphrase of the *a* example. 6.(27) *b* describes an event; 6.(27) *a*, a state. Correlated with this is the possibility of ordinary modifiers of degree with the first but not the second:

> 6.(28) *a* I was very surprised at that.
>   *b* *I was very surprised by that.

This phenomenon is quite general:

> 6.(29) *a* I was awfully frightened of that dog.
>   *b* *I was awfully frightened by that dog.

Moreover, the passives and true adjectivals have in some cases different selectional restrictions:

> 6.(30) *a* *I was mystified at Harry.
>   *b* I was mystified by Harry.

> 6.(31) *a* *I was nauseated at Louise.
>   *b* I was nauseated by Louise.

Observe that the passives correspond in selections with actives:

> 6.(32) *a* Harry mystified me.
>   *b* Louise nauseated me.

---

[2]Chapin (1967:80–82) explicitly argues that the forms in question are *not* passives. He gives among other arguments one based on instrumental adverbs. He observes that an active:

> (i)   Jerry amused Irma with a harmonica solo.

has the true passive:

> (ii)   Irma was amused by Jerry with a harmonica solo.

But the form:

> (iii) *Irma was amused at Jerry with a harmonica solo.

is impossible, which is strong evidence that (iii) is not a passive at all.

We shall see below other evidence of the distinction between passives and the kind of adjectival sentences under discussion, evidence having to do directly with our chief concern of coreferentiality.

C. OTHER DATA

I view the facts brought forward so far to support the existence of the *psych*-movement rule. One fact among many which has obscured the existence of this rule is that it is subject to a great number of lexical restrictions, a property which manifests itself in several ways. First, the different choice of prepositions in the *a* type sentences of 6.(9)–6.(24) tends to obscure their basic similarity. Secondly, the rule is sometimes optional and sometimes obligatory. Thirdly, operation of the rule is linked to particular classes of verbal and adjectival forms and is hence less general than, for example, a rule like passive. [The latter rule has a more or less uniform definition in terms of general constituent categories, although it is much less general than often thought and involves many peculiar and poorly understood restrictions.] Finally, operation of *psych*-movement seems to be often linked to the operation of other mysterious rules which relate adjectival and verbal forms. Hence pairs that show the logical subject in grammatical subject and post-*to* position may reveal in addition an adjective-verb contrast:

6.(33) *a* I loathe Schwarz.
     b Schwarz is loathsome to me.

6.(34) *a* The police accepted Carter's alibi.
     b Carter's alibi was acceptable to the police.

6.(35) *a* John values Dorothea's services.
     b Dorothea's services are valuable to John.

6.(36) *a* The Devil prefers sophisticated souls.
     b Sophisticated souls are preferable to the Devil.[3]

6.(37) *a* The store agreed to my request.
     b My request was agreeable to the store.

Again the distribution of *personally* supports the postulation of *psych*-movement operation in the *b* cases.

6.(38) *a* I personally loathe Schwarz.
     b *Schwarz loathes me personally.
     c Schwarz is loathsome to me personally.
     d *I personally am loathsome to Schwarz.

---

[3] This example has, of course, an irrelevant reading analogous to:

(i) X prefers Y to Z.

with *Devil* filling the Z role, *souls* the Y role, and the unspecified "preferrer" unexpressed.

Other evidence that *psych*-movement is an operative rule in English also exists. For example, there are several cases of free variation under the rule:

6.(39) *a*   I benefited from that.
    b   That benefited me.

6.(40) *a*   I profited from that.
    b   That profited me (archaic for many).

6.(41) *a*   I am familiar with algebra.
    b   Algebra is familiar to me..

6.(42) *a*   You are lucky that Bill won⟸You are lucky [it [that Bill won]].
                           NP S   S NP

6.(42) *b*   It is lucky for you that Bill won ⟸⟸⟸ [It [that Bill won]].
                                     NP S   SNP
                                           is lucky for you.

6.(43) *a*   You are fortunate that I like owls.
    b   It is fortunate for you that I like owls.

Incidentally, the absence of post-verbal prepositions in 6.(39) *b* and 6.(40) *b* is not exceptional, but follows from a rather general rule which deletes prepositions after verbal forms that are pure verbs but not after those that are adjectival.[4] The preposition *from* as a general fact does not undergo this rule and there are many lexical exceptions (*come, occur*). There are one or two adjectives (*near, like*) which are exceptions in the opposite direction, that is, directly following prepositions drop after them despite their adjectival character. [See Chapter 18, Section E.]

I would suggest that *psych*-movement is operative for the underlined NP in all of the following sentence types. Most of these are cases where it is obligatory: These cases reveal again that the rule works for both purely verbal and adjectival predicate forms.

6.(44) *a*   *It* came to *me* that Schwarz is insane.[5]
    b   *It* hit *me* that you are wrong.
    c   *It* is clear to *me* that hippopotamuses can't fly very far.
    d   *It* is obvious to *me* that hippopotamuses can't fly very far.
    e   *It* is evident to *me* that hippopotamuses can't fly very far.

---

[4] I would suggest that in the deepest structures there are no prepositions and that at a later stage they are added to all NP. Later rules then delete some of them under certain conditions. The distinction between prepositional phrase and NP is thus purely superficial and in fact there is strong evidence [see Chapter 18, Section 3] that the node over the sequence [preposition + NP] is in fact also NP. A similar but partially distinct view has been reached independently by Fillmore (1966, 1968).

[5] In more ancestral forms of these examples, the initial *it* and final complement sentence are, of course, jointly part of one NP, the complement being moved to final position by the rule of extraposition. See Rosenbaum (1967).

> *f* *It* is plain to *me* that hippopotamuses can't fly very far.
> *g* *It* is important to *me* that hippopotamuses can't fly very far.
> *h* *It* occurs to *me* that John is a fool.
> *i* *It* strikes *me* that you are right.
> *j* *It* is vital to *me* that giraffes eat figs.
> *k* *It* concerns *me* that you are growing so slowly.
> *l* *John* impresses *me* as a fool.
> *m* *It* falls to *me* to help him.
> *n* *That* is sacred to *me*.
> *o* *That* is holy to *me*.
> *p* *This house* belongs to *me*.

The claim here is supported by the fact that the post-verbal/post-adjectival NP in these cases meet the animacy (often humanity) requirement typical of logical subjects and by the facts of *personally*-distribution.

It should be observed that postulation of *psych*-movement eliminates a certain class of examples cited by Chomsky (1965:162) as illustrations of the need for "an even more abstract notion of grammatical function and grammatical relation than any that has been developed so far in any systematic way." Chomsky cited the following examples, among others, as cases approaching paraphrase where transformational description as thus far understood cannot assign identical deep structure ("logical") relations:

6.(45) *a* *John strikes me as pompous.*—I regard John as pompous.
      b I liked the play.—*The play pleased me.*

But I would claim that the italicized cases, but not the others, are instances of the operation of *psych*-movement. Therefore, the underlying structures of the pairs are not fundamentally different, that is, very roughly they are:

6.(46) *a* I strike [it [John is pompous]]
            NP S   S NP
      b I regard [it [John is pompous]]
            NP S   S NP

6.(47) *a* I like the play.
      b I please the play.

It may well be then that the alternative to Chomsky's "more abstract notion of function," *at least for cases like these*, is highly idiosyncratic and lexically restricted transformational rules like *psych*-movement.

Evidence of the operation of *psych*-movement in such cases comes from animacy restrictions and *personally*-distribution, but most importantly from the point of view of this text as a whole, from coreferentiality restrictions, to which we finally return. The fact is that the cases we have indicated as being the result of *psych*-movement, but none of the others we have been considering, involve the same kind of nonidentity restrictions as passive, *tough*-movement, *it*-replacement, and *about*-movement. If there were no such rule as *psych*-movement, therefore, there would be no place in the grammar analogous to these four rules to state the restriction.

Let us begin with the cases cited by Chomsky:

6.(48) *a*   *I strike myself as pompous.
     b   I regard myself as pompous.

6.(49) *a*   I like myself.
     b   *I please myself. (Observe also: *I am pleased with myself.*
                                        *I am pleasing to myself.)

Observe too:

6.(50) *a*   I smelled myself.
     b   *I smelled funny to myself.

6.(51) *a*   I looked at myself.
     b   *I looked funny to myself.

6.(52) *a*   I am amused with myself.
     b   *I am amusing to myself.

6.(53) *a*   I am disgusted with myself.
     b   *I am disgusting to myself.

6.(54) *a*   I was horrified at myself.
     b   *I was horrifying to myself.

6.(55) *a*   I was irritated at myself.
     b   *I was irritating to myself.

6.(56) *a*   I loathe myself.
     b   *I am loathsome to myself.

6.(57) *a*   Schwarz accepts himself (as he is).
     b   *Schwarz is acceptable to himself (as he is).

6.(58) *a*   I am familiar with myself.
     b   *I am familiar to myself.

6.(59) *a*   I am impressed with (the fact that) I am a fool.
     b   *I impress myself as a fool. (John impresses me as a fool.)

These cases thus reveal the same general type of referential nonidentity condition as the examples under passive, *tough*-movement, *it*-replacement, and *about* movement. This similarity thus supports the postulation of *psych*-movement since the latter rule provides something in the grammar as the locus of the constraint, and furthermore something parallel in nature to other elements of the grammar already seen to involve such constraints, namely, a transformational rule which reorders NP.

In this regard we can return to a point made earlier in arguing that sentences like:

6.(60) *a*   I am annoyed with Tony.
     b   I am frightened of dogs.

are *not* passives. The strongest argument for this claim beyond those already given is the fact that such sentences permit reflexives freely:

    6.(61) *a* I am annoyed with myself.
          b Tony is frightened of himself.

If these were passives, therefore, they would be an exception to the otherwise flawless regularity that passive and reflexive are incompatible within the same minimal clause. The depth and strength of this argument will grow as we see later that this incompatibility is not simply an isolated, idiosyncratic fact about the passive rule but a function of a principle of wider scope. It would follow that taking sentences like 6.(60) as passives would thus violate not an *ad hoc* restriction on one rule but a wider principle involving an entire class of rules.

    As we have seen, although sentences like 6.(61) are well formed, those like:

    6.(62) *a* *I am annoying to myself.
          b *I am frightening to myself.

are not. This is the kind of gap we have now come to expect but for which we have, as yet, no explanation. We can observe, however, that as with passive, *it*-replacement, and *about*-movement, facts of degree of deviance immediately argue that *psych*-movement must precede reflexivization. This conclusion follows directly from the fact that although forms like 6.(62) are ill formed, those like:

    6.(63) *a* *Myself is annoying to me.
          b Myself is frightening to me.

are much worse. We attribute this to the fact that forms like 6.(63) violate the ordering while those in 6.(62) do not. What is wrong with the latter then is a violation of the pervasive kind of mysterious restriction we are studying. The violations in 6.(63) involve this phenomenon *plus* an ordering deviance, which accounts for their greater distance from well-formed English.

D. SENSATION PREDICATES

There is one final body of evidence in favor of the existence of the *psych*-movement rule that is worth mentioning. By the term in the heading of this section I refer to forms like *hurt, sore,* and so on in sentences like:

    6.(64) *a* My arm hurts.
          b Schwarz's foot is sore.
          c Your nose is numb.

I wish to argue that, surprisingly, these forms involve application of *psych*-movement, in spite of their apparent intransitive nature. In other words, it is claimed that the initial NP in such sentences are not the logical subjects of these sentences. The central point in this argument depends on two facts.

First, in all cases previously taken to be instances of *psych*-movement derivation, a special semantic property may be observed. Namely, that the NP moved into the predicate by *psych*-movement *designates the individual who experiences the psychological event, state, and so on described by the sentence.* Hence *in examples like*:

6.(65) *a* That was pleasing to me.
    b It is obvious to me that you are insane.
    c The meat tastes funny to me.

it is *me* who experiences pleasure, finds something obvious, notices a funny taste. Call this *Fact A*. We observe, however, that sentences like 6.(64) also are about psychological experiences. Here, however, the individual who undergoes the experience is denoted not by a predicate NP in the surface structure but by the "possessor" NP of a body part in the subject. Call this *Fact B*.

Secondly, in general, the verbal selection entered into by an NP is determined by the character of its head noun[6] and not by any NP inside of modifiers on this NP. In particular, selections of a genitive NP are in general not determined by the "possessor" NP. Hence a predicate like *was surprised at* requires animate, probably human, subjects. But this condition is not met by having a human possessor.

6.(66) *a* Harry was amused at what I did.
    b *The rock was amused at what I did.
    c *Harry's rock was amused at what I did.

---

[6]McCawley (1968) has argued that selectional restrictions are semantic, not syntactic, and are not fully reducible to properties of head nouns. His evidence consists of the observation that examples like (i) are no less deviant than those like (ii), while those like (iii) are fine:

    (i)   My buxom neighbor is Harry's father.
    (ii)   My mother is Harry's father.
    (iii) My neighbor is Harry's father.

Hence selectional statements must, in some way, refer to the semantic information in modifiers like *buxom*. The claim in the text here is not intended to be incompatible with McCawley's position. Notice that none of McCawley's arguments show that selections are determined *by NP embedded in modifiers*. So this is what the comment in the text really excludes. In other words, what is excluded are cases of a predicational element P, whose combination with NP is selectionally distinct in:

    (iv) My neighbor who is fond of *the woman* P
    (v)   My neighbor who is fond of *the man*   P

In such a case it is the properties of the embedded NP which would determine selectional compatibility with P, and clear cases of such are unknown. But exactly this is the *apparent* property of the examples discussed immediately below in the text.

Call this point about selection *Fact C*.

The crucial observation is that sensation predicates are an apparent exception to Fact C, just as they are to Fact A. Hence:

6.(67) *a*   My arm is sore.
       b   *The statue's arm is sore. *The arm of the statue is sore.[7]

6.(68) *a*   My leg is numb.
       b   *The table's leg is numb. *The leg of the table is numb.

6.(69) *a*   My face hurts.
       b   *The face of the clock hurts.

6.(70) *a*   My whole body aches.
       b   *The whole body of the airplane aches.

Quite exceptionally then, verbal/adjectival selection with sensation predicates is apparently being determined by the "possessor" NP, not the head NP. The general rule would predict that nouns like *arm, leg, face, body*, should determine selections, not their "possessors."

We can, I think, account for these facts, eliminating the apparent exceptions to both the generalizations Fact A and Fact C, by assuming that *psych*-movement is involved in the derivation of sentences involving sensation predicates. Together with this assumption, we will require use of another rule I shall refer to as *predicate possessive identity*.

The claim of *psych*-movement involvement seems dubious at first, if for no other reason than because of the absence of an NP in the relevant sentences which would have been the original logical subject. It is interesting therefore to observe that while the sentences in 6.(71) are ungrammatical for most people,

---

[7] The contrast between:

  (i) *a*   *The face of Harry's   *The face of Harry
       b   Harry's face
  (ii) *a*   The face of the clock   *The face of the clock's
        b   *The clock's face

illustrate that the *genitive preposing* rule [see Chapter 15, Section D] is in part conditoned by animacy of the "possessed" element and that there is a rule of *degenitivization*, also conditioned by this property. These two rules interact in a highly complex and possibly idiosyncratic way. Compare for example:

  (iii) *a*   The mountains of France
        b   *The mountains of France's
        c   France's mountains

Such constructions are, I believe, also the source of the pseudoadjectives like:

  (iv)   the French mountains

they present no difficulties of interpretation and are understood as exact paraphrases of the corresponding sentences of 6.(72):

6.(71) *a* *My arm is sore to me.
    b *The dog's leg is numb to it.
    c *Schwarz's face hurts him.[8]
    d *The elephant's body aches him.

6.(72) *a* My arm is sore.
    b The dog's leg is numb.
    c Schwarz's face hurts.
    d The elephant's body aches.

The inserted NP which yield the ungrammaticality of 6.(71) have an interesting property. They are exactly such as would be determined by application of pronominalization from underlying NP coreferential to the possessive NP in the grammatical subject position. This coreference is an important indicator of the role of *psych*-movement because there is quite clearly some rule of English, operative for many predicational forms, which requires a possessive NP in the predicate to be coreferential to the logical subject. This is the rule called earlier predicate possessive identity.
    Thus consider:

6.(73) *a* Bill$_i$ is out of Bill$_i$'s mind $\Longrightarrow$ his mind.
    b *Bill is out of Mary's mind.

6.(74) *a* Bill$_i$ made up Bill$_i$'s mind to go $\Longrightarrow$ his mind.
    b *Bill made up Mary's mind to go.

6.(75) *a* Bill$_i$ lost Bill$_i$'s mind $\Longrightarrow$ his mind.
    b *Bill lost Mary's mind.

6.(76) *a* Bill$_i$ took leave of Bill$_i$'s senses $\Longrightarrow$ his senses.
    b *Bill took leave of Mary's senses.

6.(77) *a* Bill$_i$ lost Bill$_i$'s will to live $\Longrightarrow$ his will.
    b *Bill lost Mary's will to live.

We can perhaps account for this by assuming predicate possessive identity substitutes the logical subject for the possessive NP. By a general principle [Katz and Postal (1964:150)] for transformational rules, such an operation is blocked if the NP are not coreferents. Hence well-formed structures only result when

---

[8] This sentence has, of course, an irrelevant causative reading under which it is perfectly well formed. Notice that on that reading *him* need not necessarily be coreferential with *Schwarz*; hence, a causative like:

   (i) Your face hurts me (when it is covered with scratchy whiskers).

is fine.

logical subject and possessive NP are coreferential, as in the *a* forms of 6.(73)–6.(77). Naturally, the relevant predicational structures must be marked as obligatorily undergoing this special rule.

By assuming the existence of predicate possessive identity, required for examples like 6.(73)–6.(77), we can subsume the apparent peculiarities of sensation predicates under otherwise valid regularities if and only if the possessive phrase in sensation predicate sentences starts out in the predicate. But it will start there if, as we claim, such predicates define a context for *psych*-movement operation. It is thus proposed that a sentence like 6.(78) *a* has an ancestor structure like 6.(78) *b* to which predicate possessive identity applies successfully:

6.(78) *a*   My foot itches.
　　　 b   To me itches in my foot.

If the structure had been:

6.(79)   To me itches in Schwarz's foot.

this operation would block.[9] At this point then, *psych*-movement applies, yielding:

6.(80)   My foot itches to me.

This will be reduced to the correct 6.(78) *a* by a special deletion, idiosyncratically operative on the old subjects of some sensation predicates, for example:

6.(81) *a*   My arm is sore.
　　　 b   My arm is sore to me.

6.(82) *a*   My arm is aching.
　　　 b   My arm is aching me.

---

[9] Actually, the description of the identity constraint in terms of *transformational* blocking may well be incorrect. The restriction seems to be a semantic one and a contrast must be drawn between restrictions with semantic bases and those without. It seems that the former should be handled by different kinds of apparatus. Thus observe the contrast between (in my dialect but not all others) the verbs *try* and *hope*. Both require that the subject of an infinitival complement be coreferential with the subject of the main verb:

(i) *a*   I tried to win.
　　 b   *I tried for Bill to win.
(ii) *a*   I hope to win.
　　 b   *I hope for Bill to win.

However, in the former case, the restriction is associated with semantic deviation. (i) *b* is uninterpretable literally and certainly not interpretable at all in a way parallel to (i) *a*. (ii) *b*, on the other hand, is not deviant semantically at all and is interpretable just like (ii) *a*. Correlated with this contrast, interestingly enough, is the fact that some dialects have (ii) *b* as grammatical but none have (i) *b*. Hence it seems quite wrong to represent both of these restrictions in the same way. The general question is studied in some detail in Perlmutter (1968).

Examples like these show that this deletion is sometimes obligatory, sometimes optional. And examples like 6.(82) *b* are the strongest argument for our analysis, since the old logical subject that we have postulated for all such sentences shows up in the surface structure just where it is predicted.[10]

The outstanding feature of the analysis involving *psych*-movement is that sensation predicates are now reduced to the regularities of Fact A and Fact C. Since the structure of 6.(78) *a* is 6.(78) *b*, it is true for sensation predicate sentences too that the "experiencer" is denoted by the logical subject. The logical subject of 6.(78) *a* is *me* and it is *me* who experiences the itching. Just so, the verbal selections are reduced to selections with heads. The fact that there is an apparent selection with the "possessor" is reduced to head selection by way of predicate possessive identity, which guarantees that the head of the logical subject is coreferential with the head of the "possessor" NP. Under this analysis, for example, a sentence like 6.(83) *a* can only be derived from a structure like 6.(83) *b*:

6.(83) *a*   *The statue's arm is sore.
     b   To the statue is sore in the statue's arm.

But the latter structure violates the selectional property of *sore* that the head of its logical subject must be animate. Hence no new principle of selection between verbal/adjectival elements and "possessor" NP is needed for this handful of cases.

Further evidence in favor of this analysis is provided by the following fact. We claim sensation predicates take animate, often human, logical subjects. But in fact these very predicates actually occur in surface structures where the animate logical subject shows up as a surface subject:

6.(84) *a*   I am sore all over (my body).
    b   I am numb all over (my body).
    c   I hurt all over (my body).
    d   I ache all over (my body).

which contrast with:

6.(85) *a*   *The statue is sore all over (its body).
    b   *The table is numb all over (its body).
    c   *The clock hurts all over (its body).
    d   *The airplane aches all over (its body).

While I do not pretend to understand such constructions in anything like full detail, it seems clear we have the basis for an account in the analysis previously given. We must add that, while in all occurrences sensation predicates require

---

[10] As already noted, the deletion of the preposition in verbal cases but not in adjectival ones is essentially regular. See Chapter 18, Section E. The loss of preposition when the NP is elided supports the statement of footnote 2 in Chapter 4.

animate logical subjects, they have several possibilities for predicate complements. When the latter are "possessive" forms, as in earlier examples, *psych*-movement is applicable. When a form like *all over* is part of the predicate complement, *psych*-movement is blocked. How to state this in detail is, of course, quite open, but the compatibility with our essential assumptions about these predicates is clear.

I have gone into exceptional detail to argue for the existence of *psych*-movement for two reasons. First, I expect its existence to be controversial, and it is not a rule with any serious previous backing[11] in the earlier transformational literature; nor has its existence been, as far as I know, discerned by traditional grammarians. Secondly, constructions derived by this rule turn out to provide a mass of evidence concerning the kind of restrictions on coreference which we are studying here. Hence it is important to recognize that these restrictions are associated with a particular transformational rule, just as in the case of the restrictions shown to be associated with passive, *about*-movement, and such.

---

[11] *Psych*-movement is mentioned in Lakoff (1965), Chapin (1967), and Rosenbaum (1967). In the former two, it is referred to as *flip*, in the latter as *subject-object inversion*.

7 SOME FURTHER COREFERENTIALITY RESTRICTIONS

We have been trying to argue that the passive-reflexive incompatibility, noticed by Lees and Klima almost at the beginning of transformational work on pronominalization, is a special case of a wider phenomenon of coreference constraints partly governing the operation of a whole set of English transformational rules. No attempt has been made thus far to state these restrictions precisely on any of the rules. It might be thought initially that this is a rather trivial matter.

For example, in the case of passive it could be suggested that the rule simply does not operate when subject and object NP are coreferential. Similar restriction types might be proposed for other rules. However, in general the situation is much more complicated. Consider the sentence:

7.(1) I bought a book for John.

This has a passive:

7.(2) A book was bought for John by me.

Here the NP interchanged by passive are *a book* and *I*, which are not coreferential. Consider, though:

7.(3) I bought a book for myself.

The passive of this is ill formed:

7.(4) *A book was bought for me by myself.

Furthermore, the deviance of 7.(4) seems to be of exactly the type exhibited by passives where subject and object are coreferents:

7.(5) *a* I betrayed myself.
     b *I was betrayed by myself.

Yet in the formation of 7.(4), just as in the well-formed passive 7.(2), the NP interchanged by the rule are *a book* and *I*, which are not coreferents. Hence it is *not* possible to formulate the restrictions on passive as simply referential nonidentity between subject and object, nor even as nonidentity between the two NP that are moved around by the rule.[1]

The same point is made by examples with *to* prepositional phrases:

7.(6) *a*   Mary made an offer to Bill.
    b   Mary made Bill an offer.
    c   An offer was made to Bill by Mary.
    d   An offer to Bill was made by Mary.

7.(7) *a*   Mary made an offer to herself.[2]
    b   Mary made herself an offer.
    c   *An offer was made to Mary by herself.
    d   *Mary was made an offer by herself.
    e   *An offer to Mary was made by herself.[3]

---

[1] This question is raised by Langacker (1969), who apparently has some doubts about the ungrammaticality of sentences like 7.(4). To quote:

> Second, there is a restriction involving passive sentences that is particular to reflexivization.
>
> (19) *The woman sitting over there* may kill *herself.*
> (20) **The woman sitting over there* may be killed by *herself.*
>
> Lees and Klima suggest accounting for this by a restriction on passivization "to the effect that the subject and object of the active verb may not be identical in the string to which the passive rule applies." Whether or not this suggestion is adequate depends on whether or not one is willing to accept sentences like 21 and 22 as fully grammatical.
>
> (21) ?A new hat was bought for *Carol* by *herself.*
> (22) ?A new hat was bought by *Carol* for *herself.*
>
> Twenty-one seems more doubtful than 22. If both are correct, Lees and Klima may be right in attributing the ungrammaticalness of 20 to a constraint on the passive rule. If 22 is correct but not 21, the restriction is rather one concerning reflexivization; the object of the passive *by* constituent cannot be reflexivized. If both 21 and 22 are rejected, the restriction on reflexivization must be slightly more complex.

It seems clear to me that both Langacker's 21 and 22 are impossible. But, as we shall see, [remembering that the reflexive word has ordinary not contrastive stress] this does not complicate the explication of these restrictions but simplifies it.

[2] This example is, of course, semantically odd and possibly even anomalous. But it seems clearly distinct from examples like 7.(7) *c*, which not only have this property but additional violations as well.

[3] Examples like 7.(6) *d* and 7.(7) *e* are completely mysterious since what one must take to be a sequence of two NP, *an offer* and *to NP*, acts as one NP under a rule, *passive*. The point here is that this mysterious process is all right in examples like 7.(6) *d* where noncoreferential NP are involved, but not in 7.(7) *e* where they are. In other words, 7.(7) *e* is not out because of the movement of the sequence of NP but because of coreferentiality restrictions.

Here also the constraints do not reduce either to subject-object referential identity or to nonidentity of interchanged NP.

Consider too the restriction on *tough*-movement. Analogous to Lees and Klima's (1963) original suggestion for passive in terms of nonidentical subjects and objects, one would suggest that *tough*-movement cannot operate on an NP of a complement if this is coreferential with the grammatical subject of that complement. This will exclude operation in cases like:

7.(8) *a*   It was tough for me to dress myself.
 b   *Myself was tough for me to dress.

But this proposal also fails to be adequate because of such sentences and nonsentences as:

7.(9) *a*   It was tough for Bill to talk to John about me.
 b   I was tough for Bill to talk to John about.

7.(10) *a*   It was tough for Bill to talk to me about myself.
 b   *Myself was tough for Bill to talk to me about.

In 7.(10) *a* the final NP in the complement and the grammatical subject of the complement are not coreferents and yet *tough*-movement is still not applicable, evidently because of another coreferential NP in the clause.

We thus see that the statement of the observed restrictions as constraints on individual rules is not the direct and straightforward matter it might seem at first. The constraints do not reduce to natural statements in terms of notions like subject and object, nor are they exclusively statable in terms of those NP which must be referred to on independent grounds in the structural descriptions of the rules. These facts support the growing suspicion that the constraints under study are not properly regarded as properties of the individual rules in the first place. This is confirming evidence of the peculiar fact noted at the outset, namely, that these restrictions would require kinds of statements in particular transformational rules of a unique and otherwise unnecessary character. We are thus led to seek some explanation of these peculiar restrictions on the distribution of coreferent NP which does not require them to be stated as idiosyncracies of individual transformational rules.

PART III

THE CROSS-OVER PRINCIPLE

8 CROSS-OVER CONSTRAINTS: INITIAL FORMULATION

We began this discussion with an apparently isolated fact about passive sentences, the absence of a subset of reflexive passives. We have now seen that this apparently idiosyncratic fact is essentially mirrored in several other transformational rules, a suspicious circumstance in itself. Furthermore, and crucially, these rules all have a fundamental feature in common, namely, *they move NP*. Finally, as is especially shown by the examples in Chapter 7, formulating the coreferentiality restrictions on these rules as part of the structure of the rules themselves will not be simple or natural since the restrictions are not representable in terms of such elementary statements as referential nonidentity of subject and object, or of two NP moved by the same rule. All this suggests that the restrictions uncovered are not special features of individual rules but rather the consequences of some general constraint on the operation of NP movement transformations in cases of coreferential nominals.

The correctness of the approach of this vague formulation is supported by the fact that it can directly be made more precise in a way that covers all of the examples presented earlier. In each of the cases where there are unexplained gaps in the output of some NP movement rule it turns out that a certain formal condition is met. Namely, *if the rule had applied, it would have crossed one NP over another with which it is coreferential*. The natural tack at this point is to posit a general linguistic constraint [either universal or English-particular] limiting the applicability of transformations which move NP to those phrase markers to which the relevant rule can apply without crossing one coreferential NP over another. Tentatively then one might propose:

8.(1) *Cross-Over I*[1]

Given a transformation T which moves NP and a phrase marker P to which T is otherwise applicable, T cannot apply to P if the operation of T on P will result in one NP in P crossing another with which it is coreferential.

Let us illustrate the applicability of this constraint to some of the cases considered so far.

What must be explained in particular is why passive does not apply to structures of the form:

8.(2) Schwarz$_i$ shaved Schwarz$_i$.

to yield:

8.(3) Schwarz$_i$ was shaved by Schwarz$_i$.

which will be turned by reflexivization into the unwanted reflexive passive. But Cross-Over I predicts that passive cannot apply to a phrase marker of which 8.(2) is the terminal sequence. This rule contains (at least) two elementary operations, one of which moves the initial NP into the predicate, the other of which moves the predicate NP into grammatical subject position. These are ordered in the way stated. Hence application of passive would mean:

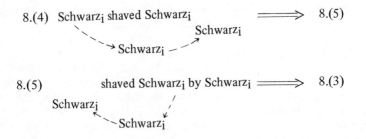

<hr>

[1] Ross (1967a: 130) refers to a cross-over condition stated by me in which it is claimed that:

  (i) No transformation can interchange two coreferential NP.

It is true that I experimented with such a formulation at the very beginning of my investigations of this problem, prompted almost entirely by passive cases. This quickly proved inadequate. However, Ross's claim (1967a: 257) that (i) was the version stated by me at the LaJolla Conference on English Syntax, February 25, 1967, is not historically accurate. (i), which we might refer to as *Cross-Over O*, had been abandoned before then. The version stated there was no doubt garbled, but amounted probably to a modified version of Cross-Over I, modified in the direction of the suggestions in the next chapter.

But in the derivation of 8.(3) from 8.(4) Cross-Over I is violated. Hence, in a theory containing this constraint, passive is not applicable to structures like 8.(4) and reflexive passives are underivable in general even though passive itself contains no statements or restrictions referring to coreferentiality.

Similarly, given:

by first cycle
reflexivization

8.(6) *a*   It was tough (for Tony$_i$ to protect Tony$_i$) ⟹

b   It was tough (for Tony$_i$ to protect himself)

It is clear that Cross-Over I prevents application of *tough*-movement to 8.(6) *b* since the predicate NP would have to cross its subject NP, to which it is referentially identical. Again this is prevented without any special restrictions on the rule itself.

Just so in the case of:

8.(7)   It seems to Tom$_i$ for Tom$_i$ to be a hero ⟹ Tom seems to $\begin{Bmatrix} \text{himself} \\ \text{him} \end{Bmatrix}$ to be a hero

where Cross-Over I prevents application of *it*-replacement since the complement subject would cross the prepositional object to which it is referentially identical. The analogous point can be seen with the rules of psych-movement and *about*-movement with respect to such structures as:

8.(8) *a*   (to) Tom$_i$ is interesting Tom$_i$ ⟹ *Tom is interesting to himself.

b   I wrote to Jane$_i$ about Jane$_i$ ⟹ *I wrote about Jane to herself.

Cross-Over I thus seems to receive a good deal of support from these *elementary cases* under the rules passive, *tough*-movement, *it*-replacement, *psych*-movement and *about*-movement. Even more interestingly, Cross-Over I predicts the facts in Chapter 7, which lie outside any simple formulation of coreferentiality restrictions on particular rules.

For instance, the passive of 8.(9) is ill formed even though passive in this case operates on subject and object which are not coreferential. But observe that nonetheless application of passive in such a case yields crossing (recall passive precedes reflexivization):

8.(9)   I bought a book for I ⟹ *A book was bought for me by myself.

Just so, Cross-Over I blocks the application of *tough*-movement in cases like 8.(10), even though subject of the complement and the NP moved by the rule are not coreferential, because again some crossing of coreferential NP results:

by first cycle
reflexivization

8.(10) *a* It was tough for me to talk to Harry$_i$ about Harry$_i$ $\implies$
       b It was tough for me to talk to Harry$_i$ about himself $\implies$

       c *Himself was tough for me to talk to Harry$_i$ about.

It is these facts, which provide the greatest difficulty for any approach to stating the restrictions *in the structure of particular rules*, that are the strongest evidence so far for Cross-Over I.

9 THE CLAUSE MATE RESTRICTION

Despite its apparent virtues, Cross-Over I is an extremely gross and inadequate formulation and cannot stand as is. This hypothetical universal constraint predicts that no rule, in particular not the several English rules considered so far, can move an NP over another with which it is coreferential. But despite earlier examples, this is obviously a false claim.

Consider for instance the structures:

9.(1) Charley$_i$ criticized the boy who annoyed Charley$_i$.
9.(2) It was tough for Charley$_i$ to visit the boy who Charley$_i$ liked.
9.(3) It seemed to Charley$_i$ for the boy who Charley$_i$ liked to be smart.
9.(4) I talked to Charley$_i$ about the boy who liked Charley$_i$.
9.(5) (to) Charley$_i$ struck the boy who hated Charley$_i$ as dumb.

According to Cross-Over I, passive, *tough*-movement, *it*-replacement, *about*-movement, and *psych*-movement should *not* respectively be applicable to 9.(1)-9.(5). But they *are* and derive respectively in conjunction with pronominalization the perfectly well-formed sentences:

9.(6) The boy who annoyed Charley$_i$ was criticized by him$_i$.
9.(7) The boy who Charley$_i$ liked was tough for him$_i$ to visit.
9.(8) The boy who Charley$_i$ liked seemed smart to him$_i$.

9.(9)   I talked about the boy who liked Charley$_i$ to him$_i$.[1]
9.(10)   The boy who hated Charley$_i$ struck him$_i$ as dumb.

What is the difference between these cases and those which initially motivated Cross-Over I? An approximation to an answer is that in these cases the

---

[1]There is obviously something unacceptable about examples like 9.(9), especially in comparison to their possible alternatives:

(i)   I talked to Charley$_i$ about the boy who liked him$_i$.

This problem, touched on by Langacker (1969) is, I believe, quite independent of the issues under discussion here. Roughly, it has to do with the fact that there are principles determining the acceptability of nonpronoun-pronoun relations in cases of coreference which are independent of crossing restrictions. While I do not know how to state these principles precisely, and could in any event not attempt to do so within the confines of a footnote, let us refer to the pair of NP entering into coreference relations as *antecedent* and *pronoun*. Roughly then, the following principles are relevant for determining acceptability:

(ii) *a*   All else equal, pronominalization is more acceptable with the antecedent on the left.
   b   All else equal, pronominalization is more acceptable if the antecedent is *less embedded* than the pronoun.
   c   All else equal, proniminalization is more acceptable if the antecedent achieves a position to the left of the pronoun without application of any transformational rule involving the movement of NP.

I shall not illustrate (ii) *a*. (ii) *b* is illustrated by the contrast between:

(iii) *a*   I sent Harry$_i$'s book to him$_i$.
   b   I sent Harry$_i$ to his father.

(iii) *a* is much clumsier because it violates (ii) *b*. (ii) *c* is illustrated by:

(iv) *a*   Charley$_i$ visited his$_i$ mother.
   b   Charley$_i$ was visited by his mother.

Here (iv) *b* is much clumsier because it violates (ii) *c*. That is, while the antecedent precedes the pronoun, it does so only by virtue of application of passive. Notice further that it is possible to violate both (ii) *b* and (ii) *c*. An example is:

(v)   Charley$_i$'s mother was visited by him$_i$.

And predictably this is worse than (iii) *a* or (iv) *b*, which violate only one of the principles.
What is particularly amazing about these principles besides their very existence and the mystery of how they fit into grammatical theory, is that there is a hierarchy of valuation of the principles and that different speakers differ on the relative positions. In particular, the present writer and most people I have questioned favor (ii) *c* over (ii) *b*. That is, a sentence which just violates the former will be chosen over one which just violates the latter. Consequently these individuals prefer (vi) *a* over (vi) *b*:

(vi) *a*   I gave Charley$_i$ his$_i$ book.
   b   I gave Charley$_i$'s book to him$_i$.

since although (vi) *a* violates application of *to-I-O-movement* [see Chapter 15] it does not violate (ii) *b*. There are, however, speakers who prefer (vi) *b* to (vi) *a* so that for them the valuation of the principles (ii) *b* and *c* is reversed. Hence not only must such principles somehow be incorporated into grammar, they must also be provided with hierarchical weightings or valuations. The whole matter deserves intensive study.

coreferential NP which cross in the derivation *are separated by a level of embedding.* For illustration, contrast:

9.(11)

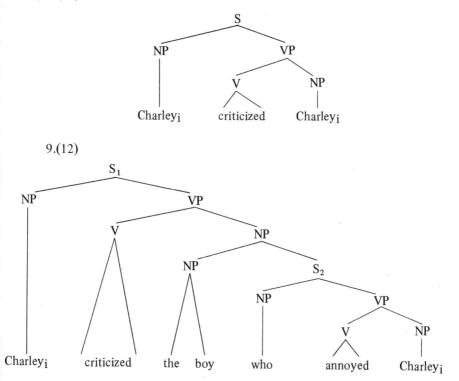

9.(12)

Here a partial bracketing of the schematic inputs to passive in the two cases has been supplied. It can be seen that in 9.(11), where Cross-Over I holds, neither of the two coreferential NP is dominated by an S which does not dominate the other. In other words, every pair of S-subscripted brackets which surrounds one, surrounds the other. Sets of NP that share all clause memberships in this way will, as noted in Chapter 2, be referred to as clause mates.

In 9.(12), on the contrary, the second occurrence of *Charley*$_i$ is inside S_2, which does not contain the first occurrence. The two NP therefore do not share all clause memberships and are not clause mates. Hence they undergo pronominalization, yielding ordinary pronoun forms, and not reflexivization. That is, one finds:

9.(13) *a*   Charley$_i$ criticized himself$_i$.
     b   *Charley$_i$ criticized him$_i$

9.(14) *a*   Charley$_i$ criticized the girl who annoyed him$_i$.
     b   *Charley$_i$ criticized the girl who annoyed himself$_i$.

This follows since, as observed in Chapter 2, reflexive forms are in general a function of the operation of reflexivization on clause mates.

These facts suggest that Cross-Over I be reformulated in such a way that *it only constrains the movement of coreferential NP which are clause mates.* Something like this will turn out to be a necessary condition for part of the formulation of proper cross-over conditions. Before considering this further, however, it would be well to clear the air of any idea that the phenomena illustrated in 9.(1)–9.(5) involve either (a) a left-right asymmetry; or (b) a moving-stationary asymmetry. By (a) I mean that it does not matter whether the more deeply embedded NP is found on the right as in 9.(1)–9.(5) or on the left as in the also perfectly well-formed 9.(20)–9.(24), derived respectively from input structures 9.(15)–9.(19):

9.(15)   The boy who annoyed Charley$_i$ criticized Charley$_i$.

9.(16)   It was tough for the boy who Charley$_i$ liked to visit Charley$_i$.

9.(17)   It seemed to the boy who Charley$_i$ liked for Charley$_i$ to be smart.

9.(18)   I talked to the boy who Charley$_i$ liked about Charley$_i$.

9.(19)   (to) The boy who hated Charley$_i$ struck Charley$_i$ as dumb.

9.(20)   Charley$_i$ was criticized by the boy who annoyed him$_i$.

9.(21)   Charley$_i$ was tough for the boy who he$_i$ liked to visit.

9.(22)   Charley$_i$ seemed to the boy who he$_i$ liked to be smart.

9.(23)   I talked about Charley$_i$ to the boy who he$_i$ liked.

9.(24)   Charley$_i$ struck the boy who hated him$_i$ as dumb.

This shows that it does not matter for these rules whether the more deeply embedded of two coreferential NP starts out on the left or right or ends up there in surface structures. In neither case does Cross-Over I apply.

Similarly, it does not matter whether it is the embedded NP which crosses the unmoving nonembedded one or vice versa. Thus in applying to 9.(2), *tough*-movement moves the embedded NP across the stationary nonembedded one; in applying to 9.(3), *it*-replacement does the same thing. In applying passive to 9.(1), however, the simple NP is moved across the embedded one, as is also the case in the application of *tough*-movement to 9.(16) or *it*-replacement to 9.(17).[2] Hence both of these matters are apparently irrelevant to the proper reformulation of Cross-Over I.

Let us return now to the suggested reformulation that Cross-Over I constrains only the movement of coreferential NP which are clause mates. We might state this as follows:

9.(25)   *Cross-Over II*

Given a transformation T which moves NP and a phrase marker P to which T is otherwise applicable, T cannot apply to P if the operation of T on P will result in one NP in P crossing another with which it is coreferential, where these NP are clause mates.

[2] It can be shown that all four possibilities of moving-stationary complex on left or right occur with no distinctions relevant to the issues at hand.

This appears to be a happy formulation since it clearly covers with no special remarks the cases of passive, *tough*-movement, and *psych*-movement. *About*-movement is also covered in a fairly clear way although here a comment is required. There is evidence [see Chapter 16, Section C] that the *about*-phrase starts out in a different clause than the rest of the sentence. But there is a rule which incorporates it into a different clause and it can be argued directly that this rule precedes the rule of *about*-movement. This incorporation is then the basis for the fact that these phrases end up with reflexive rather than ordinary pronouns in situations of coreferentiality. Hence at the time *about*-movement applies it will correctly come under the proposed clause mate condition of Cross-Over II.

A problem is immediately obvious with *it*-replacement, however. Namely, Cross-Over II with its clause mate condition does not apply to this rule. Recall that *it*-replacement, as formulated by Rosenbaum, takes the grammatical subject of a complement sentence and incorporates it into the main clause. Thus in contexts like:

9.(26) It seems to Harry for me to be sick.

which underly sentences like:

9.(27) I seem to Harry to be sick.

by way of *it*-replacement, the NP *I* and *Harry* which cross in the derivation are not clause mates. Hence Cross-Over II predicts that they can cross even if coreferential. That is, Cross-Over II predicts applicability of *it*-replacement to structures like:

9.(28) It seems to me for me to be sick.

But as observed in Chapter 4, this is impossible in such cases:

9.(29) *a*   *I seem to me to be sick.
      b   *I seem sick to me.
      c   *I seem to myself to be sick.
      d   *I seem sick to myself.

In other words, Cross-Over II, which seems to fit correctly the facts of passive, *tough*-movement, *psych*-movement, and *about*-movement, is inconsistent with the behavior of sentences under *it*-replacement. We can thus infer that either (a) Cross-Over II is wrong, specifically in its clause mate condition, a conclusion that would leave the facts under the four rules which it constrains rightly mysterious; or (b) something is wrong with the analyses of sentences involving *it*-replacement, as formulated by Rosenbaum (1967). We shall find below further evidence that the correct alternative is (b). It is interesting in this regard to note that a reanalysis of constructions involving *it*-replacement has already been proposed by Ross (1967a) and Lakoff (unpublished) on quite independent grounds. We will analyze the question in greater detail in Chapter 22, after further matters of relevance have been investigated. For the present, it must be borne in mind that either Cross-Over II is wrong or *it*-replacement must be revised in some way.

Incidentally, it should not be surprising that in attempting to formulate a condition on the movement of coreferent NP we should run across cases where previously formulated rules must be altered and revised. Remember that our knowledge of English is highly fragmentary and tentative and that past analyses, even apparently highly motivated ones, are constantly subject to modification or even rejection. This makes the search for general principles more difficult, but also more interesting. It reveals the constant interplay between the analysis of particular factual fragments in individual languages and the attempt to find general principles of grammar.

10 WH-Q-MOVEMENT AND WH-REL-MOVEMENT

A. REMARKS

Independent of any doubts about the tenability of the clause mate restriction with respect to rules already considered, cross-over phenomena are apparently complex in ways not fully captured by the reformulation of Cross-Over I in terms of co-occurrence of NP within the same minimal clause. This complexity can be seen in facts relating to rules of NP movement not yet investigated.

There are two rules, here called *Wh-Q-movement* and *Wh-Rel-movement*, that account for the special front-of-clause positioning of NP marked with the *wh* prefix [which yields morphological forms *who, what, when, where, why, how, which, that, whose*]. The first of these rules operates in question and question-like clauses; the second operates in relatives, both restrictive and appositive. Since the beginning of transformational studies, attempts have been made by many, including the present author,[1] to subsume these processes under one rule. This is quite understandable in view of their many compelling similarities. At the same time, there are some clear differences. For instance:

10.(1) *a* Charley made made a claim I discovered evidence for *wh* claim[2] *Wh-Rel*-movement

⟹

 b Charley made a claim which I discovered evidence for.
 c Charley made a claim for which I discovered evidence.
 d Charley made a claim evidence for which I discovered.

---

[1] See Katz and Postal (1964:104).

[2] This representation of the input to the rule is schematic and is not to be taken as making precise claims about the deep structure of relative phrases. In particular, I would not claim any longer [Katz and Postal (1964:129)] that the *wh* prefix is found in the underlying forms. On the contrary, I would insist that it is not and that this *wh*-marking is a function of some kind of pronominalization marking.

$Wh\text{-}Q$-movement

10.(2) *a*   Charley discovered evidence for *wh* claim =============⟹

   b   What claim did Charley discover evidence for?

   c   For what claim did Charley discover evidence?

   d   *Evidence for what claim did Charley discover?

Hence movement of the whole complex NP in such cases to forward position is a possibility in relatives, but not in question clauses. These and other facts provide some basis for assuming that there are *at least*[3] two rules, not one, involved in the movement of *wh*-clauses in English, an assumption that will be maintained from this point on.[4]

---

[3] Another possible rule is that for *wh* exclamations, which plays a role in relating such forms as:

  (i)   Harry is such an idiot!
  (ii)   What an idiot Harry is!

This rule seems to me to differ both from the rule for relatives and the rule for questions in certain ways; in particular, it does not seem natural for this rule to pull NP out of embedded clauses, while this is permitted under the other two:

  (iii) *What an idiot I thought Tom was!
  (iv)   What did you think Tom was?
  (v)   The thing you thought Tom ate

However, this may not be due to properties of the movement rule but to the source expressions since examples like:

  (vi)   I thought Tom was such an idiot!

which would reveal the underlying structure of examples like (iii), seem of dubious grammaticality.

[4] Ross (1967a:481⁻482) discusses the assumption that *Wh-Q*-movement and *Wh-Rel*-movement are the same rule, which he regards as dubious. He observes as an argument *against* this assumption the fact that the subject NP of clauses introduced by expletive *there* can undergo the former but not the latter:

  (i) *a*   There were some men in the garage.
      b   *The men who there were in the garage
      c   *Some men who there were in the garage
  (ii) *a* There were some dogs in the kennel.
      b   Which dogs were there in the kennel?
      c   Which dogs there were in the kennel is unknown.

Ross also observes that the morphological parallels between questions and relatives, while pervasive, are far from perfect. Differences involving *which*, *what*, and *that* are well known. Ross also points out, however, the less publicized fact that *whose* is restricted to human NP in questions but not in relatives:

  (iii) *a* Whose mother did you talk to?
       b   The boy whose mother you talked to
  (iv) *a*   *Whose fifth line has an error in it?
       b   The proof whose fifth line has an error in it

Notice too that manner *how* is usable in questions but not relatives:

  (v) *a*   How did you manage to start the engine?
      b   *The way how I managed to start the engine

It thus seems that the safest assumption is that there are two different, formally similar rules.

Question sentences involve many deep and unsolved problems. Fortunately, most of these problems are irrelevant to our present rather limited concerns. We can start by observing that there are *questioned NP* [that is, those marked with *wh*, which must be expanded in the answer[5]]that occur in sentences *containing other NP with which they are coreferential.* For instance:

10.(3) *a* Who shaved himself?
     b Who does Mary think hurt himself?
     c Who did the police accuse of trying to enrich himself?

In Katz and Postal (1964:116–117) it is observed that question sentences involve as a fundamental component a *presupposition.* This is a semantic notion defining just what the user of a sentence is committed to as the *assertion*[6] underlying the question. Using arbitrary letters to indicate nominals, we know that the assertions underlying 10.(3) are respectively representable roughly as:

10.(4) *a* X shaved X.
     b Y (Mary) thinks X hurt X.
     c Z (the police) accused X of X trying X to enrich X.

In each case, then, the question in 10.(3) asks for identification of the entity designated by X. It is clear therefore that the nominal which is questioned enters into relations of coreferentiality with other nominals in the same question sentence.

It can be observed that in the sentences of 10.(3), which manifest coreferentiality between a questioned NP and some other NP, the front position of each *wh*-marked NP has been achieved *without the crossing of any NP with which it is coreferential.* That is, in 10.(3) *a* the initial *wh*-NP is the subject and it moves to clause initial position by moving over no intermediate NP, since subject NP are clause initial in most cases in English. In 10.(3) *b*, the questioned NP is the subject of the embedded clause representable as *wh-X hurt X.* Hence this nominal reaches initial position in the sentence as a whole by crossing only the NP *Mary*, with which it is not coreferential. In 10.(3) *c*, the *wh*-marked NP is the subject of the verb *trying* of the embedded clause. That is, the structure at the point where *Wh-Q*-movement would apply is something like: *the police accused wh-X of X trying to enrich X.* Here the *wh*-marked NP reaches front position by crossing only the nominal *the police.* And again these are not coreferents.

------

[5] See Katz and Postal (1964:113-120) for an introductory discussion of the question-answer relation. Also Katz (to appear).

[6] It is not usual to think of questions as involving assertions. But I would insist that the presupposition of every question is in fact an assertion. Thus (ii) is just as much a contradiction as (i).

    (i)   Something is on the table and nothing is on the table.
    (ii)   Although nothing is on the table, what is on the table?

This shows that the clause *what is on the table* embodies an assertion incompatible with that of the *although*-clause.

This points up the fact that there is a hitherto unexplained property of the set of sentences containing questioned NP. There are no analogues to the sentences of 10.(3) of the form:

10.(5) *a* *Who$_i$ did himself$_i$ shave?
  b *Who$_i$ did he$_i$ shave?
  c *Who$_i$ does Mary think he$_i$ hurt?
  d *Who$_i$ did the police accuse him$_i$ of trying to enrich?

Why are there no sentences like 10.(5), which are paraphrases of the corresponding examples of 10.(3)? The difference between 10.(5) and 10.(3) is exactly that assuming structures of the form $X.......X$, where one of the occurrences of X is questioned (marked with *wh*), the 10.(3) sentences have the *wh* on the leftmost occurrence of X while those of 10.(5) have it on some other occurrence, not the leftmost. The difference in well-formedness of 10.(3) and 10.(5) illustrates the general fact of English that the latter situation is not permitted. Given a question with multiple occurrences of nominals designating the same entity, the question marker must go on the *leftmost*, where *leftmost* is defined not on surface structures, but on the structures at the point where *Wh-Q-movement* applies. All other occurrences must be pronominalized or reflexivized.

B. ORDERING ARGUMENTS

One explanation for these facts, which are not a matter of logic or a priori necessity of any known type, might be an ordering argument to the effect that both reflexivization and pronominalization *precede Who-Q*-movement. It might then be argued that application of either of the former two rules destroys the environment for the latter, possibly by causing deletion of the *wh*-prefix or [+Wh] feature marking. But this explanation is demonstrably insufficient since, although it can be strongly argued that application of reflexivization precedes that of *Wh-Q*-movement, the ordering of pronominalization and *Wh-Q*-movement must be such that the latter applies first. This conclusion follows from the left-right argument.

 Consider first reflexivization and *Wh-Q*-movement. A good deal of evidence shows that reflexivization must always apply to a clause *before Wh-Q-movement*. One argument for this is the following. There are grounds for assuming reflexivization is a cyclical rule [see Chapter 16, Section F], but we can easily show that *Wh-Q*-movement [and identically *Wh-Rel*-movement] are either postcyclical rules [rules which can only apply after the last cyclical rule has applied for the last time] or last cyclical rules [rules which can only apply during the final cycle of each derivation, even though they may apply on this cycle before other cyclical rules]. There is a variety of evidence for the last cyclical or postcyclical character of *Wh-Q*-movement and *Wh-Rel*-movement. Here I will give only one type, which might be called the *preposition dangle argument*.

We shall illustrate with *Wh-Q*-movement. Consider a structure like:

10.(6)

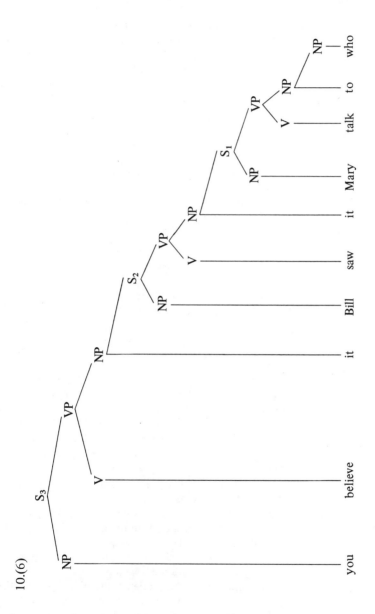

We wish to argue that *Wh-Q*-movement is not a cyclical rule. If it were, in applying to 10.(6), the *wh*-NP would be moved to the front of S_1 on the first cycle, to the front of S_2 on the second, and to the front of the whole sentence, S_3, only on the third or final cycle. If *Wh-Q*-movement is last cyclical or postcyclical, as is claimed here, the *wh*-NP, *who*, will move to the front of S_3 in a single swoop. The correctness of the latter assumption is seen from consideration of the behavior of prepositions directly preceding *wh*-marked NP. Under most conditions, these may optionally be moved forward with the *wh*-NP:

10.(7) *a*   Who were you talking to?
     b   To whom were you talking?

Ergo, under the cyclical application assumption for *Wh-Q*-movement, a preposition could be moved with an NP on one cycle, but then left behind on the next, dangling somewhere in the middle of the sentence. With respect to 10.(6) in particular, this assumption predicts that it should be possible to have all of the following outputs:

10.(8) *a*   Who do you believe Bill saw Mary talk to?
     b   To whom do you believe Bill saw Mary talk?
     c   *Who do you believe Bill saw to Mary talk?
     d   *Who do you believe to Bill saw Mary talk?

10.(8) *a* results not from taking the option of moving the preposition on the first cycle, which then automatically prevents its movement on any subsequent cycle. 10.(8) *b* results from taking the option of moving the preposition on each of the three cycles of application. 10.(8) *c* would result from taking the option of moving the preposition on the first cycle, but not on the second, preventing any movement of it on the third. 10.(8) *d* would result from moving the preposition on the first cycle, and on the second, but not taking the option on the third. Since the latter two examples are obviously severely illformed, the cyclical assumption for *Wh-Q*-movement is strongly disconfirmed.

Observe, on the other hand, that having *Wh-Q*-movement last or post cyclical means that each *wh*-marked NP moves exactly once under this rule. This assumption predicts therefore that the preposition associated with a *wh*-marked NP either remains in its original position or moves all the way to the front with the *wh*-marked NP. But, as illustrated by 10.(8), this is exactly right. Hence the conclusion that *Wh-Q*-movement is last cyclical or postcyclical is well supported both positively and negatively by the preposition dangle argument.

However, even under the assumption that reflexivization is cyclical, the result just achieved does not show that reflexivization always applies to a clause before *Wh-Q*-movement. If, as is possible even with what was shown,

Wh-Q-movement is last cyclical, it might precede reflexivization. That is, we might have the grammar:

10.(9) *Wh-Q-movement*   last cyclical
        Reflexivization   all cyclical

That this ordering is, however, *incorrect* is demonstrated by the following argument, which shows that the ordering of rules is:

10.(10) *a* *Reflexivization*   all cyclical [this is assumed, not shown by
                                           this argument]
       b *Wh-Q-movement*   last cyclical [again assumed]

The argument depends on the scope of reflexivization. Recall that this rule must be stated in such a way as to apply only to clause mates. This does not refer to deep structure clause mates but rather to those NP which are clause mates at the point where reflexivization applies. Consider then sentences like:

10.(11) *a*   You$_i$ saw someone stab you$_i$.
       b   *You$_i$ saw someone stab yourself$_i$.

We observe that reflexivization is inapplicable here, a fact which follows, I claim, from the existence of a remote structure rather like the following at the point where reflexivization becomes applicable:

10.(12)

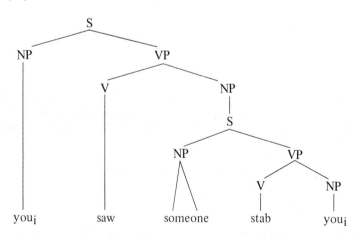

In this structure, the two occurrences of *you* are not clause mates, so that reflexivization is blocked, as is required. Suppose, however, the order of rules were, contra our claim, as in 10.(9) and not as in 10.(10), and suppose that the subject of *stab* were a *wh*-form, that is, suppose we had the structure:

10.(13)

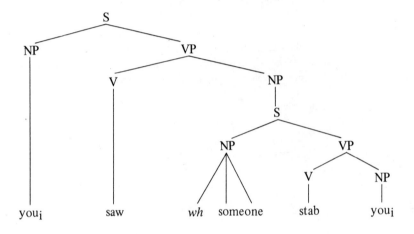

If now *Wh-Q*-movement applies to this structure before reflexivization applies on the second cycle, the grammar predicts that reflexivization is applicable on the second cycle. That is, it predicts falsely 10.(14) *a* instead of the correct 10.(14) *b*:

10.(14) *a*   *Who did you$_i$ see stab yourself$_i$?
    b   Who did you$_i$ see stab you$_i$?

The grammar predicts this for the following reason. As Ross (1967a, 1967c) has argued convincingly, there is a general principle of grammar, *the S-pruning-convention*, which has the effect of *pruning or eliminating any embedded S-node which does not branch*. That is, unary branching S-nodes are eliminated. Therefore, when *Wh-Q*-movement applies to 10.(13), ripping out the subject of *stab*, it causes the pruning of the S-node of the embedded sentence. This means that the structure which results from this rule application is essentially:

10.(15)

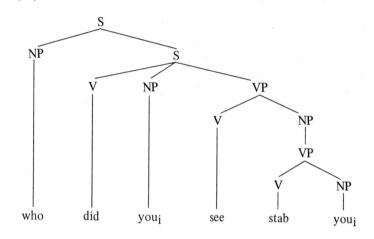

But this structure meets the clause mate condition for reflexivization. Hence the order of rules in 10.(9), together with the *S-pruning*-convention, wrongly predicts the possibility of reflexivization in these cases. To prevent reflexivization one requires the order in 10.(10). Given the latter order, reflexivization is tested for application in such derivations at the stage represented by 10.(13). And it is there blocked by the failure of the clause mate condition.

Hence these arguments show with some strength that reflexivization does in fact precede *Wh-Q*-movement, and identical arguments show the same thing for the ordering of *Wh-Rel*-movement. With these facts concerning ordering established, we can return to the consideration of the ill-formed sequences of 10.(5), repeated here for convenience:

10.(5) *a*   *Who$_i$ did himself$_i$ shave?
   b   *Who$_i$ did he$_i$ shave?
   c   *Who$_i$ does Mary think he$_i$ hurt?
   d   *Who$_i$ did the police accuse him$_i$ of trying to enrich?

We can now explain the ill-formedness of 10.(5) *a* with no further special assumptions or conditions.[7] Given the fact that reflexivization and *Wh-Q*-movement are ordered as in 10.(10), 10.(5) *a* could only be derived if reflexivization applied right-to-left, which it never does. That is, since the

---

[7] 10.(5) *b* is then to be explained by the obligatoriness of reflexivization on coreferent NP meeting its conditions. That is, 10.(5) *b* is impossible for the same reason as:

   (i)   *He$_i$ likes him$_i$.

question rule applies after reflexivization, 10.(5) *a* could only be derived by the operation of *Wh-Q*-movement on a structure like:

10.(16)   Himself shaved who?

But such structures are underivable by a left-to-right operating rule of reflexivization. Hence ordering is sufficient to explain 10.(5) *a*.

Consider then 10.(5) *c* and *d*. Here reflexivization is irrelevant since under no conditions are the coreferents clause mates. Hence the relevant rule is pronominalization. The question is, therefore, whether these cases can be explained analogously to 10.(5) *a* by arguing that the order of rules is:

10.(17)   Pronominalization
              Wh-Q-movement

That this is impossible is shown by the left-right argument of Chapter 2, which reveals clearly that the order of rules is necessarily:

10.(18)   *Wh-Q*-movement
              pronominalization

The argument is illustrated by such examples as:

10.(19) *a*   [Which of the men who hated Charley$_i$] did he$_i$ attack
        b   [Which of the men who hated him$_i$] did Charley$_i$ attack

In each case the bracketed NP achieves front position by virtue of the operation of *Wh-Q*-movement. The fact that these environments permit backwards pronominalization follows from the backwards condition if pronominalization applies on structures which are the output of *Wh-Q*-movement, that is:

10.(20)   Which of the men who hated Charley$_i$ did Charley$_i$ attack

But the permitted backwards pronominalization is completely anomalous if it is defined, as required by the ordering in 10.(17), on the structure before application of *Wh-Q*-movement, namely:

10.(21)   Charley$_i$ attacked *wh* some of the men who hated Charley$_i$

Notice that this kind of structure does not permit backwards pronominalization:

10.(22) *a*   Charley$_i$ attacked some of the men who hated him$_i$.
        b   *He$_i$ attacked some of the men who hated Charley$_i$.

This shows clearly that the order of rules is given by 10.(18) and not by 10.(17).

C. CONSEQUENCES

From the validity of 10.(18), it follows that there is no ordering explanation for 10.(5) c and d, as there is for 10.(5) a. Taking this conclusion together with what was established in earlier chapters with respect to rules like *passive*, it is natural to consider some kind of cross-over explanation for such examples. This approach would seem attractive since the *wh*-rules both move NP to the left. It follows therefore that the contrast between the ill-formedness of 10.(5) c and d, and the well-formedness of the parallel examples in 10.(3) correlates with the fact that in the former the operation of *Wh-Q*-movement crosses coreferents but in the latter its operation has no such effect. One might therefore suggest that these facts are a function of cross-over restrictions.

This suggestion may be correct, which would permit the addition of *Wh-Q*-movement to the list of rules subject to such restrictions. But such an addition is too simple. For *Wh-Q*-movement is apparently subject to cross-over constraints of a much more severe type than any of the rules previously considered. First of all, the clause mate formulation clearly does not limit the restriction on crossing of coreferents by this rule:

> 10.(21) a She$_i$ knows that Bill hates her$_i$.
> b Who$_i$ knows that Bill hates her$_i$?
> c *Who$_i$ does she$_i$ know that Bill hates?[8]

Here no question exists in which a *wh*-NP is moved out of a *that*-clause across a coreferential NP in the main clause.
Similarly:

> 10.(22) a The bird who she$_i$ found left her$_i$.
> b *Who$_i$ did the bird who she$_i$ found leave?

> 10.(23) a You talked to the boy who she$_i$ liked about her$_i$.
> b *Who$_i$ did you talk to the boy who she$_i$ liked about?
> c *About whom$_i$ did you talk to the boy who she$_i$ liked?[9]

Hence while the rules passive, *tough*-movement, *about*-movement, and *psych*-movement permit crossing of coreferent NP that are not clause mates, *Wh-Q*-movement, for at the moment unknown reasons, not only does not cross

---

[8] The *that*-clause here is of course a complement and not a moved relative phrase, that is, 10.(21) c is not intended as a paraphrase of:

 (i)   *Who$_i$ does she$_i$ know who Bill hates?

[9] The ungrammaticality of sentences like:

 (i)   *Who did you talk to the boy who liked about her?

has nothing to do with coreferentiality but rather with general constraints on the movement of NP, as discussed in Ross (1967a). In particular, one constraint is that nothing may be moved out of a relative clause.

clause mates but also does not cross certain other coreferential NP that are *not* clause mates.

The question immediately arises whether one can say simply that *Wh-Q*-movement does not permit any coreferential NP to cross regardless of what structural conditions their positions meet. The answer is negative.

10.(24) *a* Charley$_i$ visited some of the men who criticized him$_i$.
      b [Which of the men who criticized Charley$_i$] did he$_i$ visit?
      c [Which of the men who criticized him$_i$] did Charley$_i$ visit?

The perfectly well-formed character of the *b* and *c* sentences, formed by a crossing of the complex NP over the simple NP subject, reveals that the crossing restrictions for *Wh-Q*-movement are more structured than a simple ban on "path" intersections for all coreferents.

Before attempting to provide some account of these facts and their contrast with the behavior of structures under previously discussed rules, it would be well to document their generality. First of all, they are true not only of independent question sentences derived with *Wh-Q*-movement but also of embedded question clauses. This will be illustrated by providing the appropriate analogues of earlier independent question clauses:

10.(25) *a* I know who shaved himself.
      b I know who Charley thinks hurt himself.
      c I know who the police accused of trying to enrich himself.

10.(26) *a* *I know who$_i$ himself$_i$ shaved.
      b *I know who$_i$ he$_i$ shaved.
      c *I know who$_i$ Charley thinks he$_i$ hurt.
      d *I know who$_i$ the police accused him$_i$ of trying to enrich.

10.(27) *a* I found out she$_i$ knows that Bill hates her$_i$.
      b I found out who$_i$ knows that Bill hates her$_i$.
      c *I found out who$_i$ she$_i$ knows that Bill hates.

10.(28) *a* The bird who she$_i$ found left her$_i$.
      b *I found out who$_i$ the bird who she$_i$ found left.

10.(29) *a* You talked to the boy who she$_i$ liked about her$_i$.
      b *I found out who$_i$ you talked to the boy she$_i$ liked about.
      c *I found out about whom$_i$ you talked to the boy she$_i$ liked.

10.(30) *a* I know Charley$_i$ visited some of the men who criticized him$_i$.
      b I know which of the men who criticized Charley$_i$ he$_i$ visited.
      c I know which of the men who criticized him$_i$ Charley$_i$ visited.

Secondly, it can be shown that exactly the same restrictions govern the rule of *Wh-Rel*-movement, in its application to both restrictive and appositive relative clauses, that is, in structures like 10.(31) *a* and 10.(31) *b* respectively:

10.(31) *a* The Harry Schwarz who I know is a German.
      b Harry Schwarz, who I know, is a German.

As before we can illustrate with the analogues of question sentences given earlier. We shall consistently use restrictive relatives for illustration.

10.(32) a The man who shaved himself
        b The man who Charley thinks hurt himself
        c The man who the police accused of trying to enrich himself

10.(33) a *The one$_i$ who himself$_i$ shaved
        b *The one$_i$ who he$_i$ shaved
        c *The one$_i$ who Charley thinks he$_i$ hurt
        d *The one$_i$ who the police accused him$_i$ of trying to enrich

10.(34) a The one$_i$ who knows that Bill hates her$_i$
        b *The one$_i$ who she$_i$ knows Bill hates

10.(35) a The bird who she$_i$ found left her$_i$.
        b *The one$_i$ who the bird who she$_i$ found left.

10.(36) a You talked to the boy who she$_i$ liked about her$_i$.
        b *The one$_i$ who you talked to the boy she$_i$ liked about
        c *The one$_i$ about whom you talked to the boy she$_i$ liked

In summing up our findings so far, let us refer to all rules like the five discussed in previous chapters as *A-movements* and those like the two brought up in this chapter as *B-movements*. One sees that there is a general contrast in cross-over behavior between these two classes of rules. *A*-movements appear to be constrained by coreferentiality limitations only in the case of clause mates; *B*-movements seem to be governed by more severe restrictions. Thus far we have no precise characterization of the differences, no explanation of why they should exist, in fact not even any characterization beyond lists of the two types of rules. It is clear, however, that even if the clause mate reformulation of Cross-Over I is adequate for *A*-movements, it fails for *B*-movements and thus such a statement is not as it stands a possible formulation of the correct principle for the general phenomenon.

D. THE NONCYCLICAL CHARACTER OF PRONOMINALIZATION

In Section B of this chapter it was shown that the order of rules must be:

10.(37) *Wh-Q*-movement, *Wh-Rel*-movement
         Pronominalization

and that *Wh-Q*-movement and *Wh-Rel*-movement cannot be cyclical. These conclusions permit us to show rather directly that pronominalization cannot be cyclical. Consider sentences like:

10.(38) a Which of the men who hated Harry$_i$ did he$_i$ talk to?
        b Which of the men who hated him$_i$ did Harry$_i$ talk to?

The underlying structure of these is one in which the option of backwards pronominalization is possible, and realized, in *b*. This follows from the backwards condition if the *wh*-nominal in such examples has been moved forward before pronominalization applies, that is, it follows from this condition given the ordering of 10.(37). No difficulties appear in examples like 10.(38), where there are only two cycles and pronominalization could only become applicable on the last.

   Consider, however, what will happen under the assumption that pronominalization is cyclical when rules are applied to a structure like:

10.(39)

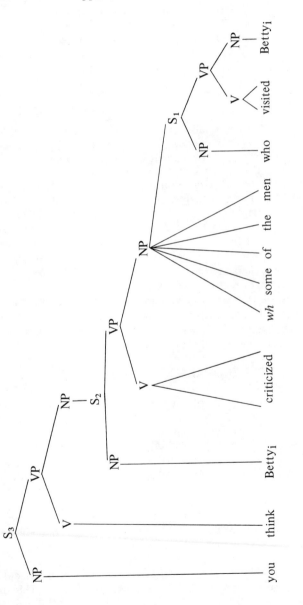

Here nothing of interest will happen on the S_1 cycle. On S_2, however, there are two coreferent occurrences of Betty$_i$. However, the one on the left is not in a subordinate clause [with respect to the structure S_2].[10] Consequently, according to the backwards condition, only forwards pronominalization is possible here and must obligatorily take place. Wh-Q-movement, even though earlier in the ordering of rules than pronominalization, cannot yet have applied since it is either last cyclical or postcyclical and the last cycle has not yet been reached. Therefore the object of visited is turned into an anaphoric proniminal and when the wh-movement finally takes place the grammar will derive from the structure 10.(39) only the sentence:

10.(40)   Which of the men who visited her$_i$ do you think Betty$_i$ criticized?

This is a fine sentence. But the trouble is that 10.(39) has an equally fine alternative realization, namely:

10.(41)   Which of the men who visited Betty$_i$ do you think she$_i$ criticized?

But this cannot be derived by the grammar 10.(37) under the assumption that pronominalization is cyclical.

To derive 10.(41) it is necessary that pronominalization not apply on the S_2 cycle and then apply on S_3 after Wh-Q-movement has, as in examples like 10.(38). But there is no way to prevent pronominalization from applying on S_2 under the cyclical assumption, since the meaning of cyclical application is exactly application on every applicable cycle in succession.

It follows then that pronominalization is *not* a cyclical rule and that some other explanation must be found for the data which originally motivated Ross's (1967b) claim that this rule is cyclical. This question is pursued by Lakoff (to appear), who provides much additional evidence of the noncyclical character of pronominalization. Another argument to the same effect is provided in Chapter 20, footnote 3.

---

[10]Examples like this show, of course, that the notion *subordinate clause* must be defined *relatively*. With respect to the whole sentence, S_3, the subject of the verb *criticized* is in a subordinate clause. But with respect to just the substructure S_2 it is in a main clause. Hence the notion must be defined along the lines: S_a is subordinate to S_b with respect to S_c.

11 ROSS'S SUGGESTION

One suggested modification of both Cross-Over I and Cross-Over II is due to John Ross. He observes (1967a:132) that it is important whether or not the NP being moved by some transformation is "mentioned" in the structure index of that transformation. This is not a property referred to in either Cross-Over I or Cross-Over II.

Ross does not provide any extensive discussion of the motivation for reference to whether or not the NP being moved is "mentioned" in the relevant transformation. But a basis for this idea seems initially clear. Consider the following possible inputs to passive:

11.(1) a (Bill$_i$) criticized (Bill$_i$)

b (Bill$_i$) criticized (the girl who liked Bill$_i$)

c (the girl who liked Bill$_i$) criticized (Bill$_i$)

The fact is, as seen earlier, that passive cannot apply to the a form although its application to b and c is permitted. Yet under the action of passive in both b and c cases, an NP$_i$ must cross another one to which it is coreferential. Our initial approach to differentiating 11.(1) a from b and c was to refer to the fact that in a the two occurences of *Bill*$_i$ are clause mates, while in b and c they are not. But it might be argued instead that reference to the structure index is what is relevant.

Very roughly, the index of passive is given by something like:

11.(2) X, NP, Verb, NP, Y
      1 2   3   4 5

In 11.(1) those NP which correspond to the NP symbols in this structure index are circled. It can be seen that only in the a case are the circled NP themselves coreferential. Assuming then a definition of the notion "circled NP with respect to rule T" in the intuitively obvious sense, one might propose a formulation of the cross-over principle such that:

11.(3)   "Circled" coreferential NP may not be crossed by the rule with respect to which they are "circled."

This formulation, like Cross-Over II with its reference to the clause mate condition, correctly predicts that passive may apply to 11.(1) b and c but not to 11.(1) a.[1]

Ross, however, does not suggest a principle like 11.(3), which, as we will see, is not adequate for the cases under *Wh-Q*-movement and *Wh-Rel*-movement. Instead, based on certain instances relevant to *these* rules, he proposes what is intended as a much stronger condition, namely:

11.(4) = Ross's (4.30)

> No NP mentioned in the structure index of a transformation may be reordered by that rule in such a way as to cross over a coreferential NP.

This formulation is explicitly motivated by examples like:

11.(5) = Ross's (4.29)

> *The pudding$_i$ (which) the man who ordered it$_i$ said would be tasty was a horror show.

Here the circled *which*, whose underlying structure is coreferential with that of the object of *ordered, it$_i$*, has crossed the latter under *Wh-Rel*-movement, with resulting violation. While Cross-Over II predicts that 11.(5) should be well formed, since the relevant coreferent NP are not clause mates, as does 11.(3) since the *it$_i$* of the relative corresponds to no NP mentioned in the rule *Wh-Rel*-movement, the intention of 11.(4) blocks it since the NP that ends up as *which* in 11.(5) is exactly the one "mentioned" in the structure index of *Wh-Rel*-movement.

I say here "the intention of 11.(4) blocks it" since, although intuitively clear, 11.(4) is not given precisely. Taken literally, 11.(4) is vacuous and

---

[1]Observe, however, that 11.(3) does not correctly predict the inapplicability of *tough*-movement to structures like:

(i) It was tough for Tony$_i$ to shave himself$_i$.

since only the final NP corresponds to one mentioned in the structure index of *tough*-movement. The difference is that passive mentions two NP; *tough*-movement, only one. A similar remark could be made for *it*-replacement, which is like *tough*-movement in this regard. Hence 11.(3) is immediately seen to be inadequate, even with respect to covering the class of *A*-movements. This is of no real importance since we quickly pass on to more complex and sophisticated versions of the idea under discussion.

excludes no crossing whatever. It speaks of moving an NP that is mentioned in the structure index of a transformation. But literally speaking no *particular* NP occurrence is mentioned in any transformation. However, this is a minor technical difficulty and 11.(4) can easily be reformulated more precisely incorporating Ross's suggestion. It is necessary only to define briefly Chomsky's (1961) notion of *proper analysis.*

Very roughly, the proper analysis of a phrase marker P with respect to a fixed transformation T is that segmentation of P which is such that it meets the condition defined by the structure index of T. That is, the proper analysis defines the fragmentation of P into the successive parts corresponding to the analysis condition in the structure index. If the structure index of T has n terms, then P must be divisible into n segments, each meeting the condition of the corresponding term in the structure index. Hence a phrase marker P being analyzed with respect to the transformation whose structure index is 11.(2) must be segmentable into five segments such that the first is anything, the second an NP, the third a verb, the fourth an NP, and the fifth anything.[2] If this can be done, the phrase marker may undergo the rule; if not, it cannot.

With this rather crude account of proper analysis in mind, we can reformulate 11.(4) more literally as follows:

11.(6) *Cross-Over III*

A transformation T with a structure index whose ith term is NP does not apply to any phrase marker P whose proper analysis with respect to T is such that its ith term is an NP, NP_j, where T is such that it reorders proper analyses with respect to it in such a way that, in applying to P, NP_j must cross some other NP in P, NP_k, and NP_j and NP_k are coreferential.

However, Ross notes that his version of Cross-Over III is too strong since it is incompatible with the existence of sentences like:

11.(7) = Ross's (4.32) *b*

That gangsters had bribed him$_i$ was denied by the sheriff$_i$.

---

[2] This account is a little misleading in that it fails to indicate that severe, hopefully universal, constraints must be placed on the way variables determine the proper analyses of phrase markers. For instance, if nothing is said about this, a structure like:

(i)   I met Johnson's brother.

could be analyzed into terms with respect to 11.(2) as follows:

(ii) $\emptyset$, I, met, Johnson's, $\emptyset$
       1   2   3   4   5

When passive applies this would yield the impossible:

(iii) *Johnson's was met brother by me.

No published statement of the appropriate conditions exists, although the problem has been studied by Ross. See Chapter 18.

Such sentences are the direct analogues of our 11.(1) *b*. Ross does not note that 11.(4), and hence its more precise version 11.(6), is also incompatible with all analogues of 11.(1) *c*. In both of these respects, then, 11.(4)–11.(6) are too strong, that is, exclude the application of rules in cases where they are in fact applicable.

Before throwing out Ross's suggestion too hastily, one should note that the suggestion to permit reference to whether an NP being moved is one "mentioned" in the structure index of the rule moving it receives further support from examples not considered by him. In particular, reference to this property accounts for the contrast between:

11.(8) *a* (What claims which referred to Bill$_j$) did he$_j$ deny?

   b * (Whom$_i$) were claims which referred to him$_i$ denied by?

   c *By (whom$_i$) were claims which referred to him$_i$ denied?

In 11.(8) *a* the NP which is "mentioned" in the structure index of *Wh-Q* movement is circled. This NP is the large one with *claims* as its head and it is not coreferential with any NP over which it moves, in particular, not with the subject of *deny*. In 11.(8) *b* and *c*, however, the NP "mentioned" in the rule is that underlying *whom$_i$*, and this does cross one with which it is coreferential when *Wh-Q*-movement applies. Hence the crucial feature of Cross-Over III suggested by Ross predicts this otherwise puzzling difference.

Nonetheless we have seen that Cross-Over III is inadequate since it is too strong. And this is hardly surprising at this point. Cross-Over III is perfectly general and makes no distinction between *A*-movements and *B*-movements. But it has been shown that the crossing constraints for these two types of movement rule are in contrast. Hence Cross-Over III seems to work for *B*-movements but is too strong in falsely preventing the operation of *A*-movements on a whole set of structures to which they in fact apply. Cross-Over II, on the other hand, works for *A*-movements but is too weak in the case of *B* movements, allowing the operation of these in a whole class of cases where this is in reality blocked. Evidently some reformulation is required which distinguishes the two classes of rules and associates the not entirely identical restrictions with each.

12 APPARENT COUNTEREXAMPLES TO ROSS'S "MENTION" PROPOSAL

A. THE DIFFICULTY

There are significant examples not considered by Ross which seem to show that his proposal about whether a moved NP is the one "mentioned" in the transformation doing the moving cannot stand, even for B-movements. Among these are genitive questions like:

$\quad$ 12.(1) a $\quad$ * (Whose$_i$ father) did he$_i$ disagree with?

$\quad\quad\quad\quad b$ $\quad$ * (Whose$_i$ mother's brother) did she$_i$ marry?

Here in each case it is the entire circled NP which has been moved by the rule of *Wh-Q*-movement out of the predicate. These "large" NP are, however, not coreferential with the NP they cross. Hence, on the assumption that it is these "large" NP which correspond to the NP symbol mentioned in this rule, Ross's proposal is not only *too strong* with respect to the behavior of A-movements, but also *too weak* with respect to the behavior of B-movements. That is, it does not block applications yielding structures like 12.(1), when these must be blocked.

$\quad$ The apparent difficulty is illustrated in 12.(1) only for *Wh-Q*-movement. But it is equally manifest with *Wh-Rel*-movement:

$\quad$ 12.(2) a $\quad$ The man whose$_i$ son loved him$_i$
$\quad\quad\quad\quad b$ $\quad$ *The man whose$_i$ son he$_i$ loved
$\quad\quad\quad\quad c$ $\quad$ The man who$_i$ loved his$_i$ son

Moreover, it is not restricted to genitive constructions:

$\quad$ 12.(3) a $\quad$ The girl who hated him$_i$ spread rumors about the man$_i$.
$\quad\quad\quad\quad b$ $\quad$ *The man$_i$ about whom$_i$ the girl who hated him$_i$ spread rumors.
$\quad\quad\quad\quad c$ $\quad$ *The man$_i$ whom$_i$ the girl who hated him$_i$ spread rumors about.
$\quad\quad\quad\quad d$ $\quad$ *The man$_i$ rumors about whom$_i$ the girl who hated him$_i$ spread.

12.(4) *a* The doctor who studied it$_i$ discovered a cure for that disease$_j$.

    b *The disease$_j$ for which$_j$ the doctor who studied it$_i$ discovered a cure.

    c *The disease$_j$ which$_j$ the doctor who studied it$_i$ discovered a cure for.

    d *The disease$_j$ a cure for which$_j$ the doctor who studied it$_i$ discovered.

In these examples, it is the *d* forms which directly illustrate the phenomenon under discussion, that is, cases where "large" NP containing other NP cross NP with violations, but where the only coreference is between the contained NP and those crossed. The problem is, then, that the *d* forms reveal the same violations as the *c* forms which do meet Ross's "mention" condition, since in these it is the *wh* form alone which is moved and this is coreferential to an NP which is crossed.

12.(1)–12.(4) seem to illustrate cases where there are coreference crossing restrictions involving an NP which is not itself moved but is rather *inside of a larger NP which is moved*. Such restrictions are, it should be emphasized, by no means the general case, even for the rules under discussion, as already partly illustrated. For example, the following reveal no violations:

12.(5) *a* Which of the men who visited him$_i$ did Tony$_i$ disagree with?

    b What man who insulted Mary$_i$ did she$_i$ end up dating?

The examples of this chapter so far illustrate two types of contrast with respect to coreference crossing constraints on B-movement. There is the contrast between examples like 12.(3) *c* and *d*. The former meets Ross's condition and properly involves a crossing violation. The latter apparently does not meet it and yet mysteriously involves the same kind of violation. Then there is the contrast between examples like 12.(1), 12.(2), 12.(3) *d*, 12.(4) *d* on the one hand and ones like 12.(5) on the other. There is a fundamental property in which these two sets of examples differ, besides the fact that the former manifest crossing violations and the latter do not. In the set involving violations, one of the NP involved in coreference relations is a *wh*-form, while this is not the case in the latter type of example.

The question is, then, whether some statement can be formulated which covers these facts and which, in particular, reduces this data to consistency with Ross's proposal about "mention" correspondences. I think that the answer is "yes" and that the basis for such a formulation is Ross's notion of Pied Piping.

B. PIED PIPING: INITIAL DISCUSSION

I would like to claim that examples like 12.(1)–12.(4) do not contradict the "mention" proposal since the assumption that the "large" NP, which have moved, are those "mentioned" in the rule is false. In fact, only the "little" initial, *wh*-marked NP are "mentioned" and these are coreferential to the NP over which the large NP crosses, explaining the deviance under the condition suggested by Ross. Of course, the claim that only the "small" initial NP is "mentioned" in these cases requires justification.

That is, normally an NP in a phrase marker can be operated on only if it is "mentioned" in the transformation which is to operate on it. Hence to move the "large" NP in examples like 12.(1) it would normally be necessary to mention an NP in the structure index of the appropriate rule "corresponding" to this "large" NP and not to one of its "smaller" NP constituents. That this is not necessary in these cases is not a completely unique fact but is a property of certain transformational rules uncovered by Ross (1967a:196–240) and designated by him the *Pied Piping convention*. I shall not try to justify this condition very deeply, since this matter is dealt with by Ross at some length.

Recall, however, that, as pointed out in Chapter 10, there are often *alternative movement possibilities* for complex NP in contexts where *Wh-Rel*-movement is applicable. Thus given a structure like:

12.(6) Charley made [a claim [I discovered [evidence for
$$\text{NP}_3 \qquad\qquad \text{S} \qquad\qquad \text{NP}_2$$

[wh claim]]]]
$$\text{NP}_1 \qquad\qquad \text{NP}_1\ \text{NP}_2\ \text{S}\ \text{NP}_3$$

the grammar must derive either:

12.(7) *a* Charley made a claim for which I discovered evidence.
   b Charley made a claim which I discovered evidence for.
   c Charley made a claim evidence for which I discovered.

12.(7) *a* and *b* illustrate "normal" movements under *Wh-Rel*-movement, cases where just the *wh*-word, or just this word plus its preceding preposition, are moved.[1]. 12.(7) *c* shows, however, that the whole larger NP may be moved. The question arises, therefore, how this movement of the "larger" NP (NP$_2$ in 12.(6)) in such cases can be accounted for in terms of *Wh-Rel*-movement. This rule would very roughly have a structure index of the form:

12.(8) W, [NP, [X, $\begin{bmatrix}\text{NP}\\ \text{+wh}\end{bmatrix}$, Y]] Z
   NP   S   S NP
   1   2   3   4   5   6

and would adjoin the fourth term to the left of the third, thus effecting placement of the *wh*-marked NP in the front of its relative clause. Normally then, only the constituent which ends up in the surface structure as the *wh*-word is moved.

Ross shows, with arguments I will not repeat, that modification of a rule like 12.(8) to cover the movement of "larger" NP in cases like 12.(7) requires some addition to the theory of grammar. No simple addition of constituent symbols to the structure index suffices, principally because of the productivity of the

---

[1] This preposition movement is discussed in Section C below.

phenomenon. That is, as the constructions become more and more complex, larger and larger NP may optionally be moved *and in fact there is no bound on this process*. Hence as the constructions grow more complex, the number of alternative surface structures increases correspondingly:

12.(9) *a* I overheard the discussion of the reason for the failure of that proposal.

b The proposal the discussion of the reason for the failure of which I overheard

c The proposal the reason for the failure of which I overheard the discussion of

d The proposal the failure of which I overheard the discussion of the reason for

e The proposal which I overheard the discussion of the reason for the failure of

There are, moreover, other variants of these where the prepositions move.

In the face of facts like these, Ross proposes, in what I believe is a fundamental insight, that the alternative movements are to be accounted for not by modifications of the structure index of 12.(8) but rather by the addition of a condition on some reordering transformations, a condition he calls the *Pied Piping convention*. Roughly, this convention says that a transformation which reorders an NP can, if its structure index meets certain conditions, also optionally reorder not only that NP but any "larger" NP, that is, one which dominates it, provided no S-node or coordinate node intervenes between the one to be moved and the one actually "mentioned" in the structure index.[2] Given such a condition, by stating the rules to which it applies in terms of the "smallest" NP, one automatically accounts for the optional possibilities of moving the larger ones.

Wh-Rel-movement is obviously a rule of the type subject to this convention. In fact, as Ross states this principle of grammar, it would be a general property of the rules of the type called *B*-movements, a type not yet characterized generally here [see Chapter 13], and of almost no others. However, there are good grounds, many already presented in Ross's discussion, to doubt that a fully general statement of the conditions under which Pied Piping operates is possible.

This question of generality will be dealt with briefly immediately below in Section C, and again in Chapter 18. Before dealing with problems in the formulation of Pied Piping, however, it would be well to consider first how this condition does provide a basis for explaining the apparent anomalies of Section A of this chapter with respect to Ross's proposal about the role of NP "mentioning" in coreferent crossing restrictions.

---

[2] Ross states the Pied Piping convention as follows (1967a:206):

Any transformation which is stated in such a way as to effect the reordering of some specified node NP, where this node is preceded and followed by variables in the structural index of the rule, may apply to this NP or to any noncoordinate NP which dominates it, as long as there are no occurrences of any coordinate node, nor of the node S, on the branch connecting the higher node and the specified node.

Let us refer to those NP which dominate other NP[3] as *complex NP*. The first point to observe is that the notion of Pied Piping provides a bifurcation of complex NP into two types:

12.(10) *a*   those where the complex NP-node itself and an NP-node it dominates are separated by either an S-node or a coordinate node

       b   those not meeting the condition of 12.(10) *a*

The division is such that the former type of complex NP are never subject to Pied Piping, the latter type often are.[4]

Returning now to the original examples of this chapter which provide a problem for the "mention" hypothesis, we see that they involve exclusively complex NP of the type that are subject in principle to Pied Piping. For example, in 12.(1) *a* there is the complex NP *whose father*, which contains the embedded NP *whose*. Yet no S-node or coordinate node intervenes between the "large" and "small" NP-nodes. The same thing is true of 12.(1) *b*, 12.(2), 12.(3), and 12.(4). All the NP that move in these examples are of the type whose movement is accountable as a function of Pied Piping.

This fact naturally suggests that examples like 12.(1)–12.(4) are *not* true counterexamples at all to the principle that NP "mentioning" is relevant for crossing restrictions. Given the Pied Piping condition, the movement of the "large" NP in these examples is due not to the fact that it is the "large" NP which is "mentioned" in the rule of *Wh-Rel*-movement or *Wh-Q*-movement but rather to Pied Piping with respect to rules which "mention" what is in fact the "small" or embedded NP. In short, the movement of the dominating NP in these cases is due not to their correspondence to the NP mentioned in the structure index of the movement rule but to the fact that they are dragged along by Pied Piping.

Strong evidence for this is the fact, remarked in section A, that examples 12.(1)–12.(4) all have as one of the coreferent NP a *wh* form, which is not

---

[3] This definition is not really adequate. For example, an NP like

    (i)   this boy

may well have the structure:

    (ii)   [this [boy]]
         NP   NP   NP NP

and yet we would not wish this to be a complex NP. A closer specification can be achieved by requiring not only domination of one NP node by another but also that these nodes correspond to two distinct references. Thus the structure in (i) involves only one reference while that in the kind of NP discussed in the text involves multiple references. Of course to state this condition precisely would require some account of how the reference of NP-nodes is to be represented formally, a question largely ignored throughout this study.

[4] This division of NP corresponds essentially to that drawn in Chapter 17 between *nominally-complex NP* and *sententially-complex NP*, with the exception that the latter division does not refer to notions of coordination and in fact places coordinate NP in the former category.

moved as such but is inside a larger NP which is moved. But both *Wh-Q*-movement and *Wh-Rel*-movement [as illustrated in 12.(8)], will have a *wh*-marked NP as the one mentioned in the structure index, and indicated as the NP to be moved. Hence in examples like 12.(1)–12.(4) that NP which cannot cross a coreferent, namely the "small" *wh*-marked one, is exactly the one corresponding to the NP mentioned in the appropriate rule of movement.

Let us illustrate this argument by considering application of 12.(8) to the structure underlying the impossible 12.(2) *b*:

12.(11)   [the man$_i$ [man$_i$ loved [$\begin{bmatrix} \text{man}_i\text{'s} \\ +wh \end{bmatrix}$ son]]]
        NP   S   NP   NP S NP
                                              NP   NP

Given 12.(8), 12.(11) must have a proper analysis providing a fragmentation into six segments if it is to undergo the rule, and, in particular, the fourth segment must be an NP marked with the feature [+wh]. The only analysis of 12.(11) meeting 12.(8) is:

12.(12) $\emptyset$,   the+man$_i$,   man$_i$+loved, $\begin{bmatrix} \text{man}_i\text{'s} \\ +wh \end{bmatrix}$,   son, $\emptyset$
          1   2   3   4   5   6

But this analysis predicts that the NP of the fourth term should be the one moved. In fact, however, it is the "larger" NP of which this is the leftmost constituent that is actually moved. The *possibility* of moving the "larger" NP is of course due to Pied Piping. Its *obligatory character* is another question, discussed in the next section. The crucial point then is that although the "large" NP [man$_i$'s son] moves, it is the "small" NP [man$_i$'s] which is "mentioned."
   [+wh]   [+wh]
Hence the fact that the "small NP is not allowed to cross a coreferent, even when moving inside the "large" one, follows from Ross's "mention" proposal, taken in conjunction with a Pied Piping analysis of the movement of the dominating NP in such cases. That is, the crossing violation in 12.(2) *b* follows directly from Cross-Over III, given the proper analysis 12.(12).

The notion of Pied Piping provides for a kind of derivative movement of dominating NP by rules whose statements as such would lead only to the reordering of embedded, dominated NP. Taken together with Ross's "mention" proposal, as embodied in Cross-Over III, this provides an explanation for the otherwise mysterious and anomalous crossing restrictions manifested by 12.(1)–12.(4), where certain NP traveling inside other NP are not allowed to cross their coreferents. This explanation yields a striking support for the correctness of Ross's notion of Pied Piping, arrived at originally on grounds totally independent of crossing restrictions or coreference generally. But the evidence in favor of Pied Piping here is even stronger. For not only does this notion predict the violations in 12.(1)–12.(4), it also predicts *the absence of crossing violations in examples like 12.(5)*. In these, it is not the *wh*-word itself which is a coreferent of a crossed NP but rather some NP inside the relative clause. For instance, the inner structure for 12.(5) *a* would look something like:

$$12.(13) \quad \text{Tony}_i \text{ disagree with } \left[\begin{array}{c} \text{some men} \\ +\text{wh} \end{array} \right] \text{ of the men } [\text{ who visited}$$

$$\text{Tony}_i] \,] \qquad \qquad NP \qquad \qquad NP$$
$$S \, NP$$

And this must be analyzed under *Wh-Q*-movement into the proper analysis:

$$12.(14) \quad \text{Tony}_i + \text{disagree} + \text{with}, \left[\begin{array}{c} \text{some men} \\ +\text{wh} \end{array} \right], \text{ of} + \text{the} + \text{men} + \text{who} + \text{visited}$$
$$+ \text{Tony}_i$$
$$1 \qquad \qquad \qquad 2 \qquad \qquad \qquad 3$$

Hence the NP "mentioned" in the second term, which ends up as the word *which*, is not coreferential with any NP that is crossed. Hence even though Pied Piping is applicable here,[5] one predicts rightly that no crossing violations will ensue if the theory of crossing restrictions incorporates Ross's proposal about "mention." The striking fact is that the structure in 12.(12) meets the condition of Cross-Over III, while that in 12.(14) does not since it is not the NP in term 2 which crosses a coreferent.

The Pied Piping cases illustrated in this chapter all deal with rules that come under the heading of *B*-movements. It is important to observe that their behavior contrasts with the facts for *A*-movements, where NP coreferential to the elements of larger NP may cross them freely [but see footnote 1 of Chapter 9]:

12.(15) *a* John$_i$ was punished by his$_i$ father.
      b John$_i$'s father was visited by him.

12.(16) *a* John$_i$ was tough for his$_i$ father to punish.
      b John$_i$'s father was tough for him$_i$ to visit.

These facts confirm the contrast between *A*-movements and *B*-movements, but they do more. They raise important questions of rule ordering and underlying structure with respect to properties defined by conditions on clause mates such as cross-over constraints for *A*-movements. That is, observe that if *A*-movements operate on structures which actually contain genitives in essentially the forms found in 12.(15)–12.(16), the clause mate constraint falsely predicts nonapplication of *A*-movements to such structures since the coreferents are clause mates.

---

[5] Of course, it is not only applicable but obligatory. That is, the small NP cannot be moved alone:

    (i)   *Which did Tony disagree with of the men who visited him?

This is a general fact about such constructions which follows from the principle called by Ross the left-branch condition. This condition, the general question of Pied Piping obligatoriness, and other restrictions on this principle are discussed in Section C.

We return to this problem of genitive and other nominalization structures in cross-over cases below in Chapter 17.

C. PROBLEMS WITH THE SCOPE OF PIED PIPING

Ross's discussion of Pied Piping is somewhat less convincing that it might otherwise have been because he does not sharply distinguish between two really quite distinct aspects of his proposal. I would distinguish these as follows:

12.(17) *a*   *Pied Piping Function*

It is a functional property of some transformational rules that they operate on the proper analyses of phrase markers in such a way as to reorder not an NP_a mentioned in *some term T* of the proper analysis but rather some NP in the phrase marker which dominates NP_a.

b   *Pied Piping Scope*

Those rules which manifest this property are characterizable by the condition X and operate in the class of contexts Y.

We might state 12.(17) *a* informally in terms of the remark that some reordering rules drag along dominating NP in a way not predicted by the structure of the rule statement itself. It seems to me that this is the crucial insight involved in the notion of Pied Piping. An independent concern, which Ross places on an equal or possibly even superior footing, is the question of which rules in which contexts will manifest this functional property. Ross's concern with the latter question, whose fundamental importance I am obviously not denying, is natural in view of the fact that all of the other conditions he studied in his investigations of constituent movement turned out to be governed by a particular type of rule property or set of properties. And it was natural to try and assimilate Pied Piping to this apparently general characterization.

However, it is evident from Ross's discussion itself and from certain other immediately evident facts that the scope aspect of Pied Piping is not completely statable in a very general way. Other than the condition that the Pied Piping NP not be separated from the dominated NP by S-nodes or by coordinate nodes and that it not be itself coordinate, it is not clear that anything can be said in universal grammar about the scope of Pied Piping.

Only two rules in English, *Wh-Q*-movement and *Wh-Rel*-movement, provide a clear basis for the principle of Pied Piping.[6] And for both of these rules there are constraints on Pied Piping of a type not provided in the principle itself. As stated, for instance, the condition should predict 12.(19) as well as 12.(18) type structures:

12.(18) *a*   Whose father did you visit?

b   The boy whose father you visited

---

[6]However, we argue in Chapter 18 that certain other rules of English must be taken to manifest this property if a general account of crossing restrictions is to be given.

12.(19) *a*   *Whose did you visit father?
      b   *The boy whose you visited father

But these are ill formed. To explain such facts Ross proposes a principle, relevant for English, but not, for example, for Russian or Latin,[7] and called by him *the left-branch condition*:

12.(20) = Ross's (4.181)
      No NP which is the leftmost constituent of a larger NP can be reordered out of this NP by a transformational rule.

This condition predicts in effect that, for English, Pied Piping is obligatory whenever the dominating NP has an embedded NP as its leftmost constituent. What is important about 12.(20) is that it is language dependent, showing that no fully universal statement of the scope of Pied Piping is possible. That is, it is not possible to give a completely universal characterization of the X or Y in 12.(17) *b*. Notice, however, that the left-branch condition has no effect on 12.(17) *a*. This condition thus supports the point made earlier: the functional effect of Pied Piping and its scope are distinct notions. The validity of 12.(20) for English but not Russian or Latin shows that scope conditions cannot fully be part of universal grammar. But nothing shows this for the statement of the functional effect of Pied Piping. These two aspects should thus be sharply distinguished.

      Further evidence for this separation resides in the fact not, to say the least, emphasized by Ross, that *Wh-Q*-movement and *Wh-Rel*-movement are not fully alike in their Pied Piping behavior. The difference has already been illustrated in Chapter 10, where it was shown that Pied Piping is possible under the latter rule in a class of contexts where it is blocked under the former. This was the chief argument given there for distinguishing the two rules in the first place. Let us repeat the relevant examples:

12.(15) *a*   Charley made a claim which I discovered evidence for.
      b   Charley made a claim for which I discovered evidence.
      c   Charley made a claim evidence for which I discovered.

12.(22) *a*   What claim did Charley discover evidence for?
      b   For what claim did Charley discover evidence?
      c   *Evidence for what claim did Charley discover?

The ill-formedness of 12.(22) *c* shows that there is a Pied Piping limitation on *Wh-Q*-movement. We might state the limitation roughly as follows: Pied Piping is

---

[7] Ross (1967a:236–238) gives examples showing that both Latin and Russian are not fully subject to the left-branch condition.

blocked for *Wh-Q*-movement when that NP in the proper analysis which is marked [+wh] is the rightmost constituent of some higher NP [which does not directly dominate a preposition]. Here then is further evidence of the idiosyncratic nature of the scope of Pied Piping, which is seen now not only to be language-particular, but rule-limited. That is, one must state for particular rules restrictions having to do with things like right branch applicability and the like. But again the functional effect of Pied Piping is unaffected and can be given in the universal statement, so that the basis for distinguishing it from the conditions of applicability is strengthened.

The same conclusion is intensified when we observe that Pied Piping is limited not only by language-particular constraints and rule-particular constraints, but also by construction-particular constraints. We have, for instance, already illustrated cases where Pied Piping is *optional* for constructions where the "mentioned" NP is on a right branch. There are, however, constructions where Pied Piping is *obligatory* for such NP. For instance:

12.(23) *a* The men, all of whom I visited
        b *The men, of whom I visited all
        c *The men, whom I visited all of

12.(24) *a* The children, relatives of whom I investigated
        b *The children, of whom I investigated relatives
        c *The children, whom I investigated relatives of

Further evidence of the highly idiosyncratic character of the scope limitations on Pied Piping comes from the facts of preposition movement under *Wh-Q*-movement and *Wh-Rel*-movement. Such facts have been illustrated by many previous examples but not explicitly discussed. The facts are these. In general in English a preposition which precedes a *wh* form may be optionally fronted with it under the application of either of these two rules:

12.(25) *a* I talked to someone.
        b Who did you talk to?
        c To whom did you talk?

12.(26) *a* I wrote a letter for someone.
        b The one who I wrote a letter for
        c The one for whom I wrote a letter

The first point to be made is that, given what Ross has already established, and especially given the conclusions of sections A and B of this chapter, one wishes to account for this phenomenon by way of the notion of Pied Piping. But in fact such an explanation follows directly *if it is recognized that prepositional phrase nodes should properly be taken as NP.* Looked at the other way, this behavior of prepositions is one of the most striking arguments for an NP analysis of traditional prepositional phrases. There is other evidence for such an analysis, some briefly discussed in Chapter 18.

However, there are many contexts in English where the optionality of Pied Piping is eliminated by constraint of obligatory applicability. This is true for a large class of prepositional phrases of roughly the type which would be called adverbial:

12.(27) *a*   I left France during that month.
      b   *What month did you leave France during?
      c   During what month did you leave France?

12.(28) *a*   He said that in a funny way.
      b   *What way did he say that in?
      c   In what way did he say that?

12.(29) *a*   He called her for a definite reason.
      b   *What reason did he call her for?
      c   For what reason did he call her?

Ross (1967a:214-217) discusses this special constraint, noting the observation of S. Y. Kuroda that it correlates with the property of the following noun of prohibiting pronominalizations [in certain contexts]. For present purposes, however, the key point is that again there are construction-specific constraints on the scope of Pied Piping, although its functional effect is once more uniform. Other similar cases are discussed by Ross (1967a:217-223), in particular, some where Pied Piping is blocked in an *ad hoc* class of contexts.

Taken all together then, these facts showing the varied, highly specific constraints on the scope of Pied Piping suggest several things. First, again, that Pied Piping scope and Pied Piping functional effect are quite distinct. The importance of this from the present viewpoint is that the complex and varied constraints on the applicability of Pied Piping do not in any way disconfirm the basic notion. Secondly, that knowledge of the restrictions on Pied Piping, even for English, is still highly limited and fragmentary. This topic could still be the basis for a whole study in itself. Thirdly, it may be correct to state these applicability features not in the rules of movement, *Wh-Rel*-movement, *Wh-Q*-movement, and so on, but rather in terms of a marking of NP-nodes by other rules. That is, there may be a syntactic property, call it [Pied Pipe], which can be assigned to NP-nodes and whose presence requires Pied Piping, that is, movement of an NP dominating one "mentioned" in the rule of movement. By having the rules which assign the feature [Pied Pipe] optional in some contexts, obligatory in others, and so on, conditions like the left-branch condition, those on right branches, and so on, may be reducible to a uniform framework, *and one which makes no use of language-particular conditions which are not rules* [for example, Ross's left-branch condition]. Since such conditions have no natural place in a grammer, this would be a relevant gain.[8]

Pied Piping will be discussed further in Chapter 18, where the conclusions of this section will be further supported. In particular, idiosyncratic constraints on

---

[8]This problem relates to the suggestion made by Ross (1967a:238-240) that each language has not only rules but a "conditions box" stating general constraints on all of its rules.

the contexts in which Pied Piping operates will again attract attention, but again nothing will be found interfering with a universal statement of the effects of Pied Piping.

We conclude therefore that despite difficulties in stating the contexts for Pied Piping, its obligatory versus optional character, and so on, the basic idea is correct and reveals that examples like 12.(1)–12.(4) are not true counterinstances to Ross's "mention" proposal, which is thus on the basis of known data valid for *B*-movements. Putting matters the other way, the data about crossing restrictions for *B*-movements is among the most impressive evidence for Ross's notion of Pied Piping.

13 TRANSFORMATIONS MAKING ESSENTIAL USE OF VARIABLES

A. TWO FUNDAMENTAL CLASSES OF RULES

Our aim is to formulate a general condition in linguistic theory which, together with the independently required structure of individual grammars, has as consequences the observed restrictions on the movement of NP involved in coreferentiality relations. This is a strong aim and possibly an unachievable one. That is, ultimately it might be necessary to accept highly idiosyncratic restrictions for particular languages or even for particular rules within them. But there is no reason to abandon the stronger and consequently more interesting aim without the most stringent attempts at success. Moreover, what has been said already takes us a good distance in the direction of success, at least as far as the facts of English are concerned.

Immediate problems in reaching the strong goal are two. First, it is necessary to distinguish formally between those rules which behave like English passive, *tough*-movement, and so on and those which behave like English *Wh-Rel*-movement. That is, it is necessary to find an independent, formal differentia of *A*- and *B*-movements, thus providing a precise characterization of each type. This formal feature must be referred to in the universal constraints, which obviously cannot refer to lists of the particular English [Chinese, Urdu] rules themselves. Secondly, assuming the first requirement can be met, one must state precisely under what conditions rules of these two types constrain the movement of NP with respect to other NP in the same phrase marker with which they are coreferential. But important strides toward the solution of this second class of problems have been achieved, since what seems necessary is a combination of the clause mate constraint, Ross's device of reference to "mention," and the differentia of the two classes of rules.[1] Hence the chief immediate problem

---

[1] We shall see in later chapters, however, that other problems remain and further conceptual apparatus is in the end certainly required for an adequate overall statement of coreferent crossing constraints.

standing in the way of a general formalization of crossing restrictions is the
A-movement/*B*-movement difference.

Fortunately, important parts of a solution here are suggested by insights of
Ross (1967a). Ross studied in great detail constraints on the movement of NP
under transformational rules, constraints having to do not with coreferentiality
but with the general structural form of the phrase markers in which these NP lie.
He was able to isolate a number of general principles of differing degrees of
universality and scope, one of which, the Pied Piping convention, has already
been mentioned. I shall not list the others here. The key fact from our point of
view is Ross's insight that these constraints are applicable not to *any*
transformational rules which reposition NP but only to a certain subset. He was
able to specify properties which determine whether a rule falls into one class or
another. Crucially, this categorization of rules into types corresponds in essence[2]
to the difference between *A*- and *B*-movements. The relevant properties chiefly
concern whether or not the movement transformation moves an NP over
structure represented in the rule by *constants* or *variables*, where each of these
terms has a special sense and not that of logic, although there is a definite
parallelism. This distinction requires a good deal of discussion since it is far from
fully precise, and it is doubtful that enough is known at the moment to
formulate it with complete precision.

Perhaps the easiest way to begin is indirectly. One can distinguish what must
be the formal *results* of the operation of *A*-movements and *B*-movements rather
than the structure of the rules themselves. Each of the *A*-movements considered
does one of two things. It either moves an NP from one place in a clause to
another without crossing *higher* clause boundaries, or it moves an NP from a
subordinate clause into the *immediately* higher clause which contains it. By
higher clause boundaries I refer to those which are the end points of sentence
constituents which dominate the NP whose movement is under discussion. Thus,
for instance, if an NP is moved across another NP, and the latter contains a
relative clause, the former crosses a clause boundary. But this is not a higher
clause boundary since the embedded sentence which makes up this clause does
not contain the moved NP. A higher clause boundary is crossed if, for example,
an NP moves out of a subordinate clause into the main clause of some complex
sentence. In the latter case, the NP crosses the boundary of a clause which
contains it. Passive, *psych*-movement, and *about*-movement are rules which
shift NP in such a way that they remain internal to the clause of origin.
Tough-movement and *it*-replacement are of the type which take an NP from a
subordinate clause and insert it in the immediately containing clause. General-
izing, it can be said on the basis of present evidence that *A*-movements are rules
which transport NP in a highly bounded or restricted way with respect to higher
clause boundaries. There is a maximum of exactly one such boundary over
which an *A*-movement repositions an element.

B-movements have entirely different consequences. It is true that in *certain*
cases a rule like *Wh-Q*-movement moves an NP from one point in a clause to

---

[2] Actually, Ross's categorization of rules and the one proposed here are not simply
comparable for reasons discussed below in Section D.

another point in that clause, and hence operates without crossing a higher clause boundary:

13.(1) Who did you vote for?

It is also true that *in certain cases Wh-Q*-movement moves an NP from an embedded clause into the next higher clause:

13.(2) Who did Bill say that you voted for?

Restricting attention to cases like these, then, one might claim that *Wh-Q*-movement also is subject to a bound of one on the number of higher clause boundaries over which it may move an element. But a restriction to such cases is totally arbitrary. One can immediately find as many examples as desired where this rule crosses an element over two, three, four, or more higher clause boundaries:

13.(3) *a* Who did you see?
   b Who did you think$_1$ that you saw?
   c Who did Bill say$_2$ that you thought$_1$ that you saw?
   d Who did Mary believe$_3$ that Bill said$_2$ that you thought$_1$ that you saw?
   e Who did Jack find out$_4$ that Mary believed$_3$ that Bill said$_2$ that you thought$_1$ that you saw?

In each I have marked the higher clause boundaries which the moved *who* has crossed. In 13.(3) *a* the *who* has simply been moved to the front of the minimal clause which contains it. In 13.(3) *b* it has moved out of one sentential complement to the front of the main sentence in which that complement is embedded. In 13.(3) *c* it has moved out of a complement sentence, over the next higher sentence, and to the front of a third sentence in which the second is embedded. In 13.(3) *d* a third level of embedding is present and an NP has moved from the end of the most deeply embedded clause to the front of the main, nonembedded sentence. In 13.(3) *e* the moved NP crosses four higher clause boundaries.

Exactly similar examples are found for the other *B*-movement we have dealt with, *Wh-Rel*-movement:

13.(4) *a* The boy who you saw
   b The boy who you thought you saw
   c The boy who Bill said that you thought that you saw
   d The boy who Mary believed that Bill said that you thought that you saw
   e The boy who Jack found out that Mary believed that Bill said that you thought that you saw

It is clear that there are exactly analogous examples for both rules in which the moved element crosses five, six, seven, and so on higher clause boundaries.

What is revealed, in other words, is that *B*-movements reposition NP across an unbounded number of higher clause boundaries. Stated differently, if one compares the deep structure position of particular NP occurrences with the surface structure location of the same NP, the distance between the two must be highly restricted in terms of intervening clause structures if repositioning is a function of one operation of one *A*-movement. At most, the NP can have been moved one clause away. But if *B*-movements are involved, there is no bound on the distance in terms of clauses which an arbitrary NP can have been moved. This difference is the formal distinction in rule *results* between *A*-movements and *B*-movements. It is, as far as I can see, quite clear and definite.

B. CONSTANTS AND VARIABLES

It is necessary to distinguish formally between *A*-movements and *B*-movements in order to state the cross-over restrictions properly. However, for this purpose one needs a categorization of rules *not by their results* but *by the formal structure of their descriptions*. That is, it must be said that if a rule is a formal structure of one type, it behaves one way under crossing constraints; if not of that type, it behaves another way. But here is where there is a lack of knowledge. Although it is clear that in order to state rules which have the differing formal effects of *A*-movements versus *B*-movements they *must* have contrasting formal properties, it is not so clear just how these differences are manifested. This follows from our present limited knowledge of the real form of grammatical rules and the concomitant significant degree of arbitrariness present in all rules we actually construct. It does seem evident, however, that the distinction between the two rule types has to do with the difference between the occurrence of variables and constants in descriptions of transformational rules, a statement which brings us back to the opening remarks of the previous section.

By *constants* in the structural indexes of transformations I mean occurrences of the names of particular constituents, NP, VP, Verb, Sentence, Preposition, and so on. By *variables* I refer to elements *X, Y, Z*, which occur in such rules to designate arbitrary sequences. The contrast can be illustrated by a hypothetical transformational description:

13.(5) X, NP, Verb + Preposition, NP, Y
      1   2   3   4 5

In this structure index there are four constants and two variables. Recalling Chomsky's notion of proper analysis [Chapter 11], which defines the relation between a transformation and the class of structures which can undergo it, we can say the following. 13.(5) is applicable to any phrase marker which is segmentable into five consecutive, nonoverlapping, exhaustive parts such that the first is anything at all, the second an NP, the third a Verb + Preposition, the fourth an NP, and the fifth anything at all.

The variables *X* and *Y* in 13.(5) fulfill a frequently required function. If they were left off, that is, if the structure index were given as:

13.(6) NP, Verb + Preposition, NP
      1   2   3

it would apply only to sentences consisting wholly of a single clause of this form. It could not, for example, apply to embedded clauses or conjoined ones. Stating the rule as in 13.(5) allows application to any clause, independent, embedded, or conjoined. This is the function of initial and final variables, henceforth *end variables*.[3]

Suppose now 13.(5) were a rule of NP movement which placed the fourth term in front of the third, that is, suppose its operation were:

$$13.(7) \quad 1, 2, 3, 4, 5 \implies 1, 2 + 4, 3, \emptyset, 5$$

What kind of rule would it be? Clearly an A-movement, since the NP moved by the rule would remain wholly within a single clause. No higher clause boundaries would ever be crossed. What properties of the formal structure of the rule itself correlate with the restriction on the operation of the rule? The answer to this is partly given by consideration of the structure over which the moving element is transported. In any phrase marker which 13.(5) applies to there will be some NP_i moved. This NP must move over structure to its left which has the analysis Verb + Preposition. That is, the *path* traveled by NP_i in its phrase marker is characterized in the rule by a sequence of *constants*. Moreover, this sequence is such as not to apply to any string of elements not contained within one clause (making reasonable assumptions about the phrase structure of the language involved).

An example of a real rule of this type is English passive, the first A-movement we investigated. Very roughly, this rule can be stated something like:

$$13.(8) \quad \begin{array}{ccccc} X, & NP, & Verb, & NP, & Y \\ 1 & 2 & 3 & 4 & 5 \end{array} \implies 1, 4, 3, 2, 5$$

In this case the path traveled by the fourth term NP is defined exclusively by the constant in the third term. Furthermore, this string is such that any string analyzed according to it must be clause internal.

The fact that A-movements seem so far to manifest structure indexes in which the movement path of the transported NP is characterized by constants directly suggests possible formal differentia of A-movements and B-movements. Conceivably, an A-movement is a rule which transports an NP over a path characterized in the structure index by constants alone while a B-movement is a rule which transports an NP over a path characterized in its structure index by one or more variables. This preliminary characterization approaches the

---

[3] Such variables may ultimately correctly be dispensed with in favor of conventions for applying rules to subsections of phrase markers. What is crucial here is the fact that there is a contrast in rules. Some are applicable to all clauses, main, embedded, conjoined, and so on. Passive is an example. Others are restricted just to application on nonembedded clauses. An example is the rule called Y-movement, discussed in Chapter 16 below. One possible way of partially representing this contrast is the distinction between rules constructed with end variables, like passive, and those without at least one such, such as, possibly, Y-movement.

formulation given by Ross (1967a), which, however, differs from it in some important ways.[4]

The difference between these two kinds of rules in the terms now being suggested can be seen in the contrast between the hypothetical A-movement, 13.(5), and the *hypothetical B*-movement:

13.(9) X, NP, Y, Sentence Boundary
        1   2   3   4

Suppose 13.(9) is the structure index of a rule which throws the second term NP to the left of the sentence boundary. The path of any NP moved by this rule is thus not characterized exclusively by constants since the NP hops over structure represented in 13.(9) by the third term variable Y.

Observe that in contrast to 13.(5), there is nothing to prevent this new rule from yanking an NP across higher clause boundaries. For example, 13.(9) applies to structures like:

13.(10)

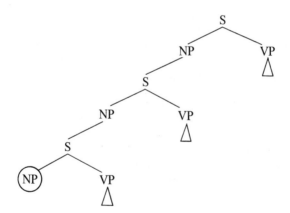

and would move the circled NP to the extreme right boundary. Hence 13.(9) has the property shown to be required in *Wh-Q*-movement and *Wh-Rel*-movement, namely, moving an NP across an unbounded number of higher clause boundaries.

----

[4] See footnote 2.

Roughly again, the structure index of *Wh-Q*-movement could be formulated as:[5]

13.(11)   Sentence Boundary, X, $\begin{bmatrix} NP \\ +wh \end{bmatrix}$, Z

      1   2   3   4

Here the third term *wh*-marked NP moves to the left over the variable in the second term.

Now a question arises. *Wh-Q*-movement has been stated with a variable in its second term and this permits a formal differentiation of it from, for example, passive, in a way desirable for our purposes with respect to different cross-over constraints for the two. It might be wondered, however, whether this is not simply an empty trick, since possibly we are free to use variables as we wish. It might be said, for instance, that it is possible to state *Wh-Q*-movement without such variables. Although such a claim might be made, it is, as far as I can see, false. For in fact there is no known way to do this. It seems that this rule *must* be stated with variables.

There are two reasons why variables are indispensable for *B*-movements: (a) As we have seen, such rules move NP an unbounded number of clauses away from their initial positions; (b) Such rules move NP over structure which cannot be characterized by any constant, or finite string of constants. Reason (b) is of course the crucial point here. After all, even *A*-movements transport elements across structures of unbounded length. For instance, passive crosses one NP over another, and there is no bound on the length of NP. But the key fact about these structures of boundless length over which passive moves NP is that they are characterizable as constituents, that is, NP. Hence the unbounded length is recursively specified by a single symbol in the structure index of passive. But this exact situation is not possible in the case of the *B*-movements because they cross elements over structure which is not any single constituent. Moreover, this structure is not characterizable by any finite string of constituents.[6] The fact is that the element is moved over whatever stands between it and some piece of structure which indicates its stopping point. In 13.(11) the stopping point is sentence boundary.

---

[5] This statement of the rule ignores, among other things, the fact that the rule must apply on embedded question clauses:

    (i) I wondered who John spoke to.

Hence it is incorrect to have the *wh*-marked NP always move to absolute sentence initial position and some way must be found of characterizing the "stopping point" precisely for both absolute and embedded question clauses.

[6] Of course, there is no available proof in the strong sense for this claim. It is obviously true given anything like the structures heretofore proposed or imagined for English sentences. The key point is that the burden of demonstration is on anyone who would argue that a finite constituent characterization of the intervening structure is possible.

The apparently insurmountable difficulties in the way of a finite constant formulation of the path are easily seen by recalling examples like 13.(3). Given 13.(3) *a* types alone, one could formulate the rule like:

13.(12)   Sentence Boundary, NP + Verb, $\begin{bmatrix} NP \\ +wh \end{bmatrix}$, Y

1   2   3 4

where the path is given by the constants of term 2. But this fails for examples like 13.(3) *b* which have a more remote structure like:

13.(13)

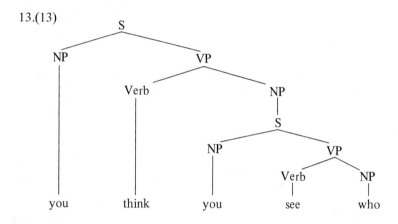

To get a rule stated in such a way that the NP moves only over a path defined by constants to apply to structures like this and those like 13.(3) *a* requires already a monster something like:

13.(14)   Sentence Boundary, NP + Verb + (NP + Verb), $\begin{bmatrix} NP \\ +wh \end{bmatrix}$, Y

1   2   3 4

And as far as one can see, as longer and longer examples like 13.(3) *c, d*, and *e* are taken into account, the rule [specifically the second term] must become longer and longer.[7] But this is hopeless since there is no bound on the length of examples, and hence this procedure cannot yield a finite rule. In order to get around this difficulty, one must use variables, as in 13.(11). Consequently, it is not an empty trick to state *Wh-Q*-movement with variables in the movement path. This is the only way known to state the rule.

---

[7]Note, furthermore, that we are artificially simplifying things enormously by pretending that all predicates have a verb for their head and by restricting application of the rule to what is in effect grammatical object position when, in reality, it must apply to NP in all positions.

We have now come across two different types of variable usage in transformational rules. The internal variables in rules like 13.(11) are essential. There is no way to state the rules without them. Let us refer to such internal variables as *essential variables*, and to rules which contain at least one such as *variable rules*. End variables also occur and these might be dispensed with in favor of certain conventions for applying rules to subparts of structures. This need not concern us here. What is of importance is that it is not the mere presence of variables in rules which is relevant to the distinction between *A*-movements and *B*-movements but rather their function. We have isolated two functions of variables in transformational statements. Fortunately, these two are formally distinguishable in a trivial way. A variable occurrence is an end variable if it occurs at either extreme of a rule description; this yields a definition of essential variable as any other variable occurrence. However, this definition does not provide much content to the notion of essential variable, and this lack of content becomes a problem since there are other functions of variables not yet dealt with. To distinguish these other functions from that of essential variables involves greater structural specificity in the characterization of variable functions. It can be observed that this is the case by examining rules which must be characterized as *A*-movements and yet whose statements naturally come to contain variable occurrences which are not end variables.

C. ABBREVIATORY VARIABLES

Recall *tough*-movement. This rule takes an NP from the complement sentence and sticks it in place of a main clause grammatical subject, *it*. The structure index might be given at first as:

13.(15) X, it, be + Adjective$_{tough}$ + for + NP + $\begin{Bmatrix} \text{Adjective} \\ \text{Verb} \end{Bmatrix}$

$$+ (\text{Preposition}) + (\text{NP}) + (\text{Preposition}) , \ \text{NP}, \ \text{Y}$$

1 2   3   4 5

Stated in this fashion, the rule is grossly complicated and inelegant and thus rather dubious. A very minor amount of the complexity arises, I think, from having ignored up till now the possibility that Adjective$_{tough}$ obligatorily undergo *psych*-movement[8] as well as *tough*-movement. What this means is that

---

[8]Some evidence for the correctness of this assumption, which is not crucial to the present argument, however, is derivable from the fact that the posited underlying organization shows up sporadically with certain "nominal predicates":

(i) *a* I have difficulty in digesting whale meat.
    b Whale meat is difficult for me to digest.

That is, the relations in (i) *a* and *b* seem identical. But under the *psych*-movement analysis (i) *a* and *b* have parallel structures.

the sentential complement starts out in the object position and the logical subjects of these adjectives are animate. Hence a sentence like:

13.(16)   It is tough for me to go.

has a more remote structure:

13.(17)   NP be tough [it [for I to go]]
                NP S   S NP

Therefore if *tough*-movement is specified to precede *psych*-movement, *tough*-movement can be defined slightly more compactly:

13.(18)   X, Adjective$_{tough}$, it, for + NP + $\begin{Bmatrix} \text{Adjective} \\ \text{Verb} \end{Bmatrix}$ + (Preposition)

                                              +(NP)+(Preposition), NP, Y
        1   2   3   4   5 6

This reformulation has no effect on crossing restrictions proper since the complement NP must still cross its subject NP when it substitutes for the *it*. Observe that in 13.(18), as in 13.(15), the moving NP travels a path represented in the rule exclusively by constants.

However, 13.(18) is still quite unwieldy and in particular seems to require listing of irrelevant elements, namely, those in term 4. These are listed simply because, "accidentally," they intervene between the *it* and the movable NP, and because no single constituent characterizes the gap. Perhaps this notion of "accidental" occurrence of elements in rules can be made clearer and more precise in terms of the notion of contrast. Imagine a rule which deletes prepositions directly following adjectives, but not following verbs, adverbs, and such. The structure index of this rule might look something like:

13.(19)   X, Adjective, Preposition, Y
        1   2   3   4

There is a clear sense in which the symbol Adjective in such a rule is nonaccidental. Namely, its presence there is a function of contrast. Prepositions do not drop when directly preceded by verbs, adverbs, and such. Hence the rule described by 13.(19) mentions an element relevant to the operation which is in contrast with other elements that can occur before prepositions.

Contrast this, however, with the situation in term 4 of 13.(18). The symbols mentioned in term 4 do not contrast with anything. In fact, to the extent that the formulation is descriptively adequate (and obviously it is not), it must be the case that term 4 mentions every possible sequence of symbols which can intervene in English phrase markers between an *it* directly following a member of the class Adjective$_{tough}$ and an NP which can be substituted for such an *it*. Hence the occurrence of the symbols in term 4 of 13.(18) is not a representation of contrast at all in the sense that Adjective in term 2 of 13.(19) contrasts with verb, adverb, or other elements which do not determine the deletion of prepositions in the hypothetical situation there described.

This division of symbol occurrences in rules into those which are in contrast versus those which are stated in order to exhaustively characterize what can, accidentally, intervene between two other elements, suggests that present notations for expressing rules are inadequate, since these two different situations are apparently not formally distinguishable. One might be led, however, to note that the NP of term 5 of 13.(18) crosses *anything before it in the same clause to move into the* it-*position*. Hence one might attempt to take advantage of this fact by restating 13.(18) with variables:

13.(20)   X, Adjective$_{tough}$, it, [Y, [U, NP, W,] Z], V
$$\phantom{13.(20)\quad X, Adjective_{tough}, it, [Y, [}\ S\quad VP\qquad\quad VP\ S$$
$$\ 1\qquad 2\qquad\qquad\ 3\quad 4\ \ 5\ \ 6\quad 7\quad\ 8\ \ 9$$

This formulation indicates directly that the rule moves an NP in the complement sentence VP regardless of what elements stand in front of it within the complement clause. This seems to be the maximally general formulation. If so, it should certainly be maintained as against 13.(18), with its reference to irrelevant elements. It would suggest the general principle that noncontrastive constant occurrences, such as those in term 4 of 13.(18), are replaced in correctly formulated rules by variables.

But now the problem is clear. *Tough*-movement must be an *A*-movement. Yet 13.(20) moves the NP of the sixth term over a path defined in part by the variables of the fourth and fifth terms. Hence, by the definitions so far, 13.(20) would characterize a variable rule, entailing that its cross-over properties should, for example, be like those of *Wh-Q*-movement and not like passive. But this is false. Somewhere something is obviously wrong.

It is not hard, moreover, to see what the problem is. The variables Y and U in 13.(20) are intended to serve an abbreviatory function. But the discussion so far is sufficiently vague that nothing points this out and indicates that these are different from essential variables like the internal occurrence in 13.(11). That such a distinction is necessary is indicated not merely by the fact that 13.(20) as is makes false cross-over predictions, but also by the more gross fact that, as is, 13.(20) yields completely ungrammatical structures of other sorts.

Despite appearances, 13.(20) fails to embody the restriction that an NP under *tough*-movement operation is transported only from the *immediately lower*[9] clause into the main clause. 13.(20) can in fact move an NP which is

---

[9] Ross (personal communication) has observed that there are apparent cases where NP under a putative rule of *tough*-movement must be regarded as moving from more deeply embedded structures:

  (i) Harriet is tough for me to stop looking at.

Here it seems that the NP *Harriet* must be taken to have moved out of complement sentence of the verb *stop*, which would have an ancestor form *I look at Harriet*. There are at least two things to be said about such examples which suggest that they are not true counterexamples to the claim in the text. First, observe that the complement sentence loses its subject by deletion through identity to the subject of *stop*. However, it is not required that the subject of the complement of *stop* be identical, that is, both of the following are possible:

  (ii) *a* I stopped looking at Harriet.
       b I stopped Bill's looking at Harriet.

Observe, however, that the analogue of (i) when the subject of *looking at* is not suitable for deletion is:

  (iii) *Harriet is tough for me to stop Bill's looking at.

The implication is, then, that deletion of the subject, which is known to prune the S-node of a sentence, permits other NP in the clause to be moved. This implies an ordering such that deletion takes place before *tough*-movement, and while I have no evidence to support this I also know of nothing to preclude it.

Secondly, it is known that gerundive complements behave specially in at least two different ways, both of which lead to exceptions to generalizations that hold for embedded sentences. That is, they do not move under extraposition:

  (iv) *a* It was disgusting for John to do that.
       b It was disgusting that John did that.
       c *It was disgusting John's doing that.

and they can occur sentence internally when exhaustively dominated by an NP without unacceptability:

  (v) *a* *Did that John came late bother you?
      b *Did for John to come late bother you?
      c Did John's coming late bother you?

These facts suggest that somehow gerundive complements are in general "desententialized" in some completely mysterious way. This fact could also account for the movability of some NP out of gerundive complements without conflict with the generalization stated in the text.

embedded arbitrarily far down. Observe, for instance, that nothing precludes the movement by 13.(20) of the circled NP in the structure:

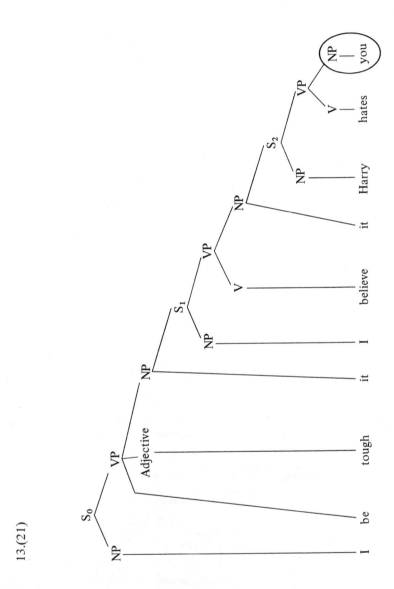

But this would ultimately yield the ill-formed:

13.(22)   *You are tough for me to believe that Harry hates.

This is ill formed just because the NP has been moved not out of the immediately embedded clause, S_1, but out of one embedded further down inside of S_1, namely, out of S_2. 13.(20) permits this straightaway since 13.(21) can be analyzed properly in terms of it as:

13.(23)   it+be, tough, it, I+believe+it+Harry+hates, $\emptyset$, you, $\emptyset$, $\emptyset$, $\emptyset$
　　　　　　1　　2　　3　　　　　4　　　　　　　　5　6　　7　8　9

That is, this proper analysis of 13.(21) meets the nine-term condition of 13.(20). Notice that the only proper application of *tough*-movement to 13.(21) is one which moves the object of *believe*, which is in the immediately lower clause:

13.(24)   That Harry hates you is tough for me to believe.

There are several conceivable ways out of this dilemma. One would be to give up 13.(20) and return to 13.(18), that is, to decide simply that no variable can be used in such cases. But this would miss the fact that 13.(18) and many other rules must list long strings of essentially irrelevant elements. That is, it would mean giving up the attempt to characterize the difference between contrastive and noncontrastive sequences in rule formulations. The natural solution to me is to propose that there is a special class of purely *abbreviatory variables*, distinct from essential variables (and from end variables). The chief property of these abbreviatory variables is that, unlike others, they do not stand for just any sequence whatever. Rather, they may be used only to represent *clause internal*[10] subsequences. In other words, they do not cover higher clause boundaries.

Suppose this class of variables is represented formally by the subscript *a*. One could then reformulate 13.(20) as:[11]

13.(25)   W, Adjective$_{\text{tough}}$, it, [Y$_a$, [Z$_a$, NP, X,] U,] Z
　　　　　　　　　　　　　　　　　S　　VP　　　　　VP　S
　　　　　　1　　　　2　　　　　3　　4　　5　　6　　7　　8　　9

Under the intended interpretation of abbreviatory variables, Y$_a$ and Z$_a$ can now stand for any sequences, as long as these do not include higher clause junctures. Hence 13.(25), unlike 13.(20), is *not* applicable to structures of the form 13.(21). This follows since the fourth term of the analysis of 13.(23), *I + believe + it + Harry + hates*, involves a higher clause juncture between *it* and *Harry*.

---

[10]It would be easy enough, and possibly correct, to extend the notion to allow variables which are exclusively NP-internal, VP-internal, and so on, that is, which do not cover higher NP boundaries, higher VP boundaries, and so forth.

[11]The cumbersome character of this rule and others could be reduced if we introduce conventions which do not require the brackets to be closed. If this is done, we could restate 13.(25) something like:

(i)   X, Adjective$_{\text{tough}}$, it, [Y$_a$, [Z$_a$, NP, Z
　　　　　　　　　　　　　　　　　　S　　VP
　　　　1　　　2　　　　　3　　4　　5　　6　　7

It can be observed that the abbreviatory variables in 13.(25) are both enclosed in brackets labeled as representing an S constituent. This is quite crucial and every usage of such variables will have to be so enclosed. That is, it will be a constraint on the formulation of rules that no occurrences of such variables are possible without the relevant subscripted brackets. This constraint is necessary in order to indicate *which clause the variable is being used to abbreviate part of.* This is determined by whatever actual constituent symbols are mentioned inside the S-subscripted brackets which contain the abbreviatory variable. In 13.(25) this is given by the NP symbol of the sixth term. It follows that Y_a and Z_a abbreviate structure in the same clause as those NP in phrase markers corresponding to the NP symbol. It is in effect the S-subscripted brackets which define the notion "higher clause boundary."

Given a structural description of a rule containing a subpart of the form:

$$13.(26) \quad [\, \ldots V_a \ldots C \ldots \,]$$
$$ S S$$

where the symbol C stands for some finite sequence of actual constituent symbols, a higher clause boundary is one at the juncture of an S which dominates the S corresponding to the subscripts on the brackets. And such an S will be one dominating the first S above the constituents corresponding to the constituent symbols[12] mentioned inside the brackets of 13.(26). Put differently, one analyzes a phrase marker with respect to a structure like 13.(26) as follows. Find the sequence in the phrase marker which is analyzable as the sequence C. Find the *first* S above this sequence. This S, call it S_j, corresponds to the subscript symbol on the brackets of 13.(26). And V_a must abbreviate exclusively structure inside of S_j.

Observe then that 13.(25) would be a quite different rule if, for example, the S-subscripted brackets enclosed the third and fourth terms instead of the fourth through the eighth. This would make Y_a abbreviate structure which is part of the same clause as the correspondents of the *it* symbol of the third term rather than part of the clause containing the correspondents of the NP symbol of the sixth term. Hence the notation of S-subscripted brackets and that of variables with subscripts are jointly necessary to define the function of abbreviatory variables[13] completely.

It seems, therefore, that abbreviatory variables provide apparatus for eliminating strings of essentially irrelevant elements in transformational rule descriptions without imposing on a rule the unbounded movement possibilities

---

[12] And of course there must always be at least one such constant mentioned inside this type of brackets for rule well-formedness.

[13] If, as suggested in footnote 10, variables abbreviating structure for constituents other than sentences are required, the formalism would naturally represent this by allowing subscripts other than S.

involved with essential variables. The latter can now be defined as variables which are distinct from abbreviatory variables and which are furthermore nonfinal and noninitial, that is, which are not end variables. It is proposed, therefore, that it is only essential variables which throw a rule in the class of *B*-movements, and that it is only the movement of an NP across structure represented by such variables which involves the typically very strong cross-over constraints associated with B-movements.

There are now several logical possibilities for a movement transformation. It may reposition an NP across a path which is characterized in the structure index exclusively by:

13.(27) *a*   Essential variables
      b   Constants and essential variables
      c   Constants and abbreviatory variables and essential variables
      d   Abbreviatory variables and essential variables
      e   Constants
      f   Abbreviatory variables
      g   Constants and abbreviatory variables

I shall now redefine a *variable movement rule* as one with the properties of any of 13.(27) *a–d*, that is, where any part of the path is characterized by essential variables.[14] All others I shall call *constant movement rules*. Rules of the former type make essential use of variables; there is no known way to state them without such. Rules of the latter type do not. Constant movement rules could be stated without variables, since the variables they contain (if any) are introduced for purposes of maximizing generalization rather than to achieve necessary formal power. Abbreviatory and end variables are, in other words, added to linguistic theory on grounds having to do with the evaluation of the complexity of grammars. Essential variables are introduced to permit the statement of rules otherwise inexpressible. It is therefore proposed with some hesitance that variable movement rules reconstruct the class hitherto given merely by enumeration as *B*-movements; constant movement rules, those given by enumeration as *A*-movements. In short, it is claimed that the differentia between weak and strong cross-over constraints is a function of whether or not a rule makes essential use of variables, that is, involves a movement path characterized in part by the occurrence of essential variables. Formally, an essential variable is a variable occurrence which is neither the initial nor the final element of the structure index and which is not a member of the specified set of abbreviatory variables. Use of essential variables involves the claim that the elements moved may, if no other structure in the rule prevents it, cross an unbounded number of higher clause boundaries.

---

[14] Ross (1967a) categorizes rules instead by whether the term to be moved is surrounded by variables. Terms which meet this condition are said to be subject to the varied movement constraints he proposes.

D. ROSS'S CATEGORIZATION OF RULES
VERSUS CATEGORIZATION IN THIS CHAPTER

Although the division of rules into constant movement rules and variable movement rules is suggested by Ross's study, there is a contrast between his approach and ours. Ross provides a division of rules into the categories:

13.(28) *a* Upward bounded
       b Downward bounded

An *upward-bounded rule* is one which cannot operate across higher clause boundaries. A *downward-bounded rule* is one which cannot operate across lower clause boundaries. An example of the former is extraposition, which throws the moving clause only to the end of the next more inclusive clause but not across its boundary. An example of the latter is reflexivization, which, for instance, cannot operate between the subject of a clause and an NP in a relative clause on the object of that clause. Reflexivization is also upward bounded of course. That is, rules which are both upward bounded and downward bounded operate only on clause mate elements.

Now, for Ross, the division of 13.(28) does not correspond fully to the characterization of rules in terms of whether the relevant term of their structure indexes is surrounded by variables. The chief reason for this is an interesting and puzzling discovery by Ross as follows.

13.(29) Rules which move elements to the right are always upward bounded.

That is, there is a contrast among rules of movement as to whether they can cross higher clause boundaries only if they move elements to the left. All rules which move elements to the right are upward bounded.

Notice, then, that in terms of the present chapter we would represent upward-bounded rules with abbreviatory variables. For example, we would have to state extraposition in these terms as:

$$13.(30) \quad X, [\ X_a, [\ it, \ S, \ ] \ Y_a, \ ] \ Y$$
$$ S \quad\ NP \quad\ NP \quad\ S$$
$$ 1 \quad\ 2 \quad\ 3 \ \ 4 \quad\ 5 \quad\quad 6 \Longrightarrow 1, 2, 3, \emptyset, 5+4, 6$$

This indicates by the abbreviatory variable occurrences that the S is moved only to the end of the next more inclusive clause, not all the way to absolute sentence final position. However, observe that if Ross's observation 13.(29) is correct, the contrast between abbreviatory variables and essential variables in such a rule moving elements to the right is meaningless. That is, given 13.(29), we can predict that any variable over which an element is moved to the right must function as an abbreviatory variable. This would seem to indicate that the present approach is by no means fully correct.

It might be asked then why Ross's system, containing only one kind of variable, with predictions as to its function by way of principles like 13.(29), is not adopted here. There are two distinct reasons. First, observe that the distinction between essential variables and abbreviatory variables or its equivalent is still needed in rules which move elements to the left. Hence in Ross's system it is necessary to simply mark such rules as being either upward bounded or not. Secondly, Ross's system does not provide any way of handling the facts of rules like *tough*-movement, which are the chief motivation for abbreviatory variables.

Observe first that *tough*-movement is *not* upward bounded in Ross's sense. It can and in fact always does cross higher clause boundaries, but only one. We were able to represent this kind of movement with abbreviatory variables but it cannot be done with markings of upward bounding. In short, our motivation for abbreviatory variables is the fact that the two characterizations:

13.(31) *a*   Rules which cross higher clause boundaries
     b   Rules which provide unbounded movement

do not coincide. Notice that the notion of upward bounding throws *tough*-movement in the same class as the unbounded movement rules, *Wh-Rel*-movement, *Wh-Q*-movement. This is a formally undesirable classification and more crucially for present purposes does not correspond to crossing behavior.

It seems clear then that problems remain in the correct categorization of rules with respect to the properties under discussion. Ross's system and the one discussed in this chapter are different in certain respects, and neither seems completely right. Much further work is required. We need to know for instance whether 13.(29) holds up as more languages are investigated. We need to know if *tough*-movement, a rule which involves considerable problems [see Chapter 16, Section D], really can be maintained in the grammar of English, and whether other languages have rules with the special property it shares with *it*-replacement, namely, movement across exactly one higher clause boundary.

At the same time, despite the problems discussed here and the differences between Ross's formulation and that of this chapter, we should not overlook the much more fundamental agreement between the two approaches and the deeper fact that crossing restrictions correlate with the division of rules into those which involve bounded movement versus those whose movement operation is unbounded. This division must be made in any linguistic theory so that, regardless of how the distinction is ultimately drawn, the cross-over principle will have available some formal properties to refer to for the proper assignment of crossing restrictions.

14 TOWARD A STATEMENT OF THE CROSS-OVER PRINCIPLE

We are now in a position to specify a closer approximation to the principle named in the title of this chapter. For this, we assume the following definitions:

14.(1) *Variable movement rule* (transformation) as in Chapter 13

14.(2) *Constant movement rule* (transformation) as in Chapter 13

14.(3) The *application path* of a transformation T with respect to a phrase marker P: the sequence of constituents in P over which a constituent is moved by T when it applies to P.

Consider then the following:

14.(4) An arbitrary movement transformation T with a structure index K, whose *ith* item is NP, and whose operation reorders the *ith* term of proper analyses.

14.(5) The set of all phrase markers S meeting the condition K (that is, having proper analyses with respect to K.[1])

14.(6) An arbitrary phrase marker P which is a member of S and whose proper analysis with respect to T has NP_k as its *ith* term.

---

[1] In fact, for application of a transformation T to a phrase marker P, it is necessary to require that P have a *unique* proper analysis with respect to T. See Chomsky (1961). This condition is seldom meetable by most of the rules normally proposed as transformations, chiefly because of the occurrence therein of variables. Hence technically, these rules are what Chomsky calls *families of transformations*, definable in such a way that they specify the relevant [usually infinite] set of transformations in the sense capable of meeting the uniqueness condition.

14.(7) *Cross-Over IV*

Despite the fact that P is a member of S, T may not apply to P if the application path of T with respect to P is such that this path contains an NP_j coreferential with NP_k and either:

a. T is a *variable movement rule*.

b. T is a *constant movement rule* and NP_k and NP_j are clause mates.

This formulation combines the clause mate constraint, Ross's insight about the structure index "mentioning" the moved NP, and the difference between constant and variable movement transformations to predict when the clause mate constraint is relevant. This formulation seems to cover all of the examples considered so far with the exception of:

14.(8) *a* The *about*-anomalies of Chapter 5

  b The clause mate problem with *It*-replacement of Chapter 9

  c The cases of constant movement crossings of coreferents inside complex nominals discussed at the end of Section B of Chapter 12.

This coverage is subject of course to the various assumptions we have made concerning particular analyses, rule ordering, and substantive general principles such as cyclical application. However, as we shall proceed, it will be found that even the far from elementary formulation of 14.(7) is too simple and unstructured to deal with the actual complexities of the domain of facts being investigated. We shall then be led to more structured and hopefully adequate versions, as well as possible revisions of certain analyses that take into account new facts and that deal with the problems of 14.(8).

PART IV
A MORE SOPHISTICATED AND MORE EMPIRICALLY GROUNDED FORMULATION

15 RULES OF LIMITED RELEVANCE

A. COMMENT

One of the limitations of the discussion so far is that it is based on only a limited number of rules, in fact at most five constant movements and two variable movements. Unfortunately, sticking to English, this is a limitation difficult to overcome. There just are not that many rules which reorder NP. A second limitation is that the rules discussed have been chosen just because they support or at least appear to support our notions about cross-over constraints. To really justify Cross-Over IV, therefore, it is necessary to show that at the least it is consistent with and explains properties of every rule in English which meets its defining conditions. There are several clear instances of rules that move NP which we have not yet considered, and a number of other possible cases which it would be well for us to consider. We will argue that a number of these rules are consistent with our formulation although they provide little positive support for it. In the next chapter, and subsequent ones as well, we will encounter other rules which provide more direct and interesting evidence.

B. *TO-I-O*-MOVEMENT

The rule of *to-I-O-movement* is involved in the ordering of direct and indirect objects. That is, it is involved in the relations between such pairs as:

15.(1) *a* I gave a book to Charley.
     b I gave Charley a book.

15.(2) *a* I threw the ball to Charley.
     b I threw Charley the ball.

15.(3) *a* I made a proposal to Tony.
     b I made Tony a proposal.

Unfortunately, there is not any really good evidence indicating whether the underlying form is more like the *a* or *b* examples.[1] However, since the rule must interchange contiguous elements of one clause, it is clear that it will be a constant movement. This means that, if there are cross-over restrictions under this rule, they will only govern clause mates. But this fact excludes *to-I-O-* movement from the set of rules which could provide strong evidence bearing on the cross-over principle since there is apparently some mysterious, independent constraint which prevents the direct and indirect objects from being coreferential[2] in such cases. Hence both of the sentence types:

15.(4) *a*   *I gave Charley to himself.
      b   *I gave Charley himself.

15.(5) *a*   *I sold the slave to himself.
      b   *I sold the slave himself.

are ill formed independently of any restrictions on crossing. We could derive direct evidence for crossing constraints only if two conditions were met. First, that although both 15.(4) *a* and *b* and 15.(5) *a* and *b* sentences are ill formed, one type was consistently worse than the other. This would indicate that this form violated both the constraint that direct and indirect object cannot be coreferential in such constructions and the cross-over principle. Secondly, there would have to be evidence that this form type, which was "doubly" ill formed, was in fact the derivative one.

For me, there is slight preference for the *a* forms. Hence if grounds could be found for believing that these were in fact more base-like, with the *b* types derivative, this might count as weak evidence for the cross-over principle's prediction that constant movements cannot cross clause mates.

---

[1] Certain weak evidence for taking the *a* forms as basic derives from the field of *exceptions*. There are many instances of verbal forms which occur only in the *a* form.

  (i)   I explained the problem to Humphrey.
  (ii)   *I explained Humphrey the problem.

There are, however, hardly any cases of verbal forms restricted to *b* structures. It seems though that in general, given an optional rule of the type under discussion, the exceptions tend to be cases where idiosyncratically a form does not permit application. Cases where the rule is idiosyncratically obligatory, although far from unknown, are rarer. This might be taken as at least a suggestion that the *a* forms are more basic.

[2] Notice that this constraint cannot be regarded as purely semantic and residing in the anomaly of the resulting sentences. The restriction holds even where the sentences are perfect semantically:

  (i)   *Harry explained himself to himself.

Independently of this, however, *to-I-O*-movement provides some weak support for Cross-Over IV in the following sense. The principle predicts not only that constant movements *cannot* cross clause mates coreferents but that such rules *can* cross coreferents which are *not* clause mates. And this prediction is of course borne out for *to-I-O*-movement:

15.(6) *a*   I gave the large book$_i$ to the boy who wanted it$_i$.
     b   I gave the boy who wanted it$_i$ the large book$_i$.

15.(7) *a*   I sent the letter he$_i$ needed to the sick man$_j$.
     b   I sent the sick man$_j$ the letter he$_i$ needed.

This fact then provides support for part of Cross-Over IV. Hence although *to-I-O*-movement does not provide very strong direct evidence in favor of our formulation, its operations are entirely consistent with it and do support one aspect of our hypothesis.

It will be relevant later to know the relative orderings of *to-I-O*-movement and the rules of reflexivization and pronominalization. With respect to the former, we can see that *to-I-O*-movement must precede reflexivization. This follows from the fact that although sentences like:

15.(8) *a*   *I sold the slave to himself.
     b   *I sold the slave himself.

are ill formed, the examples of 15.(8) are respectively much less syntactically deviant then those of:

15.(9) *a*   *I sold himself to the slave.
     b   *I sold himself the slave.

Hence regardless of which type, *a* or *b*, is treated as basic, we have an argument that *to-I-O*-movement precedes reflexivization. Similarly, we can show that *to-I-O*-movement must precede pronominalization, a conclusion which follows from the left-right argument:

15.(10) *a*   I sent the new book$_i$ to the girl who wanted it$_i$.
      b   *I sent it$_i$ to the girl who wanted the new book$_i$.
      c   I sent the girl who wanted it$_i$ the new book$_i$.[3]

Thus the operation of *to-I-O*-movement is seen to *precede* both of the rules which yield coreferential pronouns.

---

[3] For the unacceptability of parallel sentences with forwards pronominalization like:

(i)   I sent the girl who wanted the new book$_i$ it$_i$.

See footnote 1 of Chapter 9.

C. FOR-I-O-**MOVEMENT**

The rule of *for-I-O*-movement is involved in the word order of another class of direct and indirect objects. It is responsible for the relations between such pairs as:

15.(11) *a*   I bought a book for Mary.
      b   I bought Mary a book.

15.(12) *a*   I got some water for the horse.
      b   I got the horse some water.

It has been argued rather convincingly by Fillmore (1965) that this rule cannot be collapsed to form one with *to-I-O*-movement. He argued this on the basis of the fact that the two operations can be shown to have distinct ordering relations with other operations, in particular passive. Hence constructions relevant to the operation of *to-I-O*-movement have *three* passive analogues:

15.(13) *a*   I gave a book to the girl.
      b   I gave the girl a book.
      c   A book was given to the girl by me.
      d   The girl was given a book by me.
      e   A book was given by me to the girl.

Since passive operates on directly postverbal NP, these facts are naturally explained by having *to-I-O*-movement precede passive. This will permit passive to take as input both of the structures:

15.(14) *a*   I gave a book to the girl.
      b   I gave the girl a book.

Operation of passive on these yields 15.(13) *c* and *d*. 15.(13) *e* must then be derived by some rule which can shift the position of the *by* phrase.

However, this is not the case for the *for*-construction type examples. These have only *two* passives:

15.(15) *a*   I bought a book for the girl.
      b   I bought the girl a book.
      c   A book was bought for the girl by me.
      d   *The girl was bought a book by me.
      e   A book was bought by me for the girl.

That is, the indirect objects of the *for* cases, unlike those of the *to* cases, cannot be moved into subject position under passive. As Fillmore observed, this is naturally explained by placing *for-I-O*-movement after passive so that when passive applies to such constructions the only directly postverbal NP are direct objects. This yields the overall ordering:

15.(16)   *To-I-O*-movement
          Passive
          For-I-O-movement

And since a rule intervenes between the two indirect object rules, it follows apparently that they are distinct, as concluded by Fillmore.[4]

As in the case of *to* indirect objects, there is no overwhelming evidence for deciding in the *for* cases which forms, those with final indirect object preceded by preposition, or with preposed indirect object, are more basic.[5] And again there is some independent restriction precluding coreference between direct and indirect objects regardless of word order:

15.(17) *a*   *I bought a slave for himself.
        b   *I bought a slave himself.[6]

This fact thus precludes strong support for Cross-Over IV from this rule since as an obvious constant movement the most interesting prediction from the principle is that *for-I-O*-movement cannot cross clause mates. As before, weak evidence about clause mate crossing could only be forthcoming if the base form could be nonarbitrarily determined and the other form shown to be "doubly" ill

---

[4] Actually, this conclusion, which is rather unhappy in view of the great formal similarity of the two rules, follows only when given certain constraints on linguistic theory which appeared valid when Fillmore was writing but no longer seem so. Given a theory in which, for example, there are syntactic features, and syntactic features referring directly to the applicability and actual application of transformational rules [Lakoff (1965)], it becomes possible, I believe, to group these two rules together despite the facts in the text. A verbal form which can occur with an object and a *for*-phrase of the type involved in *for-I-O*-movement will have to be marked as having these properties to distinguish it from verbs that cannot occur in such an environment. Let us abbreviate these properties as [+For]. If then it is assumed that verbal forms are marked with rule features when particular transformations apply, such verbs will be assigned a certain feature, call it [+*I-O*-Movement] when this rule actually operates. The restrictions which Fillmore proposed to handle by the ordering of 15.(16) can, therefore, be represented by a statement to the effect that no verbal form can simultaneously have the features [+For], [+*I-O*-Movement], and [+Passive], where the latter is the feature assigned when passive applies. This statement requires only one movement rule and does not exclude application of both the indirect object movement rule and passive in the *to*-constructions since the verbal forms of these will not have the feature [+For]. The possibility of reducing *to-I-O*-movement and *for-I-O*-movement to one rule can be taken as an important argument in favor of syntactic features referring directly to the application of particular transformational rules, a conclusion supported by the widest variety of other evidence as well.

[5] The argument given in footnote 1 for *to*-construction holds here also.

[6] Notice that this must *not* be interpreted as a case where the *himself* is an emphatic reflexive on *slave*. On that reading, the two NP are part of a single complex NP. The intended reading, the one with the asterisk, is one where there are two independent NP.

formed. Again I have a weak preference for the *a* type in 15.(17) so that if, as seems likely, this is the more basic form, some evidence for our formulation may be derivable.

As with *to-I-O*-movement, the present rule is consistent with Cross-Over IV and does support the prediction that constant movements can cross coreferents which are not clause mates:

15.(18) *a* I bought the large book$_i$ for the boy who wanted it$_i$.
     b I bought the boy who wanted it$_i$ the large book$_i$.

Hence some limited support for our formulation of the cross-over principle is derivable from *for-I-O*-movement.

The ordering of *for-I-O*-movement and reflexivization and pronominalization should again be determined. It turns out to be exactly the same. *For-I-O*-movement must precede both of these pronominalization rules. The former ordering follows from the fact that although sentences like 15.(17) are ill formed, the examples of:

15.(19) *a* *I bought himself for a slave.
     b *I bought himself a slave.

are much more deviant syntactically. Hence regardless of whether preposed or postposed indirect object order is more basic, there is an argument that *for-I-O*-movement precedes reflexivization. The ordering *for-I-O*-movement-pronominalization follows immediately from the left-right argument:

15.(20) *a* I bought the new book$_i$ for the girl who wanted it$_i$.
     b *I bought it$_i$ for the girl who wanted the new book$_i$.
     c I bought the girl who wanted it$_i$ the new book$_i$[7]

D. GENITIVE PREPOSING

Another rule which moves NP but which provides no evidence really relevant to our concerns is that which prepositions genitive NP. That is, one finds:

15.(21) *a* A house of Harry's
     b Some house of Harry's
     c This house of Harry's
     d That house of Harry's
     e Sm houses of Harry's
     f These houses of Harry's
     g Those houses of Harry's
     h *The house of Harry's
     i *The houses of Harry's

---

[7]See footnote 3.

But corresponding to the two ungrammatical definite forms are the other structures:

15.(22) *a*   Harry's house
        b   Harry's houses

Hence, as proposed by Chomsky,[8] it is natural to derive these two otherwise orphan form types from the *h* and *i* varieties by a rule which preposes the post-prepositional genitive NP.[9] But this rule, call it *genitive preposing*, unfortunately provides no evidence for cross-over matters since it does not have the opportunity to cross coreferent NP in the most relevant cases.

Since the rule has an application path defined by a structure with the analysis:

15.(23)   NP + Preposition

it is clearly a constant movement. Hence the most interesting relevant data would have to involve clause mates. It might be thought at first that such data is excluded by the sheer dissimilarity of the head NP and the genitive one along such dimensions as animate, human, and so on. But this is *not* the case. Cases similar or even identical along these dimensions occur freely:

15.(24) *a*   John's friend
        b   Your father
        c   Their critics
        d   Her victim
        e   Carter's killer
        f   Schwarz's employee

However, there is some kind of independent constraint which prevents a coreferential interpretation in these cases. That is, for instance, 15.(24) *e* is not understandable as descriptive of a suicide. This fact is not explained by anything said above or anywhere else previously.

That this mysterious constraint is fully independent of crossing restrictions is shown by its presence in the analogues of 15.(21). That is, coreferentiality

---

[8] In unpublished work.

[9] This proposal receives strong support from the fact that unpreposed genitives are possible with definite articles if there is a following relative:

(i)   *The house of the woman's
(ii)   The house of the woman's which was burned by the raiders

It also receives support from the fact that the unpreposed order shows up with definite articles in certain cases where a "degenitivization" rule [referred to in footnote 7 of Chapter 6] operates:

(iii) *a*   The president of Chile
      b   Chile's president

between underlined elements is barred just as clearly in the phrases of 15.(25) as it is in those of 15.(26):

15.(25) *a*   That *critic* of *his*
     b   A *critic* of *hers*

15.(26) *a*   *His critic*
     b   *Her critic*

But nominal movement by genitive preposing only occurs in the derivations of 15.(26). The explanation of the coreferentiality constraint in preposed genitives is, therefore, its existence in the underlying source expressions parallel to 15.(25). The absence of coreferential interpretations in 15.(25) is thus a function of a more general constraint on the whole genitive construction.[10] It has nothing to do with crossing constraints.

Like *to-I-O*-movement and *for-I-O*-movement, which provided some support for Cross-Over IV by being consistent with its predictions about the possibilities for their crossing coreferents which are *not* clause mates, genitive preposing yields this kind of weak support. This follows because the constraints which independently ban coreference in examples like 15.(25) and 15.(26), which involve clause mates, are inoperative in examples like:

15.(27) *a*   A *critic* of the man who raped *her* repeatedly
     b   One *victim* of the villain who assaulted *him* viciously

15.(28) *a*   The man who raped *her* repeatedly's *critic*
     b   The villain who assaulted *him* viciously's *victim*

Here the italicized NP *can* be understood as coreferents. Hence genitive preposing has a chance to cross coreferents which are nonclause mates. It is thus consistent with the predictions about constraints on nominal movement provided by Cross-Over IV with respect to constant movements and clause mates, and it weakly supports the predictions about nonclause mates with such rules.

E. COMPLEX-NP-SHIFT

Another rule weakly relevant to the study of cross-over phenomena has been discovered by Ross (1967a:56) and is called *complex-NP-shift*. This rule moves an NP to the right end of the next more inclusive sentence. Some of Ross's examples of the operation of this rule include:

15.(29) = Ross's (3.15)
     a   He attributed the fire to a short circuit.
     b   *He attributed to a short circuit the fire.
     c   He attributed to a short circuit the fire which destroyed most of my factory.

---

[10] I have discussed this general constraint briefly and not entirely adequately in Postal (1969).

This example suggests that the condition on movement under complex-NP-shift is that the relevant NP dominate an S and this turns out to be the case in general. Observe, too:

15.(30) = Ross's (3.18)
  a They dismissed the proposal as too costly.
  b *They dismissed as too costly the proposal.
  c They dismissed as too costly the proposal for the State to build a sidewalk from Dartmouth to Smith.

Consider now cases where the moved NP contains an NP coreferential to one over which it moves:

15.(31) a Charley threw the bomb which the man$_i$ who I know invented at him$_i$.[11]
  b Charley threw at the man$_i$ who I know the bomb which he$_i$ invented.

Since the b form, which results from application of complex-NP-shift, is well formed, it follows that the cross-over principle must not be applicable. The coreferential NP here are not clause mates; therefore, if the formulation of Chapter 14 is to hold, the explanation must lie in the fact that complex-NP-shift is a constant movement. And this raises some difficulties.

Ross states this rule (1967a:56) in the form:

15.(32) X, NP, Y
          1   2 3

with certain subsidiary conditions on the second term, namely that it dominate an S, and on the third, which we ignore. But it must be remembered that Ross does not operate with the notion of abbreviatory variables and there is every reason to assume, I think, that the correct version of this grammatical rule involves movement over a variable of this type.

The formulation of complex-NP-shift involves many difficulties, some of which are discussed at considerable length by Ross. It is not my intention to go into them here. It should be pointed out, however, that the rule really only works on predicate NP. Subjects are excluded:

15.(33) a The man who I know who Charley hates is ugly.
  b *Is ugly the man who I know who Charley hates?

15.(34) a I think that Charley bought a book from Jack.
  b *I think that Charley bought from Jack a book.
  c I think that Charley bought from Jack a huge house which is worth nothing.

---

[11] See footnote 1 of Chapter 9 for the unacceptability of such sentences.

    d I think that an enormous man who owned six green Jaguars bought a house from Jack.

    e *I think that bought a house from Jack an enormous man who owned six green Jaguars.

These facts suggest to me that the proper formulation of the rule takes it to move an NP from a predicate over an abbreviatory variable occurrence defining the rest of that sentence. Roughly:

$$15.(35)\quad X,\ [\ Y,\ \text{Verb/Adjective}+(NP,\ NP,\ Z_a,\ ]\ ,\ \ Z \Longrightarrow 1,2,3,5,4,6$$

$$
\begin{array}{ccccccc}
 & S & & & & S & \\
1 & 2 & & 3 & & 4\ 5 & 6
\end{array}
$$

As this formulation brings out, complex-NP-shift moves an NP over a sequence of structures which can be given in a finite list of constants and abbreviatory variables. The rule does not make essential use of variables in the sense that rules like *Wh-Q*-movement do. And by the formulation of Cross-Over IV, this predicts the observed result that it can cross coreferential NP if these are not clause mates. I take it then that this rule provides the same kind of weak evidence in favor of one aspect of the formulation given in Chapter 14 as is given by *to-I-O*-movement, *for I-O*-movement, and genitive preposing.

    Incidentally, this conclusion follows even if the formulation of 15.(35) is not accepted. It is clear independently that complex-NP-shift must be a constant movement in view of its functional properties. It does not have the unbounded movement properties of true variable movements like the *wh*-movement rules.

    I can find no cases where it would be possible for complex-NP-shift to have the opportunity to cross clause mates since in all cases where it applies independent constraints[12] seem to preclude the identity. The only exceptions are the *about* constructions discussed earlier in Chapter 5. But these yield no argument since exactly the sentences which would be used to show something about complex-NP-shift are produced independently by *about*-movement. That is, there is no argument that sentences like:

    15.(36) *I talked about the man who wanted to be president to himself.

are ill formed due to Cross-Over IV constraining complex-NP-shift since the ill-formedness independently follows from this principle and *about*-movement.

---

[12]This is not entirely accidental but follows from what is an unexplained regularity of English. Namely, there are no cases, other than those with *about*, where multiple NP in the predicate can be coreferential. We have already seen this in the case of both *for* and *to* indirect object types. See also:

    (i)   *I bought myself from myself.

    (ii) *I cut the knife with itself.

    (iii) *Harry fought with me over myself.

This constraint again cannot be regarded as semantic since many if not all of the blocked sentences have nonanomalous readings.

Recall that *about*-movement precedes reflexivization so that the ancestor of the pronoun, *himself*, here could, with appropriate assumptions,[13] have been complex.

F. LEFT DISLOCATION AND RIGHT DISLOCATION

Ross (1967a) discusses two putative rules that have the effect of placing an NP at the extremes of a sentence, leaving a pronominal form in the original position. *Left dislocation* is the rule he formulates to derive sentences such as:

15.(37) *a* Charley$_i$, he$_i$'s out of his mind.[14]
     b Schwarz$_i$, Mary will never marry him$_i$.
     c Thor$_i$, Tony thinks he$_i$ was a good god.

According to Ross, these are respectively derived from structures like:

15.(38) *a* Charley's out of his mind.
     b Mary will never marry Schwarz.
     c Tony thinks Thor was a good god.

by a rule which places a double of the relevant NP in sentence initial position, while pronominalizing the original.[15] As 15.(37) *c* and 15.(39) show, the operations of this proposed rule must not be limited by higher clause boundaries:

15.(39) *a* Charley$_i$, I like him$_i$.
     b Charley$_i$, I think Bill likes him$_i$.
     c Charley$_i$, I think Mary said Bill likes him$_i$.
     d Charley$_i$, I think Jones knew Mary said Bill likes him$_i$.

In other words the operation involved would have to involve the use of essential variables.

---

[13] Actually, these assumptions are impossible since arguments first constructed by E. Bach, S. Peters, and W. Woods show that an identity of constituent condition on complex NP leads to inconsistent assertions about some sentences given an assumption of the finiteness of deep structures.

[14] This sentence must not be confused with sentences where the initial NP is a vocative and designates the person to whom it is addressed.

[15] Ross (1967a) builds the pronominalization into the rule itself but this might follow automatically from pronominalization if left dislocation were to precede pronominalization, an ordering which is suggested by the left-right argument.

The question is whether left dislocation can move an NP across one with which it is coreferential. Since its movement path[16] is represented in part by essential variables, left dislocation should, according to Cross-Over IV, involve crossing constraints of the strict kind, that is, not limited to clause mates. Unfortunately, it seems impossible to tell if this is the case. Consider a structure like:

15.(40)   Charley$_i$ thinks that Mary hates Charley$_i$.

Suppose now the rule applies to the first occurrence of *Charley$_i$*, which it can do with no crossing. The result will be 15.(41)*a* converted to 15.(41)*b* by pronominalization.

15.(41)*a*   Charley$_i$, Charley$_i$ thinks that Mary hates Charley$_i$.
   b   Charley, he thinks that Mary hates him.

If, however, the rule applied to the second occurrence, which would involve crossing, the result would be identical. That is, because the rule *copies* NP rather than chopping them out and moving them proper, it leaves no traces of its action in cases of multiple occurrences of NP which are coreferents.[17] Hence this putative rule seems irrelevant to the study of cross-over phenomena.

Moreover, it is not even clear to me that there *is* such a rule since examples like 15.(37) seem related to sentences like:

15.(42)*a*   As for Charley$_i$, he$_i$'s out of his$_i$ mind.
   b   As for Schwarz$_i$, Mary will never marry him$_i$.
   c   As for Thor$_i$, Tony thinks he$_i$ was a good god.

And it can hardly be suggested that these are derived from structures like 15.(38). It may well be, therefore, that rather than expansions of simpler structures under a copying rule, 15.(37)-type sentences are actually reductions of sentences like 15.(42) or the like. The origins of the latter are not obvious.[18]

---

[16] Actually, of course, this rule is not a movement but rather an operation which copies a constituent, that is, places a double of it somewhere else in the tree. The distinction between rules which actually rip out constituents and move them as against doubling rules is referred to by Ross (1967a) as *chopping* versus *copying*. He shows that the contrast plays an important role in governing constraints on rules. Movement constraints of the type he has uncovered apply only to chopping rules.

[17] One important constraint on such a rule is that it operate only once per sentence. Otherwise doubled NP will pile up at the front, for example,

 (i) Charley knows Betty likes Jack.
 (ii) *Charley, Betty, Jack he knows she likes him.

with, however, no known principle determining the order of elements at the front. This is a peculiar restriction and again may cast doubt on the existence of the rule in the first place.

[18] Another restriction on the proposed rule is that it operate only on main clauses, although these may be conjoined:

 (i) Charley, he's insane, and Mary, she's crazy, but they're happy together.
 (ii) *The fact that Charley, he's insane, disturbed Lucille.

Ross proposes the rule of *right dislocation* to account for sentences like:

15.(43) = Ross's (6.145)

    a They$_i$ spoke to the janitor about that robbery yesterday, the cops$_i$.

    b The cops spoke to him$_i$ about that robbery yesterday, the janitor$_i$.

    c The cops spoke to the janitor about it$_i$ yesterday, that robbery$_i$.

These are derived, Ross claims, from the structure of:

15.(44) The cops spoke to the janitor about that robbery yesterday.

As with the previous rule, I am far from convinced that this operation[19] is truly part of the grammar. But this is really irrelevant here since even if there is such a rule it provides no evidence one way or the other for cross-over phenomena. Consider:

15.(45) Charley$_i$ said that Charley$_i$ would win.

Applying the rule to the second occurrence of *Charley$_i$* one would derive by the copying:

15.(46) Charley$_i$ said that Charley$_i$ would win, Charley$_i$.

Here pronominalization application will yield:[20]

15.(47) He said he would win, Charley.

This would then be derivable without crossing. But if the rule applied instead to the leftmost occurrence of *Charley$_i$* in 15.(45) the result would again be 15.(46). Hence, again because the rule copies rather than moves elements proper, it seems to be irrelevant for the study of crossing restrictions.

---

[19] However, an important argument that it *does* exist is the fact that the putative operation is upward bounded:

    (i) He's insane, Charley.

    (ii) *The boy who hates him$_i$ is insane, Charley$_i$.

This property would follow naturally from the existence of a transformational operation. Notice additionally that the rule operates to the right, and movements to the right are in general upward bounded.

[20] Again, as with left dislocation, Ross builds the pronominalization into the rule itself. This cannot be gotten around so easily by appeal to ordering relative to pronominalization since the backwards condition would predict, falsely, that 15.(46) can be turned into:

    (i) *Charley$_i$ said that he$_i$ would win, him$_i$.

G. COMPOUND FORMATION

Another rule which moves NP is that involved in the formation of noun compounds from postposed prepositional phrases, that is, that which relates such pairs as:

15.(48) *a*   A building for monkeys
        b   A monkey building

15.(49) *a*   A serum for smallpox
        b   A smallpox serum

This rule, discussed by Lees (1960:174), is of no relevance to the study of crossing restrictions on coreferents since the moved NP never crosses anything to which it could be coreferential. It is especially important to observe here that the moving NP is typically *generic*.

16 RULES OF MORE DIRECT RELEVANCE

A. CONJUNCT MOVEMENT

There is a rule first proposed by Lakoff and Peters (1966) which moves one of a binary pair of conjoined NP to the end of the next more inclusive sentence. They propose this rule as the basis for the relations between such pairs as:

16.(1) a John and Bill wrestled.
     b John wrestled with Bill.

16.(1) a is ambiguous. It is a paraphrase of 16.(1) b on the reading where it refers to one act of wrestling in which both John and Bill took part. Lakoff and Peters provide a good deal of evidence for postulating the rule under discussion and for taking the conjoined type structures to be more basic.

Conjunct movement does apparently have the opportunity of crossing coreferent NP, even those which are clause mates. That is, there are sentences like:

16.(2) a John and Bill rescued Betty.
     b John rescued Betty with Bill.

Under the Lakoff/Peters analysis, the b form is derived by conjunct movement, which crosses the NP *Bill* over the object NP *Betty*. It would apparently be necessary only to find variants of 16.(2) where the right conjunct and the object were coreferential in order to find clause mate cases for conjunct movement. That is:

16.(3) a *John and I discussed me.
     b *John and I criticized me.

But as it turns out, all such examples are on independent grounds [briefly discussed in Chapter 17, Section B] ungrammatical.

Therefore, evidence for cross-over constraints with respect to clause mates can only be derived with respect to conjunct movement if it can be argued that while the sentences of 16.(3) are ill formed, *those of 16.(4) are much worse*:

16.(4) *a*   *John and I discussed me with myself.
    b   *John criticized me with myself.

But in this case this judgment is clearly borne out. The examples of 16.(3) are ungrammatical in a relatively subtle way. Those of 16.(4) are crashingly unacceptable. It should be emphasized that this contrast is independent of the choice of verbal element:

16.(5) *a*   *John and I amused me.
    b   **John amused me with myself[1].

16.(6) *a*   *John and I shaved me.
    b   **John shaved me with myself.

Such facts provide clear support for Cross-Over IV if the extra deviance of the *b* type forms can be attributed to crossing constraints. Cross-Over IV does predict the extra deviance since, given this principle, the *a* forms violate the restriction that one of a set of conjunct NP cannot be coreferential to some other NP in the same clause. The *b* forms violate this plus Cross-Over IV, as applied to conjunct movement. Hence in a direct way the *b* forms are predicted by Cross-Over IV to be "doubly ungrammatical," that is, to involve two violations of principles determining well-formedness in English. And this correlates with our perception of their degree of deviance from the set of completely well-formed expressions.[2]

We have been assuming in this discussion that conjunct movement is a constant movement, which reduces its interesting cross-over restrictions to those involving clause mates. That this is indeed the case is clear initially from the function of the rule, namely, that it has an intraclause domain. Hence:

16.(7) *a*   That John and Bill wrestled was disgusting.
    b   That John wrestled with Bill was disgusting.
    c   *That John wrestled was disgusting with Bill.

16.(8) *a*   The man who saw John and Harry arguing was a Communist.
    b   The man who saw John arguing with Harry was a Communist.
    c.   *The man who saw John arguing was a Communist with Harry.

---

[1] This example possibly has an irrelevant reading under which the *with*-phrase is an instrumental. This reading is also ill formed.

[2] The weakness in this argument is the generalization, discussed in footnote 12 of Chapter 15, banning coreference among the NP of predicates. It might well be claimed that the greater deviance of 16.(5) *b* over 16.(5) *a* is a function not of a crossing restriction but of a violation of the generalization of footnote 12.

What is wrong with both 16.(7) c and 16.(8) c is that the conjunct NP has been moved across a higher clause boundary. In the correct b cases, movement has been constrained to occur only within the clause of origin.

The fact that conjunct movement is *functionally* a constant movement like such rules as passive is again supportive of Cross-Over IV since this principle predicts that such rules *can* cross coreferents if these are not clause mates. And this prediction is borne out for conjunct movement:

16.(9) a John and Lucy$_i$ arrested the man who attacked her$_i$.
      b John arrested the man who attacked Lucy$_i$ with her$_i$.[3]
      c John arrested the man who attacked her$_i$ with Lucy$_i$.

16.(10) a Joan and Bob$_i$ visited the man who insulted him$_i$.
      b Joan visited the man who insulted him$_i$ with Bob$_i$.
      c Joan visited the man who insulted Bob$_i$ with him$_i$.

Consider, then, the formulation of conjunct movement in such a way that its formal structure indicates that it is in fact a constant movement, as is required if our approach to the differential crossing constraints of constant and variable movement rules is to be maintained. Ross (1967a:443) states this rule as:

16.(11) [NP, [and NP]] VP
      NP   NP   NP NP
         1   2   3

Since this formulation contains no variables at all, it certainly qualifies the rule defined as a constant movement. However, there are difficulties with this formulation. Trivially, the rule requires end variables or their equivalent to indicate that it may apply on embedded, conjoined, and such clauses as well as on the main clause of a whole sentence. More seriously, the formulation of 16.(11) apparently is suitable only for the operation of the rule on grammatical subjects. Yet evidently conjunct movement also operates on nonsubjects since one certainly wishes this rule to deal with cases like:

16.(12) a I mixed water and sand.
      b I mixed water with sand.

16.(13) a I introduced John and Mary.
      b I introduced John to Mary.

There are then two possibilities. First, it might be correct to reformulate 16.(11) in terms of an abbreviatory variable, roughly as follows:

16.(14) X, [X_a, NP, [and NP] , Y_a,] Z
         S   NP   NP   S
    1   2   3   4   5   6

---

[3] See footnote 1 of Chapter 9 for the unacceptability of such examples.

This formulation also defines a constant movement and would allow application to conjunct NP in subject or nonsubject position.[4]

Another possibility, not incompatiable with 16.(14), is that sentences like 16.(12) and 16.(13) actually have causative or causative-like analyses in which the surface structure main verbs, *mix, introduce*, and so on are actually the intransitive verbs of an embedded complement sentence. Schematically

> 16.(15)   X cause   [it   [A and B mix   ]   ]
>   NP   S   S NP

For structures like this, a restriction of conjunct movement operation to grammatical subjects would likely suffice. It is clear, however, that one way or another, conjunct movement can be formulated as a constant movement and that uncertainties in its exact description do not involve this point.

Overall then, conjunct movement provides two kinds of support for Cross-Over IV. It supports the prediction that constant movements can cross nonclause mate coreferents and it supports the claim that they cannot cross clause mate coreferents in terms of the argument that sentences like 16.(6) *b* are worse than sentences like 16.(6) *a*.

B. *Y*-MOVEMENT AND THE CRUCIAL ROLE OF ORDERING

Comparing sentences like:

> 16.(16) *a*   I like Harry.
>   *b*   I think you hate Harry.
>   *c*   I bought a book for Harry.

with sentences such as:

> 16.(17) *a*   Harry, I like.
>   *b*   Harry, I think you hate.
>   *c*   Harry, I bought a book for.
>   *d*   For Harry, I bought a book.

one begins to suspect the existence of a rule which thrusts NP to sentence initial position under certain conditions. The resulting sentences are similar to those found in Yiddish and for all I know the existence of the construction in English may owe something to contact with speakers of other Germanic languages. Let us refer to the relevant hypothetical rule, therefore, as *Y-movement*.[5]

---

[4] We ignore in this formulation any indication of the structural properties which pick out those coordinate NP that are subject to conjunct movement.

[5] Ross (1967a) refers to this rule as *topicalization*.

Y-movement is a key test for the concept of cross-over constraints, since, apparently, coreferential NP are permitted to cross under its operation:

16.(18) *a*   Harry, I can't begin to understand.
      b   Myself, I can't begin to understand.

16.(19) *a*   To Harry, I never send things.
      b   To myself, I never send things.

Furthermore, the coreferent NP which cross here meet the "mention" conditions and other constraints of Cross-Over IV. This kind of behavior makes *Y*-movement unique among all the rules of NP movement we have considered. If such facts cannot be explained, Cross-Over IV is in jeopardy. Because of *Y*-movement and other phenomena, Cross-Over IV will have to be modified and restricted. But the facts of *Y*-movement behavior will be seen not to be incompatible with the basic idea that there are constraints on the ability of transformational rules to cross coreferent NP.

The first point to make is that *Y*-movement is a variable movement. It moves NP to the front from arbitrarily deep points of embedding:

16.(20) *a*   Harry, I respect.
      b   Harry, I found out that Bill doesn't respect.
      c   Harry, I found out that Mary insinuated that Bill doesn't respect.

Hence, in this respect *Y*-movement goes in the class with *Wh-Q*-movement and *Wh-Rel*-movement. Cross-Over IV predicts, therefore, that its crossing constraints should govern any coreferents meeting the "mention" condition, not just clause mates.

Examples like 16.(18) *b* and 16.(19) *b* seem to show that *Y*-movement can cross coreferents. It might be assumed then that *Y*-movement is a rule not governed by crossing restrictions. This is quite false, however. Observe:

16.(21) *a*   Barbara claimed that Tony hated you.
      b   You, Barbara claimed that Tony hated.

16.(22) *a*   Barbara$_i$ claimed that Tony hated her$_i$.
      b   *Her$_i$, Barbara$_i$ claimed that Tony hated.
      c   *Barbara$_i$, she$_i$ claimed that Tony hated.

16.(23) *a*   Harold wanted Betty to visit Bill.
      b   Bill, Harold wanted Betty to visit.

16.(24) *a*   Harold$_i$ wanted Betty to visit him$_i$.
      b   *Him$_i$, Harold$_i$ wanted Betty to visit.
      c   *Harold$_i$, he$_i$ wanted Betty to visit.

16.(25) *a*   I told Jim to have Betty help you.
      b   You, I told Jim to have Betty help.

16.(26) *a*   I told Jim$_i$ to have Betty help him$_i$.
      b   *Him$_i$, I told Jim$_i$ to have Betty help.
      c   *Jim$_i$, I told him$_i$ to have Betty help.

It is clear, then, that the operation of Y-movement is *in part*[6] governed by the same sorts of restrictions as other rules of the variable movement[7] type. What requires explanation, therefore, is the difference between examples like 16.(18) *b* and 16.(19) *b*, in which coreferents are crossable by Y-movement, and those like 16.(22), 16.(24), and 16.(26) *b* and *c*, where they are not.

Investigation quickly reveals that examples like 16.(18) *b* and 16.(19) *b* all share a common property. In each case, that member of the coreferent pair which is moved across the other is a *reflexive pronoun*. Furthermore, this is perfectly general. Reflexive pronouns resulting from reflexivization can be crossed over coreferents by Y-movement regardless of construction type:

16.(27) *a* I talked to Bill about myself.
      b About myself, I talked to Bill.
      c Myself, I talked to Bill about.

16.(28) *a* I bought a book for myself.
      b For myself, I bought a book.
      c Myself, I bought a book for.

16.(29) *a* I made a bet on myself.
      b On myself, I made a bet.
      c Myself, I made a bet on.

The question arises, therefore, as to what can explain this peculiar behavior of reflexive pronouns under Y-movement. My approach to this problem depends on the phenomenon of rule ordering together with some assumptions about the functioning of pronominalization rules like reflexivization and pronominalization. We have assumed [see Chapter 2] that these rules, which operate on coreferent NP, mark a specified NP with certain features, including [+Pro] and [+Anaphoric]. Given the fact that transformational rules are partially ordered, it follows as a matter of logic that, given a rule which potentially crosses coreferent NP, one of the relevant NP will be marked [+Anaphoric] or not depending on the relative ordering of the crossing rule with the rules that carry out pronominalization operations.

---

[6] Bouton (1968:21) lists as well formed the example:

    (i) *Bill* the boy who hated *him* killed.

where the italicized NP are supposed to be coreferential. As of now, I take this to be a mistake, since for me and everyone else I have questioned (i) has no coreferential reading.

[7] It is rather striking that we are unable to find any examples under the *wh*-rules which correspond to Y-movement examples like:

    (i) Himself, Lyndon loves.

that is, cases where the rule can cross a reflexive over its coreferent.

Let us represent a pair of coreferent NP which might be crossed by some transformation, *T*, as A and B, where A is the leftmost of the two at the point of application of *T*. Then the following possibilities exist:

16.(30) *a* Either A or B is marked [+Anaphoric].
       b Neither A nor B is marked [+Anaphoric].

My suggestion is that the difference between these two cases is crucial in explaining the otherwise mysterious behavior of *Y*-movement with respect to reflexive pronouns on the one hand and all others on the other. So far, we have been speaking generally of constraints on crossing one NP over another with which it is coreferential. I suggest now that this is too loose a formulation. One must distinguish whether these NP have undergone operations of pronominalization or not. It will turn out, I suggest, that crossing constraints are fully in effect only for pairs of coreferent NP *which have not undergone such rules at the point when crossing becomes possible.* Let us refer to a coreferent NP which has not undergone any rule of pronominalization, that is, which is not marked [+Anaphoric], as a *pronominal virgin.*

Returning now to *Y*-movement, I wish to suggest that the ability of this rule to cross a reflexive pronoun over a coreferent but to yield no other crossings incompatible with Cross-Over IV is a function of the following generalization:

16.(31) *Y*-movement obeys Cross-Over IV insofar as the coreferent NP involved are pronominal virgins, but not otherwise.

For this principle to yield correct inferences about *Y*-movement behavior in conjunction with Cross-Over IV it is necessary that, for example, the derivation of sentences like:

16.(32) Himself, Tony always buys things for.

takes place in such a fashion that *Y*-movement applies at a point where the coreferent NP, *Tony* and *himself*, are *not* pronominal virgins, while the derivation of nonsentences like:

16.(33) *Him_i, $Tony_i$ said Harry insulted.

can only take place in such a fashion that *Y*-movement becomes applicable at a point when the coreferents here, him_i and $Tony_i$, are pronominal virgins. These conditions for 16.(32) and 16.(33) can be jointly met if and only if the order of rules is:

16.(34) *Reflexivization*
         Y-movement
         Pronominalization

It is therefore necessary to argue that this is in fact the ordering of these rules.

Let us first consider the ordering with reflexivization. We argued earlier [see Chapter 10] that both *Wh-Q*-movement and *Wh-Rel*-movement followed reflexivization, while every constant movement we have considered precedes this pronominalization rule. Perhaps it would be well to recall the argument for ordering reflexivization and the *wh*-rules. This depended crucially on such examples as:

16.(35) *a* You saw someone stab you.
       b *You saw someone stab yourself.
       c Who did you see stab you?
       d *Who did you see stab yourself?

The argument was that since moving of the subject of the embedded clause *X stab you* prunes the S-node over this clause, having *Wh-Q*-movement precede reflexivization would wrongly predict reflexivization in such cases. If, however, *Wh-Q*-movement follows reflexivization, application of reflexivization is correctly blocked in such cases. This ordering is, moreover, compatible with all other known facts about these rules.

Exactly the same argument can be given to show that *Y*-movement must follow reflexivization.

16.(36) *a* You saw Harry stab Barbara.
       b Barbara, you saw Harry stab.

16.(37) *a* You saw Harry stab you.
       b *You saw Harry stab yourself.
       c Harry, you saw stab you.
       d *Harry, you saw stab yourself.

Hence, just as with the *wh*-rules, if *Y*-movement preceded reflexivization, one would, in those cases where *Y*-movement *reorders* the subject of an embedded clause, predict application of reflexivization between elements of the main clause and elements of the embedded clause since the rule causes the S-node of the embedded clause to be pruned. But this does not happen. Ergo, the ordering must have reflexivization first.

Of course, unlike the case of the *wh*-rules, there is a much more direct argument for having reflexivization precede *Y*-movement. This is derived directly from the fact that in such *Y*-movement sentences as:

16.(38) *a* Himself, Harry loves.
       b Myself, I never buy anything for.

the reflexive pronoun occurs to the left of its coreferent. But in general reflexivization operates left-to-right. The odd ordering of reflexive pronouns in Y-movement sentences follows directly from the ordering of Y-movement after reflexivization. With another ordering, this word order would require *ad hoc* complications of reflexivization. This would be especially bad since I believe reflexivization is, in large part at least, a universal operation.[8] In particular, its left-to-right character seems language independent. Therefore it would be doubly unfortunate to add *ad hoc* right-to-left conditions to the English rule since this would involve not only giving up a generalization about this one language, but probably a deeper one about human grammar. It follows that the order of reflexivization before Y-movement is well established on these grounds.

Moreover, the above argument is even stronger than it seems at first. In fact, if reflexivization is ordered after Y-movement, not only is *ad hoc* backwards reflexivization required, but reflexivization must also be modified to allow reflexivization to operate between NP that are not clause mates. This follows because the structure of examples like 16.(39) *a* and *b* is as in 16.(39) *c*:

16.(39) *a* Himself, Harry loves.

　　 b Harriet, Joan can't stand.

　　 c

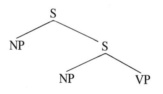

The argument for the bracketing of 16.(39) is simply that everything after the initial word in each of 16.(39) *a* and *b* is a constituent, and this is the original main S constituent of the sentence. The argument that the highest node in the tree is S is twofold. First, it keeps every tree under the condition that its single root is labeled S. Secondly, and much more importantly, this assignment of labels follows from the general principle of derived constituent structure needed for one type of adjunction operation which underlies movement rules. It follows that if reflexivization applies after Y-movement, its operation between the topicalized NP and any NP inside the original clause involves nonclause mates. Hence this ordering requires giving up another equally fundamental generaliza-

---

[8] See discussion of this in Postal (1968), Ross (1967a).

tion about reflexivization in English. Overall then, the ordering of Y-movement after reflexivization is strongly justified.[9]

We have shown that reflexivization precedes Y-movement. Now consider the ordering of Y-movement and pronominalization. That Y-movement must precede pronominalization follows more or less directly from the left-right argument:

> 16.(40) a Harry$_i$ threatened the man who insulted him$_i$.
> b The man who insulted him$_i$, Harry$_i$ threatened.
> c The man who insulted Harry$_i$, he$_i$ threatened.

Since both forwards and backwards pronominalization are possible out of NP preposed by Y-movement, it follows that Y-movement must have applied at the point where the backwards condition becomes relevant. But this point is just the point where pronominalization is checked for applicability. If Y-movement followed pronominalization, the latter would operate on already pronominalized structures like 16.(40) a. Such application would yield only results like 16.(40) b. But the perfectly well-formed structures like 16.(40) c could only be derived from pre Y-movement structures like:

> 16.(41)   *He$_i$ threatened the man who insulted Harry$_i$.

---

[9] This ordering has some interesting correlations and implications. Every constant movement we have considered, passive, *tough*-movement, *about*-movement, *psych*-movement, *it*-replacement, *to-I-O*-movement, *for-I-O*-movement, *complex-NP*-shift, genitive preposing, has been shown to precede reflexivization or is at least consistent with this assumption. It follows that Y-movement follows all of these rules in the ordering. This is, in many cases, independently determinable. For example, that Y-movement follows passive is inferrable directly from the fact that Y-movement may operate on the *by*-phrase NP which has been placed by passive in the predicate:

> (i) a Harry, Joan was insulted by.
> b Marsha, Bill was seduced by.

Consequently, a certain correlation between rule types and rule ordering emerges. All of the constant movements which rearrange NP in clauses precede reflexivization. The three variable movements which rearrange NP positions follow reflexivization. It is possible that two other features can be added here. Certainly, all of the three variable movements can be shown to be necessarily noncyclical. Probably, the constant movements can all be argued to be cyclical. In addition, the latter rules may have exceptions—verbal elements which do not permit their application. But none of the variable movements is known to induce this property. Hence an interesting correlation matrix of properties emerges of the following sort:

(ii)

	Precede Reflexivization	Cyclical	Exceptions
Constant Movements	+	+	+
Variable Movements	−	−	−

But these are ill formed. Ergo, either 16.(40) cannot be derived from a post pronominalization rule of Y-movement or the latter must be complicated in an extremely *ad hoc* and cumbersome way to work obligatorily on structures like 16.(41). However, all the facts follow naturally if the ordering is, as claimed, with Y-movement preceding. [See Lakoff (to appear) for a fuller version of this argument.]

We thus claim to have established the ordering of 16.(34). With this done, we can return to our essential problem: explaining why Y-movement can cross coreferent NP, even when the moving NP corresponds to the NP symbol "mentioned" in the rule, but only when this moving NP is a reflexive pronoun. In short, we can return to the explanation of the contrast between:

16.(42) *a*   Himself$_i$, Tony$_i$ loves.
     b   *Him$_i$, Tony$_i$ claimed I didn't love.
     c   *Tony$_i$, he$_i$ claimed I didn't love.

16.(43) *a*   Myself, I understand partially.
     b   *Me, I claimed Tony didn't understand.

16.(44) *a*   Yourself, you have betrayed.
     b   *You, I told you Bill betrayed.

The explanation to be offered is as follows. Given the ordering of rules in 16.(34), in the *a* cases here, Y-movement becomes applicable at a point *after* the reflexive pronoun has been at least partially generated, that is, after the appropriate NP has been marked [+Anaphoric]. That is, reflexivization has already applied. Hence, when Y-movement applies, it crosses coreferents, but one of these is not a pronominal virgin. Hence this crossing, although incompatible with Cross-Over IV, is compatible with the supplementary statement 16.(31). In the *b* and *c* cases, however, the situation is different. Here the coreferent NP are not clause mates. Hence reflexivization cannot apply to them. And since Y-movement applies before pronominalization, it follows that at the point this reordering becomes applicable the relevant coreferent NP are pronominal virgins. Hence the influence of Cross-Over IV is unaffected by 16.(31). We see then that 16.(31), together with the ordering of rules in 16.(33), which is independently justifiable, does suffice to explain the peculiar behavior of Y-movement. It would seem natural, therefore, to reformulate Cross-Over IV in terms of the insight of 16.(31), stating it generally without reference to the particular reordering transformation Y-movement. However, before doing this we must take account of certain other problems with Cross-Over IV, whose consideration has been delayed until now.

C. THE APPARENT *ABOUT*-ANOMALY

In Chapter 5 it was observed that there are examples like:

16.(45) *a*   I talked to Bill about himself.
     b   *I talked to himself about Bill.

    c *I talked about himself to Bill.

    d *I talked about Bill to himself.

The *b* and *c* cases here follow at least from the ordering of *about*-movement before reflexivization, together with the fact that the latter rule operates left-to-right. The *d* case follows from Cross-Over IV in its reference to constant movements. But it was noted there that there also exist the following examples:

    16.(46) *a* I talked to myself about myself.

          b I talked about myself to myself.

And the *b* form here is unexplained so far since the only derivation for it would be by way of *about*-movement. Yet this would involve the crossing of coreferent NP which are clause mates, banned by Cross-Over IV. This phenomenon is rather reminiscent of that just discussed with respect to *Y*-movement. There also we found a rule crossing a certain class of coreferents in a way not countenanced by Cross-Over IV. The question is, therefore, whether some analogue of 16.(31) for *Y*-movement can be found which will analogously distinguish acceptable from unacceptable crossing cases under *about*-movement.

    At first glance, the feasibility of this seems dim. We were able to distinguish different, apparently contrastive, cases under *Y*-movement by means of differential ordering with respect to reflexivization and pronominalization. But all the *about*-cases involve a single rule of pronominalization, reflexivization. Hence this differential ordering approach seems blocked. How, then, can one account for sentences like 16.(47) *b* and, in particular, the contrast between:

    16.(47) *a* *Harry talked about me to myself.

          b I talked about myself to myself.

    Of course, given the presence of two reflexives in the latter and only one in the former, a purely descriptive account is adequate which refers just to this difference. But this is *ad hoc* in the extreme; it is little more than a way of listing the facts. We would naturally prefer an explanation related to that for some other phenomenon, and the natural relationship is with the just explained facts of *Y*-movement. We would like to argue that the difference between the elements of 16.(47) has again to do with crossing of coreferents both of which are pronominal virgins versus crossing of coreferents at least one of which has been marked [+Anaphoric].

    I would like to suggest that such an explanation is possible and depends crucially on the notion of cyclical application of (some) transformational rules as proposed in Chomsky (1965). [See also Ross (1967b) and Lakoff (1968).] According to this proposal, which it would be well be review at this point, some of the (partially) ordered set of transformational rules are applied in a special way in cases of embedded sentences. In particular, given a structure like:

16.(48)

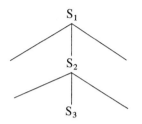

these rules, call them the *cyclical rules*, are applied in order to S_3. After the last such rule has applied, one returns to the first rule and applies it to S_2. Then again after the last relevant rule from this set has applied, one returns to the first and checks its applicability on the whole structure, S_1. When the cyclical rules have been applied in this fashion on the most inclusive clause, one proceeds to any postcyclical transformations; and the surface structure is that structure which results from application of the last applicable postcyclical rule.

This mode of applying transformational rules permits certain kinds of orderings of operations in derivations which do not correspond to the ordering of rules in the grammar proper. That is, there will be derivations in which rule Y is applied before rule Z in a derivation even though Z precedes Y in the ordering. This will happen in cases where Y is applied on an earlier cycle and Z only on a later one.

I would like to suggest that exactly this possibility explains the contrast in pairs like 16.(47) in terms of the properties uncovered in the discussion of Y-movement. There it was found that a rule can cross coreferents otherwise uncrossable if at least one of these is marked [+Anaphoric], that is, if it has at the point of crossing already undergone some pronominalization rule. Exactly this situation arises, I suggest, in 16.(47) *b* but not in 16.(47) *a*. This follows because the *about*-phrase starts out in a different clause than the rest. I do not pretend to understand the structure of these sentences in detail, but schematically we can indicate this claim of extraclause origin by:

16.(49) *a* $\quad\begin{bmatrix} & \begin{bmatrix} \text{Harry talked to me} \end{bmatrix} & \begin{bmatrix} X \text{ was about me} \end{bmatrix} & \end{bmatrix}$
$\qquad\qquad S_3 \;\; S_1 \qquad\qquad\quad S_1 \;\; S_2 \qquad\qquad S_2 \;\; S_3$

$\quad b \;\;\begin{bmatrix} & \begin{bmatrix} \text{I talked to me} \end{bmatrix} & \begin{bmatrix} X \text{ was about me} \end{bmatrix} & \end{bmatrix}$
$\qquad\quad S_3 \;\; S_1 \qquad\qquad\quad S_1 \;\; S_2 \qquad\qquad S_2 \;\; S_3$

Given such structures for 16.(47) *a* and *b*, respectively, together with the assumption that reflexivization is a cyclical transformation, reflexivization will apply on the cycle of S_1 in 16.(49) *b* but not 16.(49) *a* since only S_1 of the former contains coreferent clause mates. There must be some rule which inserts the *about*-phrase in the same clause as the rest of the structure. Call this *about*-incorporation. This rule cannot apply until the cycle of the first S inclusive enough to contain both the *about*-clause and the main clause. Since the results of this rule are subject to reflexivization, it follows that *about*-incorporation precedes reflexivization. After *about*-incorporation has applied, the structures in 16.(49) will have been converted respectively into, schematically:

> 16.(50) *a* Harry talked to me about me.
>   *b* I talked to myself about me.

And the difference here is exactly that the object of *to* in the latter but not in the former is marked [+Anaphoric] at this point. We already know that *about*-movement precedes reflexivization. Hence it will apply to structures like 16.(50) before reflexivization can apply on the main clause cycle. That is, *about*-movement will apply to structures like 16.(50) before reflexivization marks the *about*-phrase objects as [+Anaphoric]. But this means that, at the point *about*-movement operates on 16.(50)-type structures, it will deal with different kinds of elements in the two cases. In the *a* cases *about*-movement, if applied, must cross coreferent clause mates, both of which are pronominal virgins. In the *b* cases it must cross coreferent clause mates, one of which has already undergone reflexivization and has hence received the marking [+Anaphoric]. It follows that the difference in well-formedness of the results of such *about*-movement applications, revealed in 16.(47), is explained by the principle that crossing restrictions hold only for pronominal virgins. *About*-movement can apply without violation to structures like 16.(50) because in such cases the coreferents it crosses are not both pronominal virgins. It seems, therefore, that we have been able to reduce the contrast revealed in 16.(47) to the principle which explains the apparently peculiar ability of *Y*-movement to cross coreferents in those cases where the moved NP is a reflexive pronoun.[10]

---

[10] George Lakoff (personal communication) has suggested a different basis for the contrast between examples like:

> (i)   I talked about myself to myself.
> (ii) *Harry talked about me to myself.

He observes that in (ii) not only have coreferents crossed, but a pronominal form has crossed its *antecedent*. In (i) this is not the case since the antecedent of both is *I*. He proposes then a principle, which he claims has some validity in the domain of nonreferential pronominalization, that a pronominal form cannot cross its antecedent.

While this suggestion bears investigation, it runs into immediate difficulties just because of the *Y*-movement cases in which a reflexive pronoun is crossed over its antecedent:

> (iii) Himself, Harry will never criticize.

Here *himself* crosses *Harry* with no violation. These cases are thus crucial evidence in favor of the pronominal virgin explanation and, as far as I can see, against the antecedent-crossing hypothesis, at least in full generality.

The most obvious weakness[11] in this explanation is, of course, the analysis of *about*-phrase sentences. The proposal that the *about*-phrase starts out in a separate clause, which is fundamental to the whole explanation, has not been independently justified or supported. I am unable to provide much evidence of this sort. The following can be noted, however. Clauses containing *about*-phrases in the appropriate positions do occur, and in discourses where their relations to independent sentences seem identical to those required in our proposed analysis. That is:

16.(51) *a*   Harry said something to me. It was about our trip to Arabia.
      b   Louise talked to Jack. The talk was about dentifrices.

The discourses of 16.(51) seem to be equivalent respectively to the single sentences:

16.(52) *a*   Harry said something to me about our trip to Arabia.
      b   Louise talked to Jack about dentifrices.

Although such facts do not provide direct evidence of the correctness of our assumption, they do reveal its independent plausibility. In particular, they reveal that the kind of subordinate clauses postulated as containing the *about*-phrase in the analysis must be postulated anyway. At the moment, however, the chief attraction of the extraclause origin of *about*-phrases is that it does permit the pronominal virgin explanation to go through.

On the basis of these comments, we are led, therefore, to reformulate Cross-Over IV as follows:

16.(53)   *Cross-Over V*

Assumptions and definitions as in Chapter 14.

Despite the fact that P is a member of S, T may not apply to P if the application path of T with respect to P is such that this path contains an NP_j coreferential with NP_k and both NP_j and NP_k are pronominal virgins and either:

a. T is a variable movement rule.
b. T is a constant movement rule and NP_k and NP_j are clause mates.

D. THE CONFLICT WITH *TOUGH*-MOVEMENT

Cross-Over V seems to have brought the facts of Y-movement under a general statement of crossing conditions and to have explained the otherwise puzzling

---

[11] Another is the assumption, not yet independently justified, that reflexivization is a cyclical rule. See Section F.

contrast of pairs like 16.(47) involving *about*-movement. There is, however, an immediate and glaring difficulty. Namely, unlike Cross-Over IV, Cross-Over V predicts the rule *tough*-movement should be able to cross the moving NP over coreferents, when, as observed in Chapter 3, this is of course not the case.

The wrong predictions of Cross-Over V with respect to *tough*-movement follow directly from the cyclical principle and the fact that this rule, moving an NP across a higher clause boundary, can consequently not operate until the cycle of the main clause. That is, given a structure like:

$$16.(54) \quad \underset{S_2}{[} \quad \text{It is difficult} \quad \underset{S_1}{[} \quad \text{for Harry}_i \text{ to shave Harry}_i \quad \underset{S_1}{]} \quad \underset{S_2}{]}$$

reflexivization, being cyclical, will apply on the S_1 clause before *tough*-movement operates. Consequently, at the point where *tough*-movement becomes applicable, the object of *shave* will be marked [+Anaphoric] and Cross-Over V predicts that this should be movable over its coreferent, just as in *Y*-movement operations. But:

16.(55)   *Himself is difficult for Harry to shave.

As things stand, these facts are outrightly inconsistent with Cross-Over V. Given this formulation, the facts of *tough*-movement are now no longer evidence supporting the cross-over principle. On the contrary, they are now the strongest, and indeed the only, really directly inconsistent data. How then can this be resolved? I have not been able to reach a satisfactory answer to this question.

There are obviously many logical possibilities. Cross-Over V may just be wrong in some minor or even fundamental ways. Since this principle so far provides a good deal of insight into a mass of otherwise mysterious and unconnected facts, one would prefer to preserve it, or some limited modification thereof. This leads to a search for ways in which the facts of *tough*-movement behavior can be made compatible with Cross-Over V or a revision. We might, for instance, seek for formal properties which distinguish *tough*-movement from other rules whose behavior appears contrastive. This search is quickly rewarded. Of the rules we have dealt with, only *about*-movement, *Y*-movement, and *tough*-movement ever seem to have the opportunity to cross coreferents at least one of which is already pronominalized. Moreover, *tough*-movement, like *Y*-movement, operates in these cases such that the *moving* coreferent is the pronominalized one, while the pronominal virgin is stationary. In *about*-movement operations yielding sentences like:

16.(56)   I talked about myself to myself.

the stationary coreferent is already pronominalized when the rule applies. We can give a respecification consistent with all these facts by noting that *tough*-movement and *about*-movement are constant movements, while *Y*-movement is a variable movement. It is then descriptively true for our sample of rules that the peculiar behavior of *tough*-movement is formally differentiable from all other rules as follows. Like *Y*-movement, *tough*-movement has the opportunity to cross a moving, already pronominalized, NP over a coreferent.

$$Y\text{-movement}$$

16.(57) *a*   Harry likes himself $\Longrightarrow$ Himself, Harry likes

$$Tough\text{-movement}$$

 b   It is tough for Harry to like himself $\Longrightarrow$
*Himself is tough for Harry to like

The contrasting results then correlate with the fact that one rule is a variable movement, the other not. On the other hand, *about*-movement, like *tough*-movement, is a constant movement. But in yielding derivations like 16.(56), the stationary coreferent is also already pronominalized while this is not the case in either 16.(57) *a* or *b*. Ergo, it is possible to state a principle consistent with all these and previous facts by adding to 16.(53) the stipulation that, in addition, if T is a constant movement, crossing is also blocked if the leftmost of the pair NP_j and NP_k is a pronominal virgin [even when the rightmost is not].

While it is conceivable that this modification is valid, I personally do not find it in the least bit convincing. I suspect, for no really good reason, that the properties appealed to in this modification are largely accidental. Hence other possibilities for a formal differentiation of *tough*-movement from *about*-movement should be investigated. And we can find others. *Tough*-movement is, after all, one of those very rare rules which is not a variable movement, but which does move elements across higher clause boundaries. That is, it moves an NP into the next most inclusive clause. *About*-movement, like all the other constant movements we have dealt with [with the exception of *it*-replacement], operates clause internally. Rather than the left-right asymmetry of which NP is pronominalized, it may then be right to differentiate *tough*-movement from *about*-movement in terms of this property.

Still another possible formal differentiation of these two rules which could be appealed to in a possible modification of Cross-Over V would have to do with the type of operation *tough*-movement performs. We have taken this rule so far, like the other movements discussed, to detach a constituent and place it elsewhere in a tree.[12] It is conceivable, however, that what *tough*-movement does is actually double, or repeat, the constituent. That is, operating on a structure like:

16.(58)   It is easy for Harry to destroy Chicago$_i$.

the rule would yield not 16.(59) *a* but 16.(59) *b*:

16.(59) *a*   Chicago is easy for Harry to destroy.
 b   Chicago$_i$ is easy for Harry to destroy Chicago$_i$.

---

[12] That is, we have taken it to be a chopping rule rather than a copying rule in the sense of Ross (1967a).

Pronominalization would then yield:

16.(60)   Chicago is easy for Harry to destroy it.

Therefore, to derive the final forms like 16.(59) *a*, it would be necessary to add also a deletion rule, and this seems to be a drawback. In favor of the analysis, however, are two kinds of facts. First, I believe there are some dialects where sentences like 16.(60) actually exist. Secondly, even for those who, like the present writer, do not find them fully acceptable, such sentences are only deviant to a limited degree. Accordingly, it strikes me that the doubling solution deserves further study.

It appears to me than that although at the moment no really justified solution to the inconsistency of *tough*-movement behavior with Cross-Over V can be given, there are enough possible approaches to this question to suggest that the problem is properly one of lack of understanding of the constructions related to *tough*-movement, rather than a flaw in our statement of the cross-over principle as such. At any rate, we shall so assume here and below and not propose any particular modification of previous statements to handle this phenomenon, since any modification now would involve excessive arbitrariness. Those interested in these questions must then simply bear in mind that ultimate justification of the cross-over principle, even for English, depends in important respects on the analysis of *tough*-constructions.

E. *Y*-MOVEMENT AND PIED PIPING

In earlier chapters it was found that the notion of Pied Piping plays an important role in the explanation of the presence or absence of certain crossing restrictions. These cases all had to do with the rules *Wh-Q*-movement and *Wh-Rel*-movement. It should be observed then in this connection that *Y*-movement apparently meets the conditions for Pied Piping as defined by Ross.

However, unlike the two *wh*-rules, *Y*-movement does not provide any cases where Pied Piping plays a role in explaining crossing restrictions. The reason for this is quite simple. The *wh*-rules are defined in such a way that they apply directly to NP only if these are marked with the feature [+wh]. *Y*-movement involves no such condition. The consequence is that when one finds an NP like:

16.(61)   whose house

in a position which could only result from movement by one of the *wh*-rules, we know that it has moved by Pied Piping since the rule itself could only move the "small" *wh*-marked NP, *whose*. However, when one finds an NP such as:

16.(62)   John's house

in a position such that *Y*-movement operation is indicated, we cannot argue that the reordering is a function of Pied Piping. This follows because *Y*-movement is defined in such a way that it could apply directly, without Pied Piping, to either the "small" or "large" NP in such cases. That is, there is no diacritic feature like [+wh] to indicate one or the other.

The difference between the *wh*-rules and *Y*-movement with respect to Pied Piping should, if Cross-Over V is essentially correct, predict certain coreference crossing differences. In particular, given a structure of the form:

16.(63)

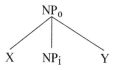

where NP_0 is of the type subject to Pied Piping, we would predict the following. If NP_0 is moved over an occurrence of NP_i by the *wh*-rules, crossing violations should ensue in those cases where it is NP_i that has the specification [+wh] since the movement of NP_0 will be a function of Pied Piping. If, however, NP_0 is moved by *Y*-movement over an occurrence of NP_i, no violation should ensue, since the movement will not be a function of Pied Piping; consider then examples like:

16.(64)   *Whose$_i$ mother did he$_i$ say I insulted?

Here the NP *whose mother* has crossed a coreferent of *whose*, with resulting violation, as predicted by the Pied Piping analysis of *Wh-Q*-movement. That is, 16.(64) is not readable as a paraphrase of:

16.(65)   Who$_i$ said I insulted his$_i$ mother?

Quite in contrast, however, is the fact that sentences like:

16.(66)   His$_i$ mother, John$_i$ said I insulted.

are fine, even though the NP *his mother* has crossed a coreferent of *his*. The reason is that *his mother* moves not by Pied Piping but by a direct application of *Y*-movement to the "large" NP.

An even more striking example of the contrast between Pied Piping with the *wh*-rules and its absence with *Y*-movement is provided perhaps by cases with prepositions. The fact is that in every case crossing restrictions are unaffected by whether or not a preposition travels with its following NP under the operation of either *Wh-Q*-movement or *Wh-Rel*-movement:

16.(67) *a*   *Who$_i$ did he$_i$ claim you were engaged to?
            b   *To whom$_i$ did he$_i$ claim you were engaged?

Neither of these is readable as a paraphrase of:

16.(68)   Who$_i$ claimed you were engaged to him$_i$?

Just so, the pair:

16.(69) *a*   *The man who$_i$ he$_i$ claimed you were engaged to
    b   *The man to whom$_i$ he$_i$ claimed you were engaged

are equally impossible and neither is a paraphrase of:

16.(70)   The man who$_i$ claimed you were engaged to him$_i$

Hence because NP of the form *Preposition + NP* move by Pied Piping under the *wh*-rules, the crossing restrictions are determined by the reference properties of the "inner" NP.

In constructions having to do with *Y*-movement, however, a quite different situation obtains.

16.(71) *a*   The man$_i$ claimed you were engaged to him$_i$.
    b   *Him$_i$, the man$_i$ claimed you were engaged to.
    c   To him$_i$, the man$_i$ claimed you were engaged.

Here accompaniment by the preposition has effects on the crossing violations. The reason is clear. Since Pied Piping does not function for *Y*-movement, only in the *b* case is Cross-Over V met. In *c*, the NP which moves is not a coreferent of any NP crossed, and it is the moving NP itself which is "mentioned" in the rule. Hence, Pied Piping in conjunction with Cross-Over V predicts exactly the contrast in crossing violations between the *wh*-rules and *Y*-movement which is observed in English sentences.

We may seem to have contradicted ourselves. At the beginning of this section, it was observed that *Y*-movement meets the conditions for Pied Piping, and yet we have just explained a whole set of facts on the assumption that Pied Piping does not function for *Y*-movement. There is no real contradiction, however. The point is we really cannot tell whether Pied Piping is operative for *Y*-movement or not because:

16.(72)   Every sentence that would be derived by *Y*-movement *with* Pied Piping is derivable by this rule *without* Pied Piping.

As a consequence of 16.(72), every sentence under *Y*-movement which would be derived with a violation because of Pied Piping [in the same way as the parallel examples under the *wh*-rules] has a nonviolation derivation because of direct application of *Y*-movement to "large" NP, impossible in the *wh*-rule cases. But it is a general principle that if a structure has a valid derivation, this is what we perceive, regardless of the number of ill-formed derivations which it has. That is, something is a sentence with the structure K if it has a valid derivation in the grammer which assigns it K. And under these conditions, we pay no attention to the fact that it failed to be derived in *n* other ways. This point can be seen in many of our other examples. For instance, 16.(69) *a* has an asterisk, indicating a lack of the coreferential interpretation. But the sentence has a valid derivation where this interpretation is lacking and if this example is presented to native speakers they find it perfectly acceptable under the noncoreferential interpretation. They do not of course notice that it "should" have a coreferential interpretation, that is, "should" under the false assumption that there is no cross-over principle.

I take these facts about *Y*-movement and its contrast with the *wh*-rules, to provide even firmer support for the conclusions of earlier sections and chapters to the effect that the Pied Piping explanation of the behavior of NP under the *wh*-rules is correct. *Y*-movement shows this further by revealing that, in the absence of the conditions which provide unique traces for Pied Piping, the relevant restrictions are not found.

F. AN ARGUMENT FOR THE CYCLICAL CHARACTER OF REFLEXIVIZATION

It is assumed in our explanation of the apparent *about*-phrase anomalies in Section C of this chapter that reflexivization is a cyclical rule. That is, this assumption, together with the pronominal virgin aspect of Cross-Over V, is used to predict the possibility of crossing in cases like 16.(73) *c* and *d:*

> 16.(73) *a*   I spoke to Bill about himself.
>   *b*   *I spoke about Bill to himself.
>   *c*   I spoke to myself about myself.
>   *d*   I spoke about myself to myself.

We have, however, given no independent argument that reflexivization is cyclical.

An apparently convincing argument for the cyclical character of reflexivization has been given by Lakoff (unpublished), and we shall consider it here. Like most arguments that transformational rules in English are cyclical, it turns to the existence of a rule (or possibly several rules) of *it*-replacement, which takes NP out of a complement sentence and substitutes them for *it* pronouns in main clauses. A rule with this property, called *it*-replacement, was discussed in Chapter 4 with respect to sentences like:

> 16.(74) *a*   It seems that Gary is ill.
>   *b*   Gary seems to be ill.

Rules like *it*-replacement have the property of moving an NP out of its clause across exactly one higher clause boundary into the next more inclusive clause. I shall refer to any NP moved in this way as a *raised NP*, and shall refer to rules which accomplish such a reordering collectively as *raising*,[13] since differences between such rules do not concern us here nor does the question of whether there is one such operation or more than one in the grammar of English.

The way cyclical arguments are derivable from such rules can be illustrated as follows, using passive. If we examine sentences like:

16.(75)   Gary seems to have been arrested by the FBI.

we note that it is the NP *Gary* which has been raised. That is, 16.(75) corresponds to the unraised version:

16.(76)   It seems that Gary has been arrested by the FBI.

We observe that the process of raising always operates on the *grammatical subject* of the complement clause. However, in the case of 16.(75), we see that the NP *Gary* is actually the underlying object of *arrested,* and achieves grammatical subject position in the complement only through the application of *Passive.* Consequently, the latter rule must have applied first. We immediately infer the ordering:

16.(77)   Passive
          Raising

Consider, however, another verb which permits raising to apply, namely, *believe*:

16.(78) *a*   I believe that Gary stole the diamond.
        b   I believe Gary to have stolen the diamond.

The fact that 16.(78) *b* has undergone raising, such that *Gary* is now the object of *believe*, is indicated by the passivizability of this NP with respect to *believe*:

16.(79)   Gary is believed to have stolen the diamond.

Notice that NP inside of *that*-clauses, like 16.(78) *a*, are not so passivizable:

16.(80)   *Gary is believed (that) stole the diamond (by me).

However, the passivizability of raised objects shows the ordering:

16.(81)   Raising
          Passive

---

[13] The term *raising* is used by Perlmutter (1968) who takes it from Kiparsky and Kiparsky (1968).

Comparison of 16.(77) and 16.(81) then seems to reveal that passive must both precede and follow raising, which is, of course, impossible.

However, investigation reveals that in all such cases when passive precedes raising it always applies to the complement sentence and when it follows raising it always applies to the main clause. Consequently, the ordering anomaly is easily eliminated by having both passive and raising cyclical, with the ordering of 16.(77). This is a striking argument for the cyclical principle, which is much strengthened by the fact that the process of successive passivization, raising, passivization, and so on is truly productive. That is, there is no bound on the number of times these rules may follow each other in this way, consequently, no bound on the number of times a fixed NP may be raised, and no bound on the distance it may travel by this process alone from its original position.

16.(82) a Louise expected that Harry would believe that Josephine kissed you.
      b Louise expected Harry to believe that Josephine kissed you.
      c Louise expected Harry to believe Josephine kissed you.
      d Louise expected Harry to believe you to have been kissed by Josephine.
      e Louise expected you to be believed to have been kissed by Josephine.
      f You were expected to be believed to have been kissed by Josephine.

However, all such facts follow naturally from having passive apply cyclically on each successive complement, followed by the application of raising on the next cycle.

Consider, then, the relation of this argument type to reflexivization. The key point is the clause mate constraint on this rule. This constraint is such that *before* an NP_i is raised it can reflexivize other NP_i in the same complement, but not after. Similarly, *after* it is raised, an NP_i can be reflexivized by other NP_i in the main clause, but not before. Consequently, sentences like:

16.(83) a Lucifer expected Marcus to kill himself.
      b Schwarz believed you to be overly proud of yourself.

show that reflexivization must apply before raising. However, sentences like:

16.(84) a I expect myself to win.
      b *I expect (that) myself will win.

show that reflexivization must follow raising. Again, however, the facts appear to fall out from an ordering of raising before reflexivization if both rules are cyclical. That is, all the cases where reflexivization applies before raising are cases where it applies on the complement sentence; cases where it applies after raising are those where it applies on main clauses.

A particularly interesting example type is provided by Lakoff here:

16.(85)   Carter was believed by everyone to have shot himself.

Here *Carter* is the underlying subject of *shot*, which caused the reflexivization of the object of this verb. This happened before the NP was raised. Consequently, although reflexivization follows raising in the ordering, it must apparently apply first in sentences like 16.(85), or else after raising has applied the clause mate condition for reflexivization will not be met. And that the simple order of rules is actually raising-reflexivization is shown clearly by examples like:

16.(86) *a*   I believe myself to be cleverer than Tony.
    b   *I believe that myself is cleverer than Tony.

which show that reflexivization must follow raising in its application to the main clause. Overall, then, these facts seem to yield a striking argument for the cyclical character of the rule reflexivization.

Unfortunately, a little deeper consideration suggests that (1) this argument is not as strong as it first appears since there is a way to account for all of the facts so far without having reflexivization cyclical; and (2) there are predictions from cyclical raising and reflexivization which are not borne out. Consider (1) first. The essence of the argument for the cyclical character of reflexivization is provided by sentences like:

16.(87) *a*   John is believed to have stabbed himself.
    b   John seems to have been believed by everyone to have stabbed himself.

in which the raised NP leaves behind a reflexivized NP in its clause of origin. Since raising must precede reflexivization and since the reflexive left behind could not be derived by reflexivization after raising takes place, due to the clause mate constraint, the assumption of cyclical ordering seems to follow. However, what is not stressed in this argument is that it assumes without justification that raising is a chopping rule rather than a copying rule. If, however, raising just puts a double of the complement subject in the main clause, leaving the original behind, then there is no argument that reflexivization must apply in the complement sentence before raising is applied. That is, if the derivation of 16.(87) *a* proceeds as:

16.(88) *a*   X believes (John$_i$ stab John$_i$) $\xrightarrow{\textit{Raising}}$
    b   X believes John$_i$ (John$_i$ stab John$_i$) $\xrightarrow{\textit{Passive}}$
    c   John$_i$ is believed (John$_i$ to stab John$_i$)

the argument for cyclical reflexivization is eliminated. Moreover, there is no counterargument *against* raising as a copying rule in terms of the necessity of a required deletion following it. The original will be deleted automatically by the same rule of identity deletion needed for ordinary complement subjects in sentences like:

16.(89) *a*   I want to go.
     b   I forced Bill to go.

In addition, there are sentences which most strongly suggest the copying nature of raising by showing both the copy and the original (in pronominal form) in the surface structure:

16.(90) *a*   It looks (to me) like John is going to win.
     b   John$_i$ looks (to me) like he$_i$ is going to win.

In sentences like 16.(90) *b* we seem to find both the original complement subject and its copy. A copying approach to raising thus seems to have some attractiveness.

   These considerations suggest that the assumption that raising is a chopping rule is debatable. If, however, this rule is a copying rule, the argument for the cyclical character of reflexivization does not go through. At the same time, it must be noted that none of the data is inconsistent with the assumption of cyclical application. We must thus consider the independent evidence for the cyclical nature of this rule to be highly tentative at best. Consequently, our use of the cyclical principle to, for example, explain the *about*-phrase data like 16.(73) must be subjected to the sharpest scrutiny. Just so, it is important to try to find other kinds of arguments either supporting or disconfirming the claim that reflexivization is cyclical.

17 NOMINALLY-COMPLEX NP AND THE NOTION OF PEER

A. NOMINALIZATIONS

I refer to those NP which contain other NP inside of them, but where the branches connecting the NP-nodes do not contain intervening S-nodes as nominally-complex NP.

> 17.(1) The vagabond who Lucille is engaged to

contains an embedded NP, *Lucille*, but this is inside of a relative clause S. Hence the NP-node for the sequence *Lucille* and that for the whole are separated by this intervening S. 17.(1) is thus not nominally complex. Among nominally-complex NP we distinguish two basic subtypes, *nominalizations* and *coordinate NP*. The present section will deal exclusively with the former type, for which we offer no attempt at a precise definition.[1] All of the examples of 17.(2) are nominally-complex NP of the nominalization variety:

> 17.(2) *a* Charley's ghost
> *b* Your claim about that
> *c* Harry's proposal concerning garbage removal
> *d* Joan's unconscious wish to be a vampire
> *e* A picture of Lucille
> *f* My story about myself
> *g* Tony's knowledge of Gzorpian rituals

---

[1] We note, however, that nominalization nominally-complex NP are essentially just those which meet Ross's definition for being in general subject to Pied Piping.

Nominally-complex NP raise important problems for any proposed principle of cross-over constraints. Their behavior with respect to coreferentiality constraints under movement transformations has not been shown to follow from any version of the cross-over principle so far.

The difficulties raised by such NP are, however, exclusively in the domain of constant movements. The behavior of these NP under variable movements follows directly from Cross-Over V. This is so because variable movements are not permitted to cross an NP over a coreferent regardless of their relative structural positions if the first is "mentioned" in the rule doing the movement, and the pronominal virgin restriction is met. Constant movements on the other hand have been taken to be subject to such constraints only with respect to coreferent NP which are clause mates.

Before considering the relations between constant movements and nominally-complex NP, it would be well to provide evidence that this class of NP does behave as provided for in Cross-Over V under the operation of variable movements. This means showing that an NP_i cannot be crossed over a coreferent NP_j even if the latter is inside of a nominally-complex NP. We can illustrate for nominalizations with analogues of the NP in 17.(2) *a*.

17.(3) *a* Someone$_i$ saw his$_i$ ghost.
   b *Whose$_i$ ghost did he$_i$ see?
   c Who$_i$ saw his$_i$ ghost?
   d *The one$_i$ whose$_i$ ghost he$_i$ saw
   e The one$_i$ who$_i$ saw his$_i$ ghost

Recall from Chapter 12 that, although in examples *b* and *d* here it is the "large," nominally-complex NP which have been moved by the rules *Wh-Q*-movement and *Wh-Rel*-movement, respectively, it is the "small" or *wh*-marked NP which are actually "mentioned" in these rules. The movement of the "large" NP follows from the Pied Piping convention.

17.(4) *a* Somebody$_i$'s ghost scared him$_i$.
   b *Who$_i$ did his$_i$ ghost scare?
   c Whose$_i$ ghost scared him$_i$?
   d *The one$_i$ who$_i$ his$_i$ ghost scared
   e The one$_i$ whose$_i$ ghost scared him$_i$

17.(5) *a* Someone$_i$ liked his$_i$ proposal about garbage removal.
   b *Whose$_i$ proposal about garbage removal did he$_i$ like?
   c Who$_i$ liked his$_i$ proposal about garbage removal?
   d *The one$_i$ whose$_i$ proposal about garbage removal he$_i$ liked
   e The one$_i$ who$_i$ liked his$_i$ proposal about garbage removal

17.(6) *a* Someone$_i$'s proposal about garbage removal enriched him$_i$.
   b *Who$_i$ did his$_i$ proposal about garbage removal enrich?
   c Whose$_i$ proposal about garbage removal enriched him$_i$?
   d *The one$_i$ who$_i$ his$_i$ proposal about garbage removal enriched
   e The one$_i$ whose$_i$ proposal about garbage removal enriched him$_i$

17.(7) a Someone$_i$ took a picture of himself$_i$.
    b *Who$_i$ did he$_i$ take a picture of?
    c Who$_i$ took a picture of himself$_i$?
    d *The one$_i$ who$_i$ he$_i$ took a picture of
    e The one$_i$ who$_i$ took a picture of himself$_i$

17.(8) a A picture of Charley$_i$[2] fell on him$_i$.
    b *Who$_i$ did a picture of him$_i$ fall on?
    c *Who$_i$ did a picture of fall on him$_i$?[3]
    d *The one$_i$ who$_i$ a picture of him$_i$ fell on
    e *The one$_i$ who$_i$ a picture of fell on him$_i$

These examples suffice to illustrate that nominally-complex NP of the nominalization sort do behave as predicted by Cross-Over V with respect to the variable movement transformations *Wh-Q*-movement and *Wh-Rel*-movement, for which Pied Piping is demonstrably functional. Cross-Over V also yields the correct results for *Y*-movement, the other rule of NP movement in English which is a variable movement. This is shown by such examples as:

17.(9) a Harry$_i$'s ghost scared him$_i$.
    b *Harry$_i$, his$_i$ ghost scared.
    c *Him$_i$, Harry$_i$'s ghost scared.

17.(10) a Harry$_i$ frightened his$_i$ ghost.
    b His$_i$ ghost, Harry$_i$ frightened.

17.(11) a Jack$_i$'s proposal about garbage removal amused him$_i$.
    b *Jack$_i$, his$_i$ proposal about garbage removal amused.
    c *Him$_i$, Jack$_i$'s proposal about garbage removal amused.

17.(12) a Jack$_i$ was amused by his$_i$ proposal about garbage removal.
    b His$_i$ proposal about garbage removal, Jack$_i$ was amused by.

17.(13) a Harry$_i$ took a picture of himself$_i$.
    b Himself$_i$, Harry$_i$ took a picture of.[4]

---

[2] Sentences like this one seem to me to deviate from perfect well-formedness for reasons mentioned in footnote 1 of Chapter 9.

[3] Examples 17.(8) c and e are included only for completeness of parallel to earlier examples. These are ill formed not because of any coreference restrictions but because of general conditions on moving the NP in such a position. Hence the grammaticality is unaffected if the pronoun *him*$_i$ is replaced by some nonpronominal NP.

[4] The grammaticality of this example is exceptional within the context of the whole class of examples which contain it, but this is explained by the pronominal virgin condition. The question is discussed further in Section D.

17.(14) *a*   ?A picture of Harry$_i$ fell on him$_i$.

      b   *Harry$_i$, a picture of him$_i$ fell on.

      c   *Him$_i$, a picture of Harry$_i$ fell on.

      d   ??A picture of himself$_i$ fell on Harry$_i$.[5]

      e   *Harry$_i$, a picture of himself$_i$ fell on.[6]

Hence, the behavior of nominalizations with respect to variable movements is that predicted by Cross-Over V.

The situation with constant movements is quite different. These constrain the crossing of coreferent NP only if these are clause mates. Recall that two NP in a phrase marker *P* are clause mates in *P* if every node S which dominates one dominates the other. By this definition, the circled NP in:

17.(15)   (Harry) can't stand (Tony's brother).

are clause mates. More importantly, however, *so are the circled NP in:*

17.(16)   (Harry) can't stand (Tony's) brother.

It apparently follows from this that in cases of coreferentiality such as:

17.(17)   Harry$_i$ can't stand Harry$_i$'s brother.

such NP should not be crossable under the operation of constant movements. But this inference is patently false.

17.(18) *a*   Harry$_i$ insulted Harry$_i$'s brother.

      b   Harry$_i$'s brother was insulted by him$_i$.[7]

      c   It was easy for Harry$_i$ to insult his$_i$ brother.

      d   Harry$_i$'s brother was easy for him$_i$ to insult.

      e   Harry$_i$ was annoyed by his$_i$ brother.

      f   Harry$_i$'s brother was annoying to him$_i$.

---

[5] Examples of this type become better with a different choice of article, and other picture nouns seem to improve them as well:

    (i)   That picture of himself fell on Harry.

    (ii)   That story about himself doesn't amuse Joe.

[6] The ill-formedness of cases such as this is unexplained under the assumption that the reflexive forms in them arise by the same rule as those in examples like 17.(13) *b*. That is, since under these conditions the NP crossed is not a pronominal virgin, no violation is predicted by Cross-Over V. The contrast between examples like 17.(13) *b* and 17.(14) *e* is discussed in some detail in Section D below.

[7] As indicated in footnote 1 of Chapter 9, there is irrelevant unacceptability in examples like this one.

17.(19) a Harry$_i$'s brother insulted him$_j$.
    b Harry$_i$ was insulted by his$_i$ brother.
    c It was easy for Harry$_i$'s brother to insult him$_j$.
    d Harry$_i$ was easy for his$_i$ brother to insult.
    e Harry$_i$'s brother was annoyed with him$_j$.
    f Harry$_i$ was annoying to his$_i$ brother.

The problem to be faced, therefore, is how these data can be shown to be compatible with that part of Cross-Over V which refers to constant movements. Several lines of attack are possible. One would involve rule ordering together with the crucial assumption that all nominalization type nominally-complex NP are in fact derivative from underlying NP which contain S-nodes[8] between those NP-nodes which are not so separated in surface structures. Let us call such NP *sententially complex*. Within a transformational grammar, it is a possibility that all surface structure nominally-complex NP have a sententially-complex ancestry. Thus, at such an earlier point, the structures of 17.(2) a–g might be, respectively, something along the lines[9] of:

17.(20) a The ghost which Charley has
    b The claim about that which you made
    c The proposal about garbage removal which Harry made
    d The unconscious wish to be a vampire which Joan has
    e The one which pictures Lucille[10]
    f The one which I storied about I
    g The knowledge of Gzorpian rituals which Tony has

This approach is attractive from the point of view of crossing restrictions since exactly what 17.(18)–17.(19) show is that under the operation of constant movements, nominally-complex NP of the nominalization variety behave like sententially-complex NP with respect to coreferential crossing behavior. This

---

[8]The claim that at least some nominalizations must be derived without underlying structures containing S-nodes is explored and supported in Chomsky (to appear). I do not, however, find his arguments particularly compelling.

[9]None of these would be the deepest structure or even very close to it.

[10]It can be seen from examples like this that a consequence of a sententially-complex ancestry for certain nominally-complex NP is the postulation of verbal elements in underlying structures which never occur as verbal forms in surface structures, that is, elements whose nominalization is obligatory. Chomsky (to appear) states that such elements are highly dubious and should be made subject to a special penalty in an evaluation measure. He gives no argument for this claim and I can imagine none. Observe that all such elements involve an inherent penalty in any event, since one must indicate in the grammar somewhere the impossibility of their appearing in verbal form in the output, a possibility predicted by the general principles of transformational grammar, given the assignment of underlying verbal form. This question is related to the much deeper one of whether there can in fact exist underlying lexical nouns at all. I regard the answer to the latter question as negative. See Bach (1968).

parallel behavior would be naturally explained by deriving the former from the latter by reduction rules ordered to *follow* the operation of all the constant movements.

Not only is a sententially-complex NP origin of nominalizations attractive from the vantage point of crossing facts, it receives additional support from the processes of reflexivization. Recall that in general reflexivization applies to coreferent NP only if these are clause mates at the point of application. But it is also a general fact that reflexivization does *not* apply between clause mate NP if one is inside of a nominally-complex NP and the other outside of it:

17.(21) *a*   Charley$_i$'s ghost frightened him$_j$.
     b   *Charley$_i$'s ghost frightened himself$_i$.

17,(22) *a*   I am worried by Bill's hatred for me.
     b   *I am worried by Bill's hatred for myself.

17.(23) *a*   My house is impoverishing me.
     b   *My house is impoverishing myself.

One exception concerns the behavior of nominally-complex NP based on so-called picture nouns, for example, *picture, story, description,* and so on, which do take reflexives in many contexts. But these are incredibly complex and unique in a number of other ways.[11] The facts illustrated by 17.(21)–17.(23) will follow automatically from the clause mate formulation of reflexivization if nominally-complex NP have a sententially-complex NP origin. If not, then on these grounds alone, reflexivization must be complicated to refer directly to the structure of nominally-complex NP [See below].

Similarly, not only do coreferent NP which are clause mates *not* undergo reflexivization if they are separated by the boundary of a nominally-complex NP, but coreferent NP inside of nominally-complex NP *do* undergo reflexivization:

17.(24) *a*   Harry$_i$'s hatred of himself$_i$
     b   Your investigation of yourself
     c   My improvement of myself

This would also follow automatically if such structures were dominated by S-nodes at the point when reflexivization applied. If they are not, then some modification of the clause mate formulation of this rule is required to ensure that reflexivization applies within nominally-complex NP (provided no S boundaries are crossed) but not across the boundaries of such NP. There are thus rather good grounds in terms of reflexivization for assuming a sententially-complex origin for nominalization nominally-complex NP. This was observed by

---

[11] See the discussion of these in Warshawsky (1965), Ross (1967a). Reflexivization in picture-noun nominalizations is discussed in greater detail in Section D.

Lees and Klima (1963:22–23) for a special case, namely, genitives, in the article where they first proposed the clause mate constraint for reflexivization:

> In still another, but opposite, type of counter-example which might arise there is a repeated nominal but no reflexive pronominalization, as in
>
> (73) Mary's father supported her.
>
> (74) Mary's father supported himself.
>
> but no:
>
> (75) *Mary's father supported herself.
>
> in which the underlying sentence must have been
>
> (76) Mary's father supported Mary.
>
> However, there is a good deal of evidence supporting the view that all genitives in English are transformational in origin, so that the underlying sentence would then be rather *The father supported Mary,* with no repetition. (The second source sentence for the genitive itself would presumably have been *Mary has a father,* with intermediate stages: *The father that Mary has supported Mary,* and *The father of Mary supported Mary.*)

It might seem that we are now justified in assuming that nominally-complex NP have a sententially-complex origin, which reduces the crossing facts for these NP with respect to constant *movements* to consistency with Cross-Over V. The validity of this approach might be taken to gain further support when it is noticed that the reflexivization justification for a sententially-complex derivation yields an ordering requirement consistent with what is required for the crossing explication. That is, in order to predict the facts for reflexivization correctly, the sententially-complex assumption must be buttressed by the assumption that the rules which reduce such NP to nominally-complex NP *follow* reflexivization. Schematically:

17.(25) Reflexivization
         Reductions

But in order to predict the crossing facts, the sententially-complex hypothesis must be associated with an ordering which places the reductions *after* all the constant movements:

17.(26) Constant movements
         Reductions

But as far as is known, 17.(25) and 17.(26) are consistent, since we have in most of the cases been able to show that each constant movement precedes reflexivization. Hence:

17.(27)   Constant movements
          Reflexivization
          Reductions

And the ordering of 17.(27) is consistent with the requirements of a sententially-complex NP origin of nominally-complex NP as a basis for a clause mate explanation of both the reflexivization behavior and crossing behavior of coreferent NP linked to nominally-complex NP.

One might therefore conclude that nominalization variety nominally-complex NP cause no problems for Cross-Over V, since the apparent inconsistency of the data in 17.(18) and 17.(19) with that part of Cross-Over V relating to constant movements is a function of rule ordering in conjunction with the fact that all nominally-complex NP have a sententially-complex origin. And perhaps this is right. However, there are so many mysterious, intricate, and not understood problems involved in the detailed derivation of nominalizations from sentential sources that this conclusion can hardly be taken to be obviously established. It is important to point out, therefore, that although such a consequence would be *convenient* for the statement of cross-over restrictions, it is by no means necessary. We can state the cross-over principle even if it turns out to be necessary to allow constant movements to apply at a point where nominally-complex NP have already been derived [regardless of how]. Before considering this alternative, however, let us turn to another class of nominally-complex NP distinct from nominalizations.

B. COORDINATE NP

An important, implicit, and unjustified constraint has governed our data base so far, not only in this chapter but in all previous ones. Namely, we have not considered crossing restrictions with respect to coordinate NP. By a coordinate node or constraint, I refer to one whose structure is as follows:

17.(28)

Examples of coordinate NP include the italicized NP in:

17.(29) *a*   *Louise and Barbara* are cousins.
   b   *Tony and I* left Chicago in 1939.
   c   *Bill and she* are getting married some day.
   d   *You and I* will never be able to beat *Jack or Arthur*.
   e   *Tony or Louise* can do it.

It is clear that coordinate NP meet the definition of nominally-complex NP.

The first point to emphasize is that coordinate nominally-complex NP do obey Cross-Over V with no further remarks, insofar as variable movements are concerned. That is, all crossing of pronominal virgin coreferents is blocked for these rules subject only to the "mention" condition.

17.(30) *a*   Joan and he$_i$ both said Barbara would marry him$_i$.
   b   *Who$_i$ did Joan and he$_i$ both say Barbara would marry?
   c   *The one who$_i$ Joan and he$_i$ both said Barbara would marry
   d   *Him$_i$, Joan and he$_i$ both said Barbara would marry.

17.(31) *a*   You told Logan and her$_i$ that I voted for her$_i$.
   b   *Who$_i$ did you tell Logan and her$_i$ that I voted for?
   c   *The one who$_i$ you told Logan and her$_i$ that I voted for
   d   *Her$_i$, you told Logan and her$_i$ that I voted for.

Hence, as with nominalizations, the problems with coordinate nominally-complex NP concern constant movements.

The evidential relevance of coordinate NP to crossing restrictions for constant movements is, however, limited by a fundamental constraint on the relations between coreference and coordination in English [and possibly universally]. [12] This constraint is briefly illustrated by the ill-formed character of the following examples, none of which involves the operation of any of the constant movement transformations:

17.(32) *a*   *John and I like $\begin{Bmatrix} \text{me} \\ \text{myself} \end{Bmatrix}$.

   b   *I praised $\begin{Bmatrix} \text{myself} \\ \text{me} \end{Bmatrix}$ and John, *I praised John and $\begin{Bmatrix} \text{myself} \\ \text{me} \end{Bmatrix}$.

17.(33) *a*   *Tony and Louise$_i$ criticized $\begin{Bmatrix} \text{her} \\ \text{herself}_i \end{Bmatrix}$.

   b   *Louise$_i$ criticized Tony and $\begin{Bmatrix} \text{her}_i \\ \text{herself}_i \end{Bmatrix}$.

17.(34) *a*   *I talked to Lois about Tony and $\begin{Bmatrix} \text{her}_i \\ \text{herself}_i \end{Bmatrix}$.

   b   *I talked to Tony and Lois about $\begin{Bmatrix} \text{her}_i \\ \text{herself}_i \end{Bmatrix}$.

---

[12] This constraint holds in exactly the same way for plural NP, a fact that suggests a deeper relation between plurals and coordinate NP than any expressed in previous or current grammars of any type.

This restriction,[13] which I have elsewhere [Postal (1969)] referred to as *the inclusion constraint*, is *not* formulatable generally as a prohibition of pronominalization between one of *n*-conjoined NP and an NP outside of that coordinate structure, a fact revealed by such perfectly well-formed structures as:

17.(35) *a* Barbara$_i$ believes that either she$_j$ or Tony will win.
     b Tony$_i$ and I simultaneously discovered that he$_i$ had cancer.
     c Tom$_i$ visited the girl who had been kind to $\begin{cases} \text{him}_i \\ \text{he}_i \end{cases}$ and his$_i$ wife.

A comparison of 17.(32)–17.(34) with 17.(35) reveals that a more narrow statement of the constraint is required, one which appeals to the notion of clause mates. In the former examples, which are ill-formed, the nominally-complex coordinate NP is in each case a clause mate of the NP which is a coreferent of one of its component NP. In 17.(35) this condition is not met. For example, in 17.(35) *a* the NP *Barbara*$_i$ is in the main clause while the nominally-complex NP *either she*$_i$ *or Tony* is in the embedded *that*-clause. It seems, then, that this very peculiar restriction will have to be formulated in terms of the clause mate notion. Although it is of great interest in itself, the inclusion constraint is not our concern here.

This constraint does, however, greatly increase the difficulty of determining the relations between crossing restrictions and coordinate NP with respect to the operation of constant movements. This follows because in all cases the source sentences, that is, those which result from the more baselike structure, are themselves ill formed. In other words, in cases where the inclusion constraint operates, sentences containing coreferents are ill formed even without the operations of any constant movements with concomitant crossing restrictions. It follows that evidence with respect to the cross-over principle can only be derived in such cases from arguments of the type involving claims that two sentences are of equal degree of deviance or that one is more deviant from English than another.

---

[13] There is a common confusion about many examples like 17.(33) *b*. I have indicated that these are ungrammatical. This ungrammaticality depends, however, on the structure. The ill-formedness holds on the reading where *Tony and herself* is a coordinate NP. Such sentences typically have, however, another reading on which the final pronominal form is not part of a coordinate NP but simply a fragment of a clause most of which has been deleted:

  (i)   [[Louise criticized Tony] . . . . . . and herself]
      S S   S   S

Here the main break is after *Tony* and the sequence *Louise criticized Tony* is a separate clause. The asterisked example thus means that there is no structure:

  (ii) *[Louise criticized [Tony [and herself]]]
       S   NP   NP   NP NP S

The general restriction under discussion thus holds for coordinate NP, not for deletion structures like those in (i), although these are frequently confused.

For instance, active sentences like:

17.(36)   *Barbara$_i$ and Tony praised $\left\{ \begin{array}{l} \text{her}_i \\ \text{herself}_i \end{array} \right\}$.

are ill formed when the reflexive is chosen and not subject to a coreferential interpretation when an ordinary pronoun is used. Therefore, to find evidence for Cross-Over V with respect to the passives of such sentences:

17.(37)   *Barbara$_i$ was praised by Tony and $\left\{ \begin{array}{l} \text{her}_i \\ \text{herself}_i \end{array} \right\}$.

one must argue either that 17.(37) is more deviant than 17.(36), attributing the extra deviance to Cross-Over V in connection with the operation of passive, or that the two are equally deviant. In short, the inclusion constraint forces us to exclusively *relative* arguments. But such arguments are based on the most difficult and weak judgements. Subtle as the distinction between:

17.(38) *a*   Harry stabbed himself.
        b   *Harry was stabbed by himself.

might be, it is crystal clear when compared to the question of whether there is any difference in degree of violation between examples like 17.(36) and 17.(37). Moreover, this difficulty of judgement is general throughout the field of sentences differentiated by the presence or absence of constant movement operations in their derivations. For instance, the following pair are differentiated by the fact that *psych*-movement applies in the derivation of the second but not the first:

17.(39) *a*   *Aren't you disgusted with Harry and you?
        b   *Aren't Harry and you disgusting to you?

Yet one is certainly hard put to decide whether one of these is worse.
    In view of this difficulty in determining the facts, I shall myself make no judgement. Rather, I shall discuss the problem conditionally, considering what the different possibilities imply about the statement of crossing restrictions.
    First, let us ask what would it mean if, in all cases where the inclusion constraint held, given pairs like 17.(39), that member which was derived by a constant movement was more ill formed than the other. Clearly, we would have to take this to be a function of cross-over violations. The question would then arise whether these violations would in fact follow from the statement of the cross-over principle that has been given. The answer to this is yes, but not obviously so. The obscurity arises from the fact that we have said nothing about how coordinate NP are derived. It is plausible, however, that a very large class of such structures are derived from coordinate sentence structures so that the surface NP coordination is transformationally derivative.

So, for instance, it is plausible that sentences like 17.(40) *a* have underlying structures essentially like those of 17.(40) *b*:

17.(40) *a*   Harry and Bill visited France.
     b   Harry visited France and Bill visited France.

If this is so, there must be rules which reduce coordinate S structures to the variety of other coordinate structures found in English surface structures, coordinate NP among them. Let us refer to these rules jointly as *coordination reduction*. And let us refer to the hypothesis that coordinate NP derive from coordinate S-nodes as *sentential compounding*. Observe then that, given sentential compounding, passive sentences like:

17.(41) *a*   Joan and Mary were arrested by the Nazi.
     b   Sloan was beaten by Jack and Louise.

could conceivably be derived in *two* different ways. One possibility is that first passive applies to the underlying conjoined actives and coordination reduction then applies to already passivized structures. The other is that coordination reduction applies first, to active structures, and then passive applies to structures already containing coordinate NP. Let us call these alternatives Method A and Method B, respectively. Schematically:

17.(42)   *Method A*

$$\text{[The Nazi arrested Joan and the Nazi arrested Mary]} \xRightarrow{\textit{Passive}}$$

[Joan was arrested by the Nazi and Mary was arrested
$$\text{by the Nazi]} \xRightarrow{\textit{Coordination Reduction}} 17.(41)\,a$$

17.(43)   *Method B*

[The Nazi arrested Joan and the Nazi arrested Mary]
$$\xRightarrow{\textit{Coordination reduction}}$$
$$\text{[The Nazi arrested Joan and Mary]} \xRightarrow{\textit{Passive}} 17.(41)\,a$$

The difference between Method A and Method B can be seen in the case of coreferent underlying structures, such as:

17.(44)   Harry$_i$ praised Harry$_i$ and Harry$_i$ praised me.

Under Method A, passive must apply directly to the first conjunct in such structures, yielding a direct violation of Cross-Over V no matter what is said about the crossing of one nominal over a coreferent inside a nominally-complex NP. In other words, under the joint assumptions of sentential compounding and

Method A, Cross-Over V definitely predicts that the pair of sentences which results from 17.(44) [depending on the application or nonapplication of passive]:

17.(45) a *Harry$_i$ praised $\left\{ \begin{array}{c} \text{him}_i \\ \text{himself}_i \end{array} \right\}$ and $\left\{ \begin{array}{c} \text{I} \\ \text{me} \end{array} \right\}$.

   b *Harry$_i$ and I were praised by $\left\{ \begin{array}{c} \text{him}_i \\ \text{himself}_i \end{array} \right\}$.

should be differentiated with respect to degree of deviance. Namely, 17.(45) b should be worse under these assumptions since 17.(45) a just violates the inclusion constraint while 17.(45) b violates this plus Cross-Over V in respect to the application of passive on the first conjunct.

On the other hand, given 17.(44), sentential compounding, and Method B, the situation is somewhat different. Here passive will not apply to 17.(44) directly but to the result of applying coordination reduction to 17.(44), namely:

17.(46)   Harry$_i$ praised Harry$_i$ and I.

Here passive will cross one NP over a coreferent, but one of the two will be inside a nominally-complex NP not containing the other. If, therefore, 17.(45) a and b are not distinguished with respect to degree of deviance, and if Method B holds, Cross-Over V is inconsistent with these facts since the coreferents in 17.(46) are clause mates, and Cross-Over V hence predicts that passive cannot cross them.

Let us sum up these rather complex considerations. The question is to what extent Cross-Over V is consistent with the data of coreferent NP insofar as coordinate nominally-complex NP are concerned. To discuss this it will be very useful to have terms for describing the relative deviance possibilities of all pairs like 17.(45) differentiated by the operation of constant movements. Let us describe the situation where such pairs are equivalently deviant, not distinguished, as *equivalence*; the situation where that member which requires operation of the relevant constant movement is more deviant as *distinction*. Here we are assuming, rather speculatively but plausibly, that the facts are constant for all rules.

What we have determined, then, is that given sentential compounding, either Method A or B is compatible with Cross-Over V only if distinction holds. Under either mode of derivation equivalence means Cross-Over V is violated, since it predicts violations not found. Given sentential compounding and Method B, Cross-Over V is violated just because it does not distinguish relations in terms of nominally-complex NP boundaries. That is, the Method B derivation of *coordinate* nominally-complex NP from sententially-compound underlying structures raises exactly the issues raised by *nominalization* type nominally-complex NP. Both involve the question of what the cross-over principle predicts in cases where a constant movement crosses an NP over a coreferent inside of a nominally-complex NP. That is, what happens in cases where, for instance, passive applies to structures like:

17.(47) *a* Harry$_i$ criticized Harry$_i$'s brother.
  b Harry$_i$ criticized Harry$_i$ and Joan.

The results are:

17.(48) *a* Harry$_i$'s brother was criticized by him$_i$.
  b *Harry$_i$ and Joan were criticized by him$_i$.

We are sure that 17.(48) *a* is well formed and just so in all analogous cases. We are sure that 17.(48) *b* is ill formed. But crucially we are not sure whether it is *more* ill formed than 17.(47) *b*. If not, only the inclusion constraint is at work.

So far then, we have seen the conditions under which Cross-Over V need not be altered to deal with nominally-complex NP of either of the two varieties. These are:

17.(49) *a* Nominalization nominally-complex NP have a sententially-complex NP ancestry and the reductions to nominally-complex NP follow the application of the constant movements.
  b Coordinate nominally-complex NP have a sentential-compounding origin and, given either Method A or B, distinction holds.

Referring back now to 17.(49), which defines the conditions under which Cross-Over V is compatible with the known facts of nominally-complex NP, we see that the chief condition of 17.(49) *b* is that coordinate NP have a sententially-compound origin. This hypothesis, while plausible for a wide class of such NP, runs into great difficulties with another class, as pointed out by several authors:[14]

17.(50) *a* John and Billy are identical.
  b *John is identical and Billy is identical.

17.(51) *a* Mary and Louise met in Florida.
  b *Mary met in Florida and Louise met in Florida.

Many now take such sentences to show that regardless of whether sentential compounding accounts for many nonsentential coordinate structures in surface forms, some coordinate NP must be derived from underlying deep structure coordinate NP. If this is true, and if cases can be found where constant movements cross such NP, then the sentential-compounding basis for maintaining Cross-Over V stated in 17.(49) will be jeopardized. But such cases do exist.

---

[14] R. B. Lees and C. Fillmore noted it in unpublished work at least as early as the summer of 1965. See also Lakoff and Peters (1966).

Thus consider:

17.(52)   Larry transferred all the money to Joan and Barbara.

The indirect object NP here is of the type which would seem to require an underlying NP coordination. But there are passives:

17.(53)   All the money was transferred to Joan and Barbara by Larry.

Thus crossing will arise in cases like:

17.(54)   Larry$_i$ transferred all the money to Larry$_i$ and Barbara.

17.(55) *a*   Larry$_i$ transferred all the money to $\begin{Bmatrix} \text{him} \\ \text{himself}_i \end{Bmatrix}$ and Barbara.

b   *All the money was transferred to Larry$_i$ and Barbara by him$_i$.

And the question is again whether 17.(55) *b* is equally deviant or more deviant than 17.(55) *a*. If it is equally deviant, and if passive truly applies to structures like 17.(54), then Cross-Over V is violated since it predicts a cross-over violation in 17.(55) *b* but not in 17.(55) *a*, while the inclusion constraint is violated in both.

Summing up overall, we see that Cross-Over V is bound up with the analysis of a wide range of constructions including nominalizations and coordination. It is difficult to draw clear conclusions in the face of our very limited knowledge of the structure of these aspects of English grammar. There are, however, many problems in the way of analyses of these phenomena that would permit Cross-Over V to stand as is in the face of nominally-complex NP. Hence it is more than worthwhile to consider what must be done to make the cross-over principle consistent with such NP if the various conditions we have brought up which permit Cross-Over V to remain as is are not ultimately met. This reduces to two subquestions: one dealing with nominalizations; the other, with coordinate NP. The latter is the more difficult since, as we have seen, the facts are very unclear. Let us assume for simplicity, therefore, that the facts of coordinate NP are consistent with those for nominalizations. What this means, then, is that in general we are claiming that just as pairs like:

17.(56) *a*   John$_i$ punched his$_i$ brother.
        b   John$_i$'s brother was punched by him$_i$.

17.(57) *a*   John$_i$'s brother punched him$_i$.
        b   John$_i$ was punched by his$_i$ brother.

are undifferentiated with respect to degree of grammaticality so that passive yields no crossing violations, just so pairs like:

17.(58) *a*   *John$_i$ punched Mary and him$_i$.
        b   *Mary and John$_i$ were punched by him$_i$.

17.(59) *a*   *Mary and John$_i$ punched him$_i$
        b   *John$_i$ was punched by Mary and him$_i$.

are not differentiated, that is, both members are equally ill formed so that again there are no crossing violations. This is to assume equivalence in our earlier terminology.

Having made such assumptions about examples like 17.(56)–17.(59), what we are asking, then, is how Cross-Over V must be modified if, contra previous suggestions, constant movements must apply directly to structures, like the *a* forms in these examples, which contain nominally-complex NP. As is, Cross-Over V will predict crossing violations in all such cases for coreferents since Cross-Over V distinguishes NP position only in terms of the notion clause mate. But all the NP here meet this condition and hence should not, by Cross-Over V, be crossable. This is clearly false in the nominalization cases and assumptively false in the coordinate ones. Hence what is required is a modification of Cross-Over V to permit application of constant movements in such cases involving nominally-complex NP.

C. THE NOTION OF PEER

My suggestion is that, if the conditions described at the end of section B obtain and Cross-Over V cannot be left as is because of nominally-complex NP, we reformulate this principle in terms of a notion I shall refer to as *peerhood*, a not completely mnemonic term for the idea. This notion will be defined in such a way that the circled NP in 17.(60) *are* peers, those in 17.(61) *not:*

17.(60) *a* (Joe) respects (his father) .

   b (Joe's father) hates (him) .

   c (Joe) saw (Tom and Mary) .

   d (Tom and Mary) saw (Joe) .

17.(61) *a* (Joe) respects (his) father.

   b (Joe's) father hates (him) .

   c (Joe) saw Tom and (Mary) .

   d (Tom) and Mary saw (Joe) .

There are several empirically possible ways to define this notion. One important question is whether it should be defined in terms of the notion of clause mates. That is, should the contrast between NP which are peers and NP which are not be restricted to the domain of clause mates? Without any real evidence, I have answered this negatively. Consequently, the following definition is offered:

17.(62)   Two NP, NP_1 and NP_2, neither of which dominates the other nor is coordinate with the other in a phrase marker P are peers with respect to a node S_i, just in case the paths between each of these NP and S_i are such that they contain no NP-nodes not separated from the starting point NP, NP_1 or NP_2, by a node S.

Consider this definition with respect to phrase markers:

17.(63)

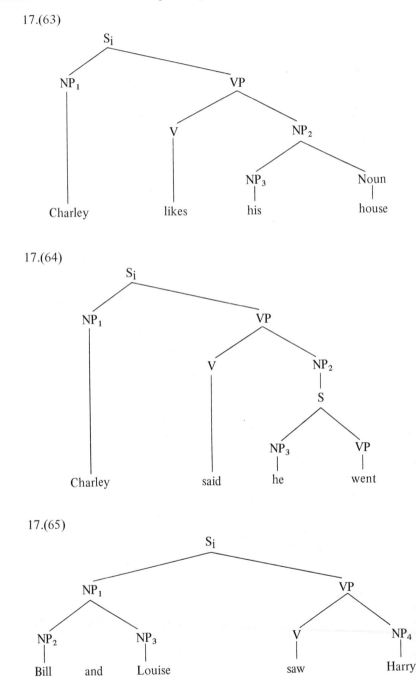

17.(64)

17.(65)

In 17.(63) NP_1 and NP_2 are peers but NP_1 and NP_3 are not, since NP_3 is separated from S_i by the NP node NP_2 and no S intervenes between NP_2 and NP_3. In 17.(64), NP_1 and NP_2 are peers as are NP_1 and NP_3. In 17.(65) NP_1 and NP_4 are peers but no other pairs are.

The reason "peer" is not completely mnemonic terminology is clear. It suggests a kind of equality between NP. But this implication would be valid only if the concept had been defined to hold between all NP of equal degree of nominal embedding. But actually it is defined so as to hold only between those of zero degree of nominal embedding. Hence the circled NP in examples like:

17.(66)   (John's) father hates (his) mother.

are not peers although they are nominally embedded to the same degree. Only the circled NP in:

17.(67)   (John's father) hates (his mother) .

are peers. "Peer" would be fully mnemonic only if it held between all NP of equal degree of nominal embedding. Another term, say "highest peer," would then be needed for the present "peer." I have not chosen this route because in this not employed usage "peer" would never play any role. One would always be referring to "highest peer."

Given the notion of peer, we are in a position to state the cross-over principle even if the facts are as in 17.(56)-17.(59) and Cross-Over V is unsalvageable in terms of rule ordering and assumptions about sentential origins. We can state the principle anew by observing that what 17.(56)-17.(59) show, under the assumptions we are now going under, is that with respect to constant movements, the cross-over principle cannot be defined exclusively in terms of the notion of clause mates. This restriction is necessary but not sufficient. However, we can give a sufficient condition by appealing to the notion of peer. Hence one can state:

17.(68)   *Cross-Over VI*

Assumptions and definitions as in Chapter 14

Despite the fact that P is a member of S, T may not apply to P if the application path of T with respect to P is such that this path contains an NP_j coreferential with NP_k and both NP_j and NP_k are pronominal virgins and either:

a. T is a variable movement rule.
b. T is a constant movement rule and NP_k and NP_j are both clause mates and peers.

Under the assumption that constant movements apply to phrase structures containing nominally-complex NP, the addition of reference to peerhood in 17.(68) predicts that coreferent NP like those in:

17.(69)   Harry$_i$ stabbed Harry$_i$.

may not be crossed, since they are both clause mates and peers. But it also predicts that NP like those in:

17.(70) *a* *Harry$_i$ stabbed Harry$_i$ and me.
      b Harry$_i$ loves Harry$_i$'s mother.

can be crossed since, although clause mates, they are not peers.

It follows, therefore, that even if constant movements must be allowed to apply to structures like 17.(70) already containing nominally-complex NP, the cross-over principle can, apparently, still be stated. The price is that we must appeal to a notion like peer.

It was observed earlier that the structural relations between NP which rightly undergo reflexivization can be stated in terms of the notion of clause mate only if reflexivization applies at a point where nominally-complex NP do not exist. If, however, reflexivization applies at a point where structures like 17.(70) have already been derived, then this notion is insufficient. However, like the insufficiency in Cross-Over V, this could immediately be remedied by reference to peer. That is, under these circumstances we could say that reflexivization applies to coreferent NP which at its point of application are both clause mates and peers.

The fact that, conceivably, peerhood might be relevant to the statement of English reflexivization is of some independent interest. As has already been suggested several times, the contrast between two types of pronominalization, reflexive and nonreflexive, is not a unique feature of English. Indeed there is some reason to regard it as essentially universal. It is quite relevant, therefore, that in Mohawk, an American Indian language of the Iroquoian group, we can give an argument showing that reflexivization *must* be stated in terms of the notion peer or some effective equivalent. This then shows that peerhood is a relation among NP which will have to be defined in linguistic theory regardless of the facts of English.

Mohawk has genitive expressions rather analogous in essential ways to those in English. And pronominalization in and out of such expressions is analogous too. That is, coreferent NP which are not peers determine nonreflexive types of structures. The question is: could this be due to rule ordering of the type that is not known to fail in English? The answer is no. Recall that the ordering argument for English depends on showing that reflexivization can apply at a point before any nominally-complex NP have been derived. In turn this depends on the assumption that all such NP have a sententially-complex origin. This lets the clause mate constraint alone predict the reflexivization contrast.

Such an ordering argument fails in Mohawk because there are cases where only the "possessor" NP of a genitive construction is left, and this undergoes the Mohawk rule of reflexivization. I shall illustrate schematically with English morpheme versions of Mohawk sentences:[15]

17.(71) I book hit I $\Longrightarrow$ 'My book hit me'
                                   *'My book hit myself'

---

[15] I have discussed these Mohawk constructions in detail in Postal (1962), more briefly in Postal (1964), and again in terms of universal grammar in Postal (1968).

Nothing thus far shows that this kind of fact could be stated exclusively in terms of the notion clause mate by assuming a sententially-complex origin for Mohawk genitives and an ordering placing the reduction to nominally-complex genitives *after* reflexivization [and having it postcyclical to prevent any applications of reflexivization on later cycles]. But this is in fact impossible because of the following facts. Under certain conditions, the object noun can be incorporated in the verb. Hence there are sentences like:

17.(72) *a*   I hit I book ⟹
     b   I bookhit I book ⟹   'I bookhit my book'
                                   *I bookhit myself's book'

And under certain conditions, the original external noun can be deleted, yielding:

17.(73)   I bookhit I.

But now these structures are not sentences. They must undergo reflexivization, yielding:

17.(74) *a*   'I bookhit myself'
     b   *'I bookhit me, my'

But this fact shows directly that reflexivization in Mohawk must be allowed to apply, regardless of how it is allowed, at a stage in derivations after nominally-complex NP have been derived. This follows since the rule of reflexivization must apply to output of the rule which deletes the "possessed" noun of genitives after this has been incorporated. But this deletion rule in turn operates on Mohawk genitive expressions, which are nominally complex.

The facts follow directly, however, even given this ordering if Mohawk reflexivization is designed to apply to coreferents which are both clause mates and peers. This approach predicts that, given a structure like:

17.(75)

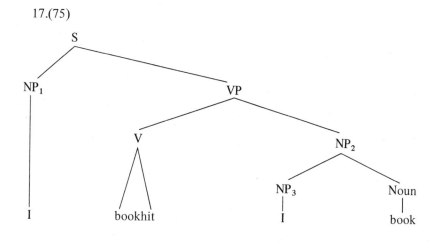

reflexivization application is blocked since NP_1 and NP_3 are not peers. This prediction is borne out by 17.(72). On the other hand, after the head noun of the object is deleted, 17.(75) is turned into the structure:

17.(76)

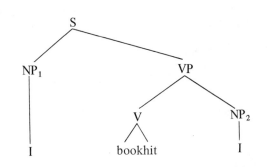

But in this, NP_1 and NP_2 are peers. Hence reflexivization will apply, and does, as shown by 17.(74). It seems, then, that the notion of peer is clearly needed to handle the facts of reflexivization in Mohawk.

Incidentally, an argument quite analogous to that just given for Mohawk *could* be constructed for English *if* one could get certain sentences of the following sort. Observe that there is a rule which drops the nonreferential pronoun *one* after a genitive:

17.(77) *a*   *John's one is on the table $\Longrightarrow$ John's is on the table
       b   *My one is on the table $\Longrightarrow$ Mine is on the table

Suppose now this rule yielded structures like:

17.(78) *a*   John$_i$'s struck John$_i$.
       b   John$_i$ dropped John$_i$'s.

Then, if reflexivization could apply to such structures, this would yield, respectively:

17.(79) *a*   *John$_i$'s struck himself$_i$.
       b   *John$_i$ dropped himself$_i$'s.

The fact that this does not happen and that the appropriate outputs are:

17.(80) *a*   John$_i$'s struck him$_i$.
       b   John$_i$ dropped his$_i$.

must then be attributed to the fact that the English rule which operates in 17.(77) to delete the "possessed" noun must follow reflexivization and the latter must never become applicable to the deletion outputs. The English rule is thus in this regard in contrast with the Mohawk genitive deletion rule discussed above. This eliminates this type of argument for the necessity of peerhood in English reflexivization. It does not, of course, show that no other types of argument will be forthcoming.

I take this discussion of Mohawk reflexivization to suggest that even if it becomes necessary to state the cross-over principle in terms of the notion of peerhood, no argument of *ad hoc* concepts can be leveled. It appears that this concept[16] must be available to transformational rules of pronominalization independently of crossing restrictions.

Summing up the overall argument of this chapter to this point, it seems that, despite the multiple mysteries and uncertainties in the analysis of nominally-complex NP of all varieties, there is nothing in the known data about them which suggests any insoluble problems for the cross-over principle as such. Those problems which do exist in fitting such a principle to the data of nominally-complex NP appear to reside exclusively in our limited knowledge of the proper structures and derivations for these nominal elements. One possible exception to this is discussed in the following section.

D. A PROBLEM WITH SOME PICTURE-NOUN DATA

Picture nouns comprise a very large class including *picture, story, description, cartoon, joke, lie, fable,* and so forth. The nominalizations based on such nouns involve a number of highly peculiar and mystifying properties. In particular, as mentioned several times previously, these permit in some contexts, and require in others, reflexive forms in positions not yet shown by anyone to follow from the operation of the rule reflexivization.

We observed in Section B [footnotes 4–6] that there are certain problems regarding the relation of picture-noun nominalizations and the Cross-Over V [or Cross-Over VI now] predictions for variable movements. One class of example is illustrated by:

17.(81) *a*   Himself, Harry took a picture of.
      b   Herself, Mary hates criticisms of.
      c   Herself, Marilyn never draws sketches of.

For me, these outputs of *Y*-movement seem grammatical, and were so indicated in the text of Section B. Since the examples illustrate coreferent crossing and crossing produced by a variable movement rule, the explanation must be that at the point of *Y*-movement application the coreferents are not both pronominal

---

[16]Strong evidence of the relevance of peerhood would show up if there exist languages in which the form of pronominal elements is systematically different when pronominalization occurs between peers and nonpeers, that is, in a language where sentences had properties like:

   (i)   John$_i$ said Mary hated him$_i$ga.
   (ii)   John$_i$ profited from Mary's proposal to him$_i$mu.

virgins. This means that whatever rule produces the reflexive forms in picture-noun nominalizations like 17.(81) and:

17.(82) *a* Harry took a picture of himself.
     b Mary hates criticisms of herself.
     c Marilyn never draws sketches of herself.

must *precede* Y-movement. If this rule is simply the ordinary reflexivization rule, this ordering has been independently established [see Chapter 16, Section B]. If, on the other hand, the possibility raised in footnote 6 of Chapter 2 is valid, that is, that this rule is distinct, then no independent justification for the ordering is known to me. At the same time, however, most facts seem consistent with this assumption.

I say "most" because we must discuss examples like those referred to in footnote 6 of this chapter:

17.(83) *a* ??A picture of himself fell on Harry the day before yesterday.
     b *Harry$_i$, a picture of himself$_i$ fell on the day before yesterday.

17.(84) *a* ??That caricature of himself annoyed Schwarz more than you realize.
     b *Schwarz$_i$, that caricature of himself$_i$ annoyed more than you realized.

What is crucial here is that while the *a* forms are of somewhat dubious acceptability, the *b* forms seem quite hopeless. In short, there is a definite distinction between the *a* and *b* forms, whose difference is just the application of Y-movement. Just as crucially, this difference seems correlated with coreference, since pairs like:

17.(85) *a* A caricature of DeGaulle annoyed Pompidou more than you realize.
     b Pompidou, a caricature of DeGaulle annoyed more than you realize.

do not seem to show such a severe difference. 17.(85) *b* does seem clumsier and less acceptable than 17.(85) *a* but not to the extent of the difference in 17.(83) and 17.(84).

If, however, there is a violation in 17.(83) *b* and 17.(84) *b*, an explanation by way of Cross-Over VI is apparently incompatible with the facts in 17.(81). The latter require that the NP inside of picture-noun nominalizations be reflexivized before Y-movement, to account for the grammaticality of 17.(81) in terms of the pronominal virgin property. But the former will require this reflexivization to follow Y-movement, in order to predict the violations in terms of the pronominal virgin condition.

There are two possible lines of attack on this situation. One would involve a revision of the cross-over principle. The other would involve the analysis of the picture-noun nominalizations involved. My own preference is the latter. And the truly crucial examples here seem to be sentences like 17.(83) *b* and 17.(84) *b*.

Observe first that examples like those in 17.(81) involve underlying picture-noun nominalizations which are *normal* in a way those in 17.(83) and 17.(84) are not. That is, the ancestor structures of 17.(81) are:

17.(86) *a* Harry took a picture of himself.
      b Mary hates criticisms of herself.
      c Marilyn never draws sketches of herself.

Whatever else can be said about the reflexivization in these cases, it at least operates in the normal direction for reflexivization, namely, *forwards*. In 17.(83) *a* and 17.(84) *a*, however, the reflexivization is backwards. Moreover, the former reflexivization is normal, while the latter is not in another sense. Namely, the process is obligatory in structures like 17.(86). There are no alternate forms of 17.(86) without reflexivization:

17.(87) *a* *$Harry_i$ took a picture of him_i.
      b *He_i took a picture of $Harry_i$.
      c *$Himself_i$ took a picture of $Harry_i$.

On the other hand, there are alternates for sentences like 17.(83) *a*:

17.(88) *a* ??A picture of him_i fell on $Harry_i$.
      b A picture of $Harry_i$ fell on him_i.

17.(88) *a* seems no worse than 17.(83) *a* and 17.(88) *b* seems better, although it is still, I think, partially deviant, for reasons that I at best only partially understand [see footnote 1 of Chapter 9]

These facts thus show the following:

17.(89) *a* The process of reflexivization in examples like 17.(81) and 17.(86) is consistent with the reflexivization produced by the rule of reflexivization with respect to the properties of (i) left-to-right application and (ii) obligatoriness, deviating only with respect to apparent violation of the (iii) peerhood constraint.
      b The process of reflexivization in examples like 17.(83) and 17.(84) deviates from that produced by the rule of reflexivization with respect to all of the properties of (i), (ii), and (iii).

The inference is then obvious. Despite the fact that both sets of examples involve peculiar reflexivization, linked to picture noun nominalizations, they are a function of different rules. The process described by 17.(89) *a* may not be a function of reflexivization, but it is at any rate interpretable as the function of a rule with the ordering properties of reflexivization, particularly, precedence over *Y*-movement. This accounts for the possibility of *Y*-movement moving the reflexive form over its antecedent in terms of the pronominal virgin condition of Cross-Over VI.

If, however, the process described in 17.(89) b is a rule distinct from that involved in 17.(89) a, the possibility opens that its ordering properties are different. And, in particular, the possibility exists that, unlike other operations of reflexivization, this one *follows* Y-movement.[17] Suppose we refer to this newly hypothesized rule of reflexivization as *late reflexivization*. Observe, then, that the suggestion is that late reflexivization has, vis-à-vis Y-movement, the same ordering as pronominalization. This predicts, then, that the crossing restrictions on the reflexive forms produced by late reflexivization should be exactly those of pronominal forms produced by pronominalization.

But this is exactly what we have observed. The violations in 17.(83) b and 17.(84) b are just those we would predict if the pronominal forms were ordinary pronouns and not reflexive pronouns. That is, the striking fact is that there is no difference in violations in such cases as:

17.(90) a That description of him$_i$ annoyed DeGaulle$_i$ more than you know.

b That description of himself$_i$ annoyed DeGaulle$_i$ more than you know.

c That description of DeGaulle$_i$ annoyed him$_i$ more than you know.

d *DeGaulle$_i$, that description of him$_i$ annoyed more than you know.

e *DeGaulle$_i$, that description of himself$_i$ annoyed more than you know.

f *Him$_i$, that description of DeGaulle$_i$ annoyed more than you know.

But this arrangement of restrictions will follow automatically from a rule of late reflexivization[18] operating after Y-movement. Hence we propose the ordering of rules:

17.(91)   Reflexivization, forwards picture-noun reflexivization (if distinct from reflexivization)
Y-movement
Pronominalization
Late reflexivization

---

[17] Y-movement is obviously not a cyclical rule; in fact it can never even apply in embedded clauses. If, therefore, there were evidence that late reflexivization were cyclical, this would mean that either it precedes Y-movement or that the latter is last cyclical. But there is no evidence whatever that late reflexivization is cyclical.

[18] This is the case referred to in Chapter 2, footnote 6 of reflexivization which cannot be attributed to a single rule of reflexivization.

Assuming that *forwards picture-noun reflexivization* marks NP with the specifications [+Pro], [+Anaphoric] like previous pronominalization operations and that late reflexivization operates only on NP already containing these specifications,[19] the observed distribution of restrictions in all the examples of this section follows directly from Cross-Over VI with its condition that only pronominal virgins are blocked from crossing.

I am assuming that late reflexivization is not only distinct from reflexivization but in fact operates on the output of pronominalization, turning what would otherwise show up as ordinary pronouns into reflexive ones in some contexts. A further argument for this analysis beyond the one already given would be possible if we could demonstrate that there were some special restrictions on pronominalization which showed up in the cases taken to result from late reflexivization, where these restrictions were not known to govern reflexivization. But just such restrictions exist. Jackendoff (1968:21) has observed that there is a constraint on *backwards* pronominalization in cases of inanimate NP:

17.(92) = Jackendoff's (52)–(55)

    a The newspaper$_i$ printed Harry's story about it$_i$.
    b *Harry's story about it$_i$ appeared in the newspaper.
    c Mary's portrait of him$_i$ hangs in the president$_i$'s bedroom.
    d *Mary's painting of it$_i$ hangs in the Pru$_i$'s main lobby.

Hence under certain conditions, the exact formulation of which need not concern us, pronominalization application is blocked between NP which

---

[19] Although all the examples in the text which we have taken to result from late reflexivization are instances of backwards operation, it is quite possible that this rule is responsible for some of the forwards cases of picture-noun reflexivization of the type most difficult to imagine being assimilated to reflexivization. Jackendoff (1968) gives a number of examples of such, for instance:

    (i) Tom made the claim that the picture of himself hanging in the post office is a fraud.

I have not, however, been able to construct any examples which would test the crossability of such reflexives, so their relevance for the question of the existence of late reflexivization is at present limited.

Similarly, we have considered late reflexivization an optional modification of ordinary pronominal forms. But Jackendoff (1968:24) gives some examples where this may be obligatory, at least for some speakers:

    (ii) = Jackendoff's (15) The picture of himself that John saw hanging in the post office was ugly.

Variants of these such as:

    (iii) *The picture of John$_i$ that he$_i$ saw hanging in the post office was ugly.

seem quite out of the question, and ones like:

    (iv) The picture of him$_i$ that John$_i$ saw hanging in the post office was ugly.

while fine for the present writer, may not be possible for some speakers.

designate inanimate objects. Just so, the same constraint holds for cases taken here to result from late reflexivization:

17.(93) = Jackendoff's (48)–(51)
    a The newspaper printed a story about itself.
    b *A story about itself appeared in the newspaper.
    c A portrait of himself hangs in the president's bedroom.
    d *A picture of itself hangs in the Pru's main lobby.

Given the claim that late reflexivization operates on the output of pronominalization, embodied in our proposal here, the restrictions in examples like 17.(93) *b* and *d* follow automatically from a restriction on pronominalization, needed to account for restrictions like those in 17.(92) *b* and *d*. That is, these restrictions need be stated only once in the grammar. If, however, late reflexivization were to be assimilated to reflexivization, which cannot be formulated to operate on the output of pronominalization, these restrictions would have to be built into this latter rule as well. There are, however, no independent reasons for so limiting reflexivization. This then is a very strong independent argument for both:

17.(94) *a* The distinctness of the rules reflexivization and late reflexivization.
      b The fact that the latter operates on the output of pronominalization.

I suggest, then, that the solution to the apparent inconsistency of examples like 17.(81) and 17.(83), when taken in conjunction with Cross-Over VI, disappears under the following conditions. One recognizes the existence of the rule of late reflexivization, an existence which is justified *independently* by the contrast between 17.(89) *a* and 17.(89) *b* and by the facts of 17.(92) and 17.(93) and which is justified nonindependently by the fact that it subsumes the facts of 17.(83)-type examples under Cross-Over VI.

Suppose, however, that contra the arguments just presented, late reflexivization cannot be maintained, and all reflexive forms of this section must be taken to be generated by a rule or several rules which precede *Y*-movement. What would this do to Cross-Over VI? Under these conditions, how could the principle be formulated to explain the contrast between 17.(81)-type examples, where crossing is allowed, and 17.(83) *b*-type examples, where crossing is blocked? The only solution I can imagine would be to take advantage of the fact that in examples of the former variety the pronominal form is moved over its nonpronominal coreferent, while in the latter it is the nonpronominal coreferent which is moved over its pronominal relative. This contrast would have to be referred to in a reformulation of the cross-over principle, at least insofar as variable movements are concerned. Let me emphasize *that I see no reason to believe this is necessary* since the solution which recognizes the existence of the rule of late reflexivization seems justified and correct. But this solution accounts for the facts with no change in Cross-Over VI. To the extent it can be maintained, therefore, we can credit Cross-Over VI with revealing the existence of this secondary reflexivization rule.

18 A PROBLEM WITH *ABOUT*-MOVEMENT AND THE FURTHER RELEVANCE OF PIED PIPING

A. A HITHERTO IGNORED DIFFICULTY

Recall that an important feature of our statement of crossing restrictions has to do with correspondence between that NP in a phrase marker which is moved and the symbol NP in the description of the rule itself. This feature of Cross-Over III, IV, V, and VI has the effect of restricting the prediction of crossing restrictions to those rules *which actually move NP*. It is a fact, at least in English, that the majority of rules which move lexical constituents seem to move NP. There are, however, some rules which move non-NP and it will be helpful to consider them with respect to the possibility of crossing constraints.

Before doing this, however, we can introduce the problem by noting that, as things stand, Cross-Over VI does not, in any obvious way at least, apply to the rule of *about*-movement, despite the fact that we have throughout taken this rule as among the strongest evidence in favor of such principles. This unhappy consequence follows from the fact that the constituents whose order is actually affected are (a) not obviously NP; and (b) in any event not those which enter into relations of coreferentiality. That is, in deriving sentences like 18.(1) *b* from structures like those underlying 18.(1) *a*:

> 18.(1) *a* I spoke to Harry about communism.
> *b* I spoke about communism to Harry.

it is clear that *about*-movement must rearrange the *to*-phrase and the *about*-phrase. Let us assume that these have the structure:

18.(2) *a*

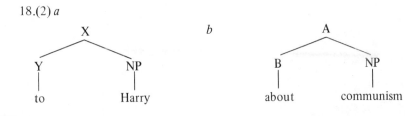

Here we indicate by the arbitrary symbols A, B, X, Y that the identity of the labels of the relevant nodes is open.

Consider first the structure of the *about*-phrase. If the node A *is not* NP, then no version of the cross-over principle is applicable at all since all versions require [see 14.(4)] that the ith term of the structure index of the relevant T be NP. Secondly, even if A *is* NP, no version of the principle really applies to *about*-constructions since it is not the constituents labeled A which enter into coreference relations but rather the NP which A dominates. That is, even if the structure of:

18.(3)   I talked to Harry$_i$ about Harry$_i$.

includes the subtree:

18.(4)

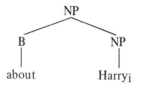

no version of the cross-over principle so far predicts that *about*-movement cannot apply to 18.(3) to yield:

18.(5)   *I talked about Harry to himself.

This follows just because the coreferent NP here does not correspond to the constituent which moves, even if it is assumed that *about* + NP is dominated by NP.

This discussion, and indeed all that has gone before, including the naming of the rule, has assumed implicitly that in the process of *about*-movement the *to*-phrase is stationary, while the *about*-constituent is reordered. There was no real basis for this.[1] But it is immediately apparent from 18.(2) that the reverse assumption *alone* will not help with the problem under discussion since the structures of the *to*- and *about*-phrases appear to be parallel.

There would seem to be two possible approaches to explaining these facts in such a way as to eliminate their apparent inconsistency with our hypothesis about crossing restrictions. We can assume that the constituents X and A are indeed NP and try to find some adjustment of analyses which will predict crossing restrictions even when the "mention" condition is not met. Or, we can assume that the constituents X and A in 18.(2) are *not* NP and can try to state a

---

[1] As we shall see below, there is, on the contrary, a good basis—derivable from Ross's discovery that reorderings to the right are upward bounded—*for requiring the reordering to operate in the reverse fashion.*

principle which predicts crossing restrictions for rules which reorder non-NP containing NP, assuming now that *about*-movement is such a rule. I shall deal with these proposals in reverse order. What I will try to show is that, in fact, every clear case of a rule which can be shown to reorder lexical constituents which are not NP is *not* subject to crossing restrictions. It follows that a solution for the problem of *about*-movement which takes the nodes A and X to be non-NP is totally *ad hoc* and without support.

B. RULES THAT REORDER THE CONSTITUENT S

There are two clear instances of rules that reorder full sentence constituents and a number of other likely candidates. The clearest and most productive rule is extraposition, mentioned several times before, especially in the discussions of *it*-replacement and *tough*-movement. Extraposition moves a sentence constituent to the end of the next more inclusive sentence:

18.(6) *a*   That Harry came late was disgusting.
     b   It was disgusting that Harry came late.

18.(7) *a*   That it was disgusting that Harry came late is obvious.
     b   *That it was disgusting is obvious that Harry came late.

18.(7) *b* is ill formed because the S constituent has been moved beyond the next more inclusive S; in other words, it has wrongly crossed a higher clause boundary. It follows that extraposition is a constant movement and further it would be naturally stated in our terms with an abbreviatory variable.

Consider, then, the question of crossing constraints for coreferent NP under this rule. That there are none follows from the equal well-formedness of such pairs as:

18.(8) *a*   That Harry ignored me was annoying to me.
     b   It was annoying to me that Harry ignored me.

18.(9) *a*   That Harry criticized me showed me something important.
     b   It showed me something important that Harry criticized me.

18.(10) *a*   That I am right seems clear to me.
      b   It seems clear to me that I am right.

It follows that extraposition is not subject to any constraint that the extraposed clause contain no NP coreferential to those over which it moves.

Another rule which reorders S constituents has been called by Ross (1967a) *extraposition from NP*. This rule is quite similar to extraposition in that it throws the moved clause just to the end of the next more inclusive clause. The rule accounts for such pairs as:

18.(11) *a*   Someone who I didn't know won the race.
      b   Someone won the race who I didn't know.

Now, in my dialect, but not some others, this rule is subject to the restriction that it not throw the relative clause over another NP. Hence it is largely restricted to intransitive verbs. This limits cross-over possibilities. We can, however, obtain a relative argument that there are no crossing constraints from the fact that sentences like 18.(12) *b*:

    18.(12) *a* Someone who hated me visited me.
           b *Someone visited me who hated me.

where the moving clause contains an NP coreferential to one over which the clause moves, are no worse than sentences like 18.(13) *b*:

    18.(13) *a* Someone who hated me visited me.
           b *Someone visited you who hated me.

Hence again there is no basis for assuming crossing restrictions.

A third rule which reorders S constituents is that involved in the derivation of sentences like 18.(14) *b*, presumably from sources like 18.(14) *a*:

    18.(14) *a* John couldn't lift it and he is no weakling.
           b John, and he is no weakling, couldn't lift it.

But again this rule, let us call it *conjunct insertion*,[2] yields no crossing restrictions, a point revealed by:

    18.(15) *a* I couldn't prevent myself from speaking and I am not loquacious.
           b I, and I am not loquacious, couldn't prevent myself from speaking.

Although there are other rules which probably move S, these three should suffice here to indicate that there are no obvious crossing constraints for such rules.

C. RULES THAT REORDER PREDICATIONAL OR ADVERBIAL CONSTITUENTS

Sentences like:

    18.(16) *a* John$_i$ kept a snake near him$_i$.
           b Near him$_i$, John$_i$ kept a snake.

    18.(17) *a* I visited Chile during October.
           b During October, I visited Chile.

---

[2]Notice that this rule is subject to the constraint that the inserted clause contain an NP coreferential to the NP next to which it is placed and that furthermore this NP must be so located in the clause that it can undergo *Wh-Rel*-movement without violation. These conditions also govern restrictive relative clause formation [see Chapter 20].

indicate the existence of a rule which throws phrases like *near him, during October*, and so forth to sentence initial position. This rule, referred to by Ross (1967a) as *adverbial preposing*,[3] is a variable movement, and hence can throw phrases across higher clause boundaries:

18.(18) *a*   John$_j$ claimed that he$_i$ always kept a snake near him$_j$.
     b   Near him$_j$ John$_j$ claimed he$_i$ always kept a snake.

18.(19) *a*   John$_j$ remembered that he$_i$ used to enjoy having snakes near him$_j$.
     b   Near him$_j$, John$_j$ remembered that he$_i$ used to enjoy having snakes.

We can see, however, that the moved adverb phrase may perfectly well contain NP coreferential to those it crosses under this rule:

18.(20) *a*   Near me, I kept a snake and a gorilla.
     b   Under him$_j$, John$_j$ wanted a pillow.

18.(21) *a*   Near my father, I saw a monkey.
     b   Near the man who attacked me, I saw a gun.

18.(22) *a*   Beneath me, I glimpsed a lot of crocodiles.
     b   Far below her$_j$, Mary$_j$ saw a gorilla.

Another rule moves predicates based on adjectival forms to sentence initial position. Call it *adjectival phrase movement*. This rule is exemplified by such pairs as:

18.(23) *a*   He is certainly ugly.
     b   Ugly, he certainly is.

18.(24) *a*   You are not more beautiful than Louise.
     b   More beautiful than Louise, you are not.

Like adverbial preposing, adjectival phrase movement is a variable movement and can thrust an adjectival phrase across an unlimited number of higher clause boundaries:

18.(25) *a*   Ugly, John said Mary certainly was not.
     b   More intelligent than Einstein, nobody ever claimed you were.
     c   Fond of grapefruit, I am sure that nobody would ever think Harry claimed I expected to be.

---

[3] It is not out of the question that adverbial preposing is a special case of Y-movement. This would follow if, among other things, it could be shown that, at the relevant quite late stage in the grammar, expressions like *near Harry* and so forth are NP.

Again, however, no crossing restrictions can be found:

18.(26) *a*   More intelligent than I, no one will believe I said you were.
    b   More radical than you, Tom should never have claimed you said Harry to be.

Incidentally, I do not know which of the two rules just discussed is to be taken to underlie the movement of adjective-based adverbial phrases in such examples as:

18.(27) *a*   I can't run faster than that train.
    b   Faster than that train I cannot run.

There are some similarities with both adverbial preposing and adjectival phrase movement.

It is particularly interesting to observe the contrast between both adverbial preposing and adjectival phrase shift, which move non-NP, with *Y*-movement, which moves NP.

18.(28) *a*   Jack$_i$ said I would someday be fond of him$_i$.
    b   *Him$_i$, Jack$_i$ said I would someday be fond of.
    c   Fond of him$_i$, Jack$_i$ said I would someday be.

18.(29) *a*   John$_i$ keeps a snake near him$_i$.
    b   *Him$_i$, John$_i$ keeps a snake near.
    c   Near him$_i$, John$_i$ keeps a snake.

In each case the *b* form, derived by *Y*-movement, is out, but the *c* form, derived by a rule which reorders non-NP, is well formed.[4]

Another rule, call it *emphasis shift*, which preposes non-NP is discussed by Ross (1967a:404–405). This rule is involved in the reordering of a verb phrase which follows an emphatically stressed auxiliary verb:

18.(30) *a*   They said Tom would win and he *did* win.
    b   They said Tom would win and win he *did*.

As Ross observes, this rule makes essential use of variables:

18.(31) *a*   They said Tom would win and I think Mary found out he *did* win.
    b   They said Tom would win and win I think Mary found out he *did*.

---

[4]The latter fact does not necessarily preclude the possibility raised in footnote 3 that adverbial preposing reduces to *Y*-movement. In cases like 18.(29) *c*, the moved constituent is *near him$_i$*, and this is not coreferential with *John$_i$*, and, most crucially, under a *Y*-movement analysis this movement is not a function of Pied Piping. Hence no violation of the cross-over principle would be involved even if *Y*-movement is the relevant operator. See Chapter 16, Section E.

However, again no coreferent crossing restrictions are found:

18.(32) *a*   John told her to be kind to me and she will *be* kind to me.
    b   John told her to be kind to me and kind to me she will *be*.

18.(33) *a*   John wants me to be helpful to you and I promise you I will try to *be* helpful to you.
    b   John wants me to be helpful to you and helpful to you I promise you I will try to *be*.

Another rule which reorders verb phrases is also discussed by Ross (1967a:406–407). This is operative in such pairs as:

18.(34) *a*   Although Harriet is lovely, I'm still going to date Betty.
    b   Lovely though Harriet is, I'm still going to date Betty.

This again is a variable movement:

18.(35) *a*   Although Harry expects me to agree Harriet is lovely, I'm still going to date Betty.
    b   Lovely though Harry expects me to agree Harriet is, I'm still going to date Betty.

This rule, call it *though-shift*, again induces no known crossing constraints on coreferents:

18.(36) *a*   Although Harry$_i$ expects me to be cruel to him$_i$, I will still help him$_i$.
    b   Cruel to him$_i$ though Harry$_i$ expects me to be, I will still help him$_i$.

18.(37) *a*   Although I$_i$ thought Harry was mean to me$_i$, I will still visit him.
    b   Mean to me$_i$ though I$_i$ thought Harry was, I will still visit him.

Although there are undoubtedly other rules which reorder non-NP lexical constituents, this brief survey of these little-studied rules should suffice for now to suggest that such rules do not impose coreferential crossing constraints on the NP inside the elements reordered by them, or over which these are moved.

D. THE *ABOUT*-MOVEMENT ANOMALY AS A CASE OF PIED PIPING

The conclusion of the last section shows that the problem of *about*-movement introduced in Section A of this chapter cannot be solved by taking this rule to reorder non-NP. In view of the discussion of Section C, this would leave the fact that *about*-movement is governed by crossing constraints totally mysterious. Consequently, we must take *about*-movement to be a rule *which reorders NP* and must find an explanation for its peculiarities within these terms.

Let us note, then, that what is odd about *about*-movement is that it does not meet the "mention" condition of Cross-Over III–VI. However, this is not a totally new problem. Recall that in Chapter 12 we dealt with a whole class of apparent anomalies with regard to the *wh*-rules. These concerned the fact that such examples as:

18.(38) *a*   **Whose$_i$ father did he$_i$ disagree with?*
     b   **The boy whose$_i$ father he$_i$ disagreed with*

are ill formed. Yet in these cases, it is the italicized NP which have crossed the pronominal forms and the italicized NP is not coreferential with the NP crossed. Consequently, this seemed to be behavior not predicted by the cross-over principle with its requirement that the "moving" NP correspond to the NP symbol mentioned in the rule producing the movement.

Our solution to this problem was to appeal to Ross's notion of Pied Piping. This permitted us to say that it was actually the "small" NP which corresponded to the NP mentioned in the *wh*-rules, and the fact that the "large" NP, not the "small" one, moved was a function of Pied Piping. We took this to be a solution, noting that it required use of the assumption, already needed by Ross, that in some contexts Pied Piping is obligatory. (See Chapter 12, Section C.)

Observe then, that if the nodes over the *about, to,* and *with* phrases are taken to be NP in examples like:

18.(39) *a*   I talked to Bill about communism.
     b   Bill argued with me about that.

the possibility of a Pied Piping explanation of the crossing restrictions of *about*-movement becomes possible. That is, in pairs like:

18.(40) *a*   I talked *to Bill about himself.*
     b   *I talked *about Bill to himself.*

it is the "large" italicized NP which have been reordered. Suppose, however, we take this behavior to be a function of Pied Piping, with only the "small" inner NP corresponding to the NP symbol mentioned in the rule itself. This would reduce *about*-movement to consistency with Cross-Over VI.

A Pied Piping approach to the behavior of NP under *about*-movement raises a number of difficulties, difficulties partially related to but partially independent of problems with the Pied Piping explanation for NP behavior under *Wh-Rel*-movement and *Wh-Q*-movement, as discussed in Chapter 12. Many of the present difficulties relate to the proper description of prepositions and prepositional phrases. The rest have to do with the scope of Pied Piping and its relation to notions like variable movement and constant movement.

The phenomenon of Pied Piping, *as specified by Ross's characterization,* is restricted essentially to that class of rules that have been referred to here as variable movements. According to this characterization, one would predict that

Pied Piping is not in general operative with constant movements.[5] It is not by any means clear that this prediction is valid [Section E below], but suppose it is. *About*-movement is a constant movement. This means that having Pied Piping relevant for *about*-movement would require an *ad hoc* statement in the grammar since this phenomenon is exceptional for rules falling in the class of constant movements. Therefore, the solution for *about*-movement in terms of Pied Piping commits us to a theory which permits *ad hoc* indications of Pied Pipeability for individual rules of the constant movement sort.[6] Given just Ross's discussion of Pied Piping, this might be taken to be a serious objection. For Ross tried to give a general statement not only of the functional effect of Pied Piping, but also of its scope. The strength of this objection is, however, mitigated [if not fully eliminated] by the fact, already discussed at length in Chapter 12, that the scope of Pied Piping is highly idiosyncratic and limited by many language-particular and rule-particular conditions, even for the class of rules covered by Ross's attempt at a general scope characterization. Hence the present proposal cannot be looked upon as giving up a fully general statement of the scope of Pied Piping, because no such statement exists.

Moreover, Ross has most perceptively discovered an intriguing property of the rule of complex-NP-shift in English, which is crucially relevant to the present discussion. This rule, discussed in Chapter 15, moves complex NP to the right boundary of the next more inclusive sentence:

18.(41) *a*   I bought the book which Mary told me I would like from him.
   b   I bought from him the book which Mary told me I would like.
   c   *I bought from him the book.

As Ross points out, however, complex-NP-shift cannot strand a preposition:

18.(42) *a*   I insisted on the fact that I was neutral throughout the discussion.
   b   I insisted throughout the discussion on the fact that I was neutral.
   c   *I insisted on throughout the discussion the fact that I was neutral.

This fact cannot be explained by stating the rule in terms of prepositional phrase movement or the like, even in the absence of previous [and subsequent Section

---

[5] Given the difference between Ross's framework of rule classifications and that of the present work, this statement cannot be precise. Ross's description of scope refers to the property that the NP in the structure index is surrounded by variables. However, this does not necessarily define a variable movement in our sense since all rules which reorder to the right are upward bounded, and Ross allows in addition *ad hoc* markings of upward-boundedness for left-moving rules.

[6] We will see as we proceed, however, that Pied Piping may be much more manifest in the domain of constant movements than appears at first glance.

E] arguments which show that such phrases are NP. This is impossible because complex-NP-shift typically moves NP:

18.(43) *a* I gave the book which Mary bought me to Margaret.
      b I gave to Margaret the book which Mary bought me.
      c *I gave to Margaret the book.

It follows, then, that the movement of prepositional phrases by complex-NP-shift in examples like 18.(42) *b* is a further strong argument for the NP character of prepositional phrases.

Ross proposes to explain the unstrandability of prepositions under complex-NP-shift by adding a special condition to *English* grammar to the effect that:

18.(44) = Ross's (4.231)

        No NP may be moved to the right out of the environment
        [P __]
         NP

In this formulation, Ross takes advantage of the special property of complex-NP-shift, that it moves NP to the right, and of the fact that no rule in English which moves elements to the right strands prepositions, although left-moving rules like *Wh-Q*-movement may do so.

However, the effect of 18.(44) can be obtained if it can be said that Pied Piping is operative for complex-NP-shift, even though it is a constant movement. This follows again on the assumption that prepositional phrases have the structure:

18.(45)

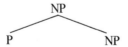

It would have to be added, of course, that in these cases Pied Piping is obligatory, that is, that it is the largest NP which must always move. Moreover, this fact, in connection with the problem about *about*-movement, suggests a possible generalization, or rather several. Like complex-NP-shift, *about*-movement is a constant movement and one for which, we seem forced to say, Pied Piping is applicable. It is then possibly true that:

18.(46) If Pied Piping is applicable for a constant movement C, then it is obligatory for C.

To complicate matters, however, 18.(46) is not the only generalization about the obligatoriness property which is available. Up to this point we have spoken of *about*-movement informally as a rule which moves an *about*-phrase to the left over preceding structures. This was quite arbitrary and, moreover, very dubious. There is evidence that the rule involved here is in fact: (a) one which is independent of *about*-phrases in particular, and (b) one which moves elements to the right. The evidence for (a) consists of the analogous alternative position possibilities for structures like:

18.(47) *a*   I fought with Harry for your sake.
   b   I fought for your sake with Harry.

18.(48) *a*   I looked for the virus with a magnifying glass.
   b   I looked with a magnifying glass for the virus.

18.(49) *a*   I talked to Harry on the telephone.
   b   I talked on the telephone to Harry.

18.(50) *a*   I walked into the room with a smile.
   b   I walked with a smile into the room.

18.(51) *a*   I snatched that from the window with a hook.
   b   I snatched that with a hook from the window.

Such data clearly suggest that there is a much more general rule which can yield alternative positions for prepositional phrases, of which the movement of *about*-phrases is just a special case.

The evidence for the claim (b) consists of the fact that it is much easier to specify the destination point of an element traveling to the right in cases like 18.(47)–18.(51) than that of one traveling to the left. This is so because an element moving to the right simply goes to the end of the clause, a stopping point guaranteed, in one way or another, by Ross's discovery that all rules moving elements to the right are upward bounded. Moreover, there is no natural characterization of a stopping point for a left-moving element. It is not true, as examples like 18.(51) show, that the element moves next to a verbal.

A final piece of evidence which shows that the rule actually moves elements to the right is important in its own right. Observe that the alternate positional possibilities illustrated previously by *about*-phrases and recently by 18.(47)–18.(51) are dependent on the presence of a preposition before the NP which starts on the left:

18.(52) *a*   I struck the table with an axe.
   b   *I struck with an axe the table.

18.(53) *a*   I warned John about Mary.
   b   *I warned about Mary John.

18.(54) *a*   I bought the car from Harry.
     b   *I bought from Harry the car.

This fact is naturally representable if we formulate the rule as one which moves an NP to the right,[7] since the preposition will simply precede the NP to be moved. With a left-moving rule, however, the preposition would be lost in the structure covered by a variable.

Roughly, then, we propose to replace *about*-movement by the more general operation:

18.(55)   *Right-NP-drift*

$$X, \quad [\ Y_a, \text{Preposition}, \text{NP}, Z_a\ ], \quad Y$$
$$ S S$$
$$1 \quad\ 2 \quad\ 3 \quad\quad\ 4 \ 5 \quad\ 6 \Longrightarrow 1, 2, 3, 0, 5+4, 6$$

Condition: Subject to Pied Piping

using again the apparatus of *abbreviatory variables* to build in the upward-bounded property of the rule. It goes without saying that this formulation ignores many restrictions of various sorts.

With respect to crossing restrictions, then, the key point is that right-NP-drift must be marked as subject to Pied Piping in order to predict the movement of the preposition with its NP, and furthermore, this Pied Piping must be made obligatory in order to gain the full effect of Ross's (4.231). This is accomplished by 18.(46). It is, however, also equally well accomplished by:

18.(56)   If Pied Piping is applicable for a rule R which reorders elements
          to the right, then it is obligatory for R.

This is now applicable since, unlike the earlier formulation of *about*-movement, right-NP-drift reorders elements to the right. The only rules for which Pied Piping is optional are *Wh-Q*-movement and *Wh-Rel*-movement, and these reorder elements to the left.

I have no basis for deciding between 18.(46) and 18.(56), but this is not our chief concern. The key point is that Ross's principle (4.231), which is an *ad hoc* condition peculiar to English and of a unique kind, can be eliminated *if* one is allowed to indicate for particular rules of the constant movement type that Pied

---

[7] At this point, I have no doubt that certain individuals will observe that the rule is much more simply statable if we have the node prepositional phrase available since this automatically limits application to those NP preceded by a preposition. The trouble with this is, of course, its incompatibility with the data on Pied Piping of the type gone over in Chapter 12, and its incompatibility with the crossing restrictions of NP under rules like *about*-movement. The fact that there is no natural way to introduce a node prepositional phrase into sentence structures is also quite relevant, especially if one bears in mind the problem of relating such a node to the diverse prepositions it must dominate together with the strictly selected NP these can precede.

Piping is applicable. This essentially reduces the special unstrandability properties of prepositions under both complex-NP-shift and right-NP-drift[8] to principles needed for an independent phenomenon of a quite different sort, namely, to Pied Piping. Hence the Pied Piping approach to the problem of *about*-movement, which seems at first totally *ad hoc*, is, on slightly deeper investigation, seen to deal with a phenomenon which requires partially *ad hoc* statement in any event, namely, the inability of complex-NP-shift to strand a preposition. Moreover, if this latter fact is stated in terms of Pied Piping, rather than as in Ross's (4.231), a generalization about the obligatoriness is available, namely, either 18.(46) or 18.(56).

I conclude that it is reasonable to assume that *about*-movement, restated as right-NP-drift, is a rule for which Pied Piping is marked as applicable by a special statement in the grammar of English,[9] a property also shared by another English constant movement, complex-NP-shift. The claim is that Pied Piping is (a) generally applicable to variable movements, although blocked in some cases and obligatory in others by special conditions [(See Ross (1967a, Chapter 4)] ; and (b) generally not applicable to constant movements although this becomes a possibility if a special condition on the rule is added.

As in Chapter 12, then, Pied Piping turns out to play a crucial role in reducing apparent coreferent crossing anomalies to regularity. Conversely, because of this, the cross-over principle turns out to yield very strong, surprising evidence in favor of the notion of Pied Piping. This conclusion is further supported by the facts of another rule, to which we turn in Section F after a digression on prepositions and the possible relevance of Pied Piping to rules like passive and *psych*-movement.

E. PREPOSITIONS

It was observed in Section D that Ross's characterization of Pied Piping scope predicts that this functional principle will not apply to constant movements. Let us consider some evidence which at first glance seems to support this prediction. Consider the behavior of prepositions in structures like:

18.(57) The committee agreed on something.

under the rules of *Wh-Q*-movement and passive. Under the former, the preposition may accompany the inner NP or not, a fact predicted by Ross's

---

[8] One might well raise the question of whether complex-NP-shift and right-NP-drift cannot be reduced to one rule. Although they both move NP to the right, this seems unlikely to me because of the complexity condition and other special restrictions on the former plus the fact that it is not restricted to moving NP directly preceded by prepositions, as is the latter. Ross (1967a) attempts to combine complex-NP-shift with other operations moving NP to the right, including that referred to below in Section F as *extraposition of prepositional phrase*.

[9] However, it is just possible, as we will see in the next section, that Pied Piping is general for all rules which reorder NP to the right.

statement of Pied Piping scope for a variable movement under the assumption of a structure such as:

18.(58)

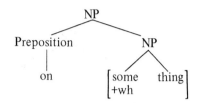

Hence:

18.(59) *a*   What did the committee agree on?
      b   On what did the committee agree?

Such behavior of prepositions is, along with the arguments of Section D, one of the chief bases for assuming prepositional phrases to have NP structure, that is, for eliminating the node prepositional phrase in favor of NP. Another is that NP structure for such phrases follows automatically from the desirable assumption that prepositions are transformationally inserted. The highest NP node is then a function of the general principle of derived constituent structure for what has been called *Chomsky adjunction*.[10]

However, when passive applies to structures like 18.(57), the preposition cannot be moved.

18.(60) *a*   Something was agreed on by the committee.
      b   *On something was agreed by the committee.
      c   *Something was agreed by the committee.[11]

It would seem to follow that Pied Piping is not applicable to passive and thus that the contrast suggested by Ross's characterization is borne out in the difference between *Wh-Q*-movement and passive in such cases. This may be wrong, however, and possibly Pied Piping *is* in part applicable to passive. This possibility is obscured by several factors.

First, it is obscured by the behavior of prepositions in examples like 18.(60), behavior which is in fact *exceptional*. Second, it is obscured by the fact that prepositions delete before NP in subject position. Third, it is obscured by the fact that prepositions generally drop directly after a verbal form which is not adjectival, a generalization to which verbs like those in 18.(60) are again exceptions.

---

[10] See Ross (1967a) and Lakoff (unpublished).

[11] This example is given because 18.(60) *b* could only be derived if one ignores the existence of a rule [to be discussed in the text presently] which deletes the preposition of subject NP under most conditions.

I suggest the following. At some stage in the grammar no NP have any prepositions. There is then a rule, call it *preposition insertion*, which assigns a preposition to every NP. This rule thus operates on structures like:

18.(61)

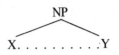

and yields new structures of the form:

18.(62)

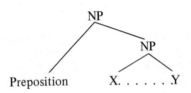

The actual shape of the preposition associated with a particular NP is determined by many factors in ways I do not pretend to understand fully. Obviously, the lexical head of the NP, its logical relation to verbal elements, lexical properties of the verbal head, and other factors play a role. I will not deal with this fundamental and difficult question further here.

Given these assumptions, consider the structure of correlative active and passive sentences such as:

18.(63) *a* Harry attacked Lucille.
     b Lucille was attacked by Harry.

This pair illustrates the general situation for such pairs. The active NP have no prepositions at all and the passive sentence has the preposition *by* on its moved former subject but no other preposition. Given a general rule of *preposition insertion*, however, our claim is that an earlier stage of sentences like 18.(63) is something like:

18.(64) *a* By Harry attacked on Lucille.
     b On Lucille was attacked by Harry.

Such structures are, I claim, converted to surface forms like 18.(63) by two rules [with different ordering relations]. One rule drops the preposition of a subject NP. This rule has, as far as I know, no exceptions whatever, a fact which is, in the context of what is known about exceptions to transformation rules, rather suspicious.[12] The other rule drops a preposition directly after a verbal form which is not adjectival. There are many exceptions to this rule, some of them possibly capable of subgeneralizations. For instance, the preposition *from* never seems to delete under this rule.

We might roughly state these rules as follows:

18.(65) *Subject preposition deletion*
X, Preposition, NP, Verbal, Y
1   2   3   4   5 ===⟹ 1, Ø, 3, 4, 5

Here I use the symbol "Verbal" as a cover term for verbs and adjectives, which I regard as members of the same category. I do not state it in terms of a constituent like VP for one reason. I would like to account for the presence of the element *for* in infinitive clauses in terms of the presence of the infinitive marker *to*, which, whatever else can be said about it, is clearly no verbal element. But it is likely that a sequence of the form *to + VP* is itself a VP, so that replacement of 18.(65) by a rule with VP as the symbol in the fourth term would predict deletion of the subject preposition in infinitives when this is in fact blocked. It is significant, perhaps, that those few verbal elements which have the infinitive marker *to* elided do not permit the subject preposition to remain:

18.(66) *a* I made John go.
        b *I made for John go.
        c I had John drive the truck.
        d *I had for John drive the truck.

Given proper ordering of the *to*-elision, this follows automatically from the analysis being suggested. It is thus insisted that the *for* of infinitive clauses is a preposition, inserted by the same rule as every other preposition, and not an *ad hoc* part of a complex "complementizer" as in Rosenbaum (1967). As noted earlier in footnote 2 of Chapter 4, this claim is supported by the fact that this *for* obeys the deletion law of other English prepositions. When its following NP is deleted, it must be deleted.

The preposition deletion rule for predicates is roughly:

18.(67) *Object preposition deletion*
X, ⎡ Verbal   ⎤ , Preposition, Y
   ⎣ Nonadjectival ⎦
1   2   3   4 ===⟹ 1, 2, Ø, 4

---

[12] That is, in general, rules of this type, rules referred to by Lakoff (1965) and elsewhere as *governed*, have exceptions. It is typically only rules which make essential use of variables like variable movements which are *ungoverned*, that is, have no lexical exceptions.

I said earlier that these two deletions were ordered differently. In particular, I would claim that they have the following positions with respect to the rule of *case marking*, which accounts in some way for *he/him, I/me*, and such contrasts.

18.(68)   Preposition insertion
Subject preposition deletion
Case marking
Object preposition deletion

With this ordering, the vast majority of "object" case forms, *him, whom, me, us,* and so on can be accounted for by case marking an NP directly following a preposition and nowhere else.

Returning now to the active-passive pair 18.(63) and such pairs generally, an immediate question is why the preposition of the active object deletes but not that of the postverbal passive object. The explanation I would offer for this is that the process of passivization involves marking the verbal form as adjectival, while active verbal forms are nonadjectival. This view receives support from the presence of *be* forms, typical of adjectival constructions, and from the special passive verbal ending, which not only can be taken to be an inflection of the adjectival marking, but actually occurs in other constructions as an adjectival ending.[13]

The crucial point here is that prepositions typically do not drop after true adjectival verbals:

18.(69) *a*   I am fond of Harry.
           b   *I am fond Harry.

18.(70) *a*   She is incapable of that.
           b   *She is incapable that.

---

[13] A further argument for the adjectivalization of verbs under the processes of passivization is provided by the fact that *do so* pro-VP replacement is blocked. That is, we find:

(i)   I punched Charley and Harry did so too.

but not:

(ii)   *Harry was punched by Jack and Charley was done so too.

However, this follows from the adjectival marking we propose since in general this process is inapplicable for adjectival verbals:

(iii)   *I was fond of Charley and Jack (was) done so too.

18.(71) *a*   He was $\left\{\begin{array}{l} \text{cruel} \\ \text{mean} \\ \text{nasty} \\ \text{unpleasant} \\ \text{nice} \end{array}\right\}$ to Barbara.

   b   *He was cruel Barbara.[14]

Notice that one of the key advantages of the present analysis of prepositional phrases as NP is that it avoids the absurdity of the prepositional phrase versus NP traditional analysis in cases like the following:

18.(72) *a*   This equals that.
   b   This is equal to that.

18.(73) *a*   Charley married Greta.
   b   Charley is married to Greta.

18.(74) *a*   Charley insisted on that.
   b   Charley was insistent on that.

18.(75) *a*   Charley amuses Betty.
   b   Charley is amusing to Betty.

18.(76) *a*   Charley threatens Harriet.
   b   Charley is threatening to Harriet.

There are dozens and dozens of such doublets and the traditional analysis forces one to say that the relation between NP and verbal is different in such pairs. The present approach permits the natural analysis of identical relations with the

---

[14] Notice that there is exceptional behavior of the adjectives *like* and *near* with respect to object preposition deletion since these forms apparently undergo this rule normally blocked for adjectives:

(i) *a*   He is like his father.
   b   *He is like (un)to his father. (but: His likeness to his father)
(ii) *a*   He is near Barbara.
   b   *He is near to Barbara. (but, strangely: How near to Barbara was he?)

The same point might be made about such elements as *in, on, under,* and so on which are often taken to be prepositions, but which can plausibly be taken as locative adjectives. However, rather than exceptionally undergoing object preposition deletion, it is conceivable that these special adjectives undergo a rule which substitutes them for the object preposition [probably *at*]. This would account for the fact that these forms manifest Pied Piping behavior under *wh*-rules:

(iii) *a*   What bridge did you kiss Mary under?
   b   Under what bridge did you kiss Mary?

preposition typically deleting in the nonadjectival cases, with *from* a common exception:

18.(77) *a*   This differs from that.
     b   This is different from that.

18.(78) *a*   This derives from that.
     b   This is derivative from that.

Consider again the active-passive pairs, but now with respect to the central issue, which is the applicability of Pied Piping. Roughly, both of the sentences of 18.(63) will have structures as follows after the application of preposition insertion:

18.(79)

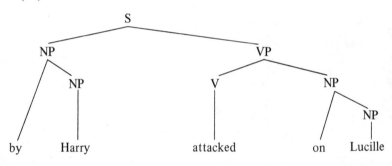

Given such a structure, it must be the case that the "large" NP are moved under the rule of passive in order to derive the appropriate sentences. This could be the case a priori for either of two reasons. First, passive itself might be formulated in such a way as to produce this result directly. Secondly, it might not be so formulated, in which case Pied Piping would be a natural explanation to investigate. Previously, we have taken the relevant aspects of the structure of passive to look something like:

18.(80)   X, NP, Verbal, NP, Y
        1 2   3   4 5

Given a structure index like this, it can be immediately claimed that the fact that the "large" preposition-containing NP moves out of the predicate follows directly from the rule, since only the "large" one will meet the rule's condition. However, as such, 18.(80) would seem to predict that the moved subject NP could be either the inner NP or the whole large NP including the subject preposition, since either analysis of sentences meets the condition of 18.(80). Suppose, however, that it is indicated that passive is subject to Pied Piping. Observe that passive consists of two distinct operations of NP movement, one moving the subject NP to the right, the other a predicate NP to the left.

According to 18.(46) or 18.(56), if passive is subject to Pied Piping, the application of Pied Piping is obligatory. With respect to the right movement aspect of passive, then, the Pied Piping approach yields exactly the right results. It predicts that passive must carry along the subject preposition *by* with the moving subject NP:

18.(81) *a*   Harry was eaten by a gorilla.
     b   *By Harry was eaten a gorilla.
     c   *Harry by was eaten a gorilla.

In short, a Pied Piping approach to passive brings out the hitherto unsuspected fact that this rule meets the condition discovered by Ross that no operation in English which reorders NP to the right can strand a preposition.

Moreover, notice that exactly the same point holds if *psych*-movement is made subject to Pied Piping. This rule would have an analysis, in the terms accepted so far, essentially like 18.(80). Hence, an analysis of a string like:

18.(82)   [to [me]] hurts [in [my arm]]
      NP   NP   NP NP   NP   NP   NP NP

under such a rule would by itself predict that either *me* or *to me* will be inserted in the predicate. But a Pied Piping analysis supported by a principle like either 18.(46) or 18.(56) predicts correctly that the *to* must always accompany the right-moving NP under *psych*-movement. A condition of Pied Piping applicability thus also brings the right movement part of *psych*-movement under Ross's generalization that right-moving rules in English cannot strand prepositions.

The striking fact, then, is that a Pied Piping analysis of passive and *psych*-movement is completely consistent with the idea that at an early stage all NP have prepositions associated with them insofar as the right movement aspects of these rules are concerned. The difficulty arises solely in the case of those exceptional verbal forms which under the operation of passive leave their object prepositions behind, that is, cases like 18.(60), repeated here for convenience:

18.(83) *a*   The committee agreed on something.
     b   Something was agreed on by the committee.
     c   *On something was agreed by the committee.
     d   *Something was agreed by the committee.

This behavior is quite incompatible with the Pied Piping suggestion for a rule like 18.(80). More fundamentally, it *seems* incompatible with the idea that the object prepositions in such structures are truly part of constituents of the form [Preposition + NP] . Observe, for instance, that given the structure for
  NP   NP
18.(83) *a*:

18.(84)

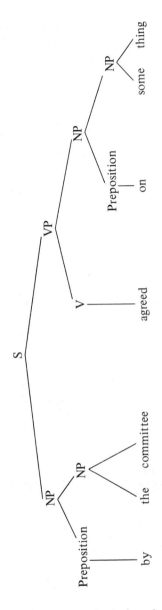

18.(80), with or without Pied Piping, predicts that the preposition *on* must accompany its following NP into subject position. Given the rule of subject preposition deletion, this predicts that the resultant sentence should be 18.(83) *d*, when in fact the only possible passive sentence is 18.(83) *b*.

What is striking here is that Pied Piping is totally useless and inapplicable. This principle deals with cases where a rule moves an NP "larger" than one predicted by the analysis of strings under the structure index of the rule. But with respect to 18.(84), passive, taken as 18.(80), moves an NP "smaller" than that which the proper analysis of 18.(84) predicts with respect to 18.(80). The only NP in 18.(84) which meets the condition of the fourth term of 18.(80) is *on something*.

There are several possible lines of attack on this problem. One would be to take *agree on* and similar cases to be complex verbals, a traditional view, with a structure such that *on* is not part of the complex object NP at the point when passive applies. The structure would then be:

18.(85)

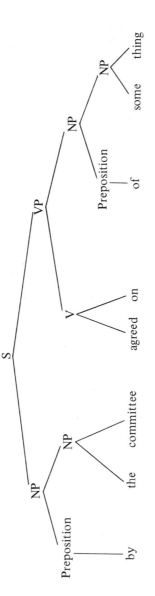

Application of passive would then move *of something* forward, the *of* later deleting by subject preposition deletion, yielding 18.(83) *b* as required.

One difficulty with this in part traditional analysis is the requirement of complex "two-word" verbals. Another is the behavior of prepositions like *on* under the *wh*-rules, where they are subject to Pied Piping, that is, where they behave like part of NP. Accounting for this behavior requires addition of a rule, call it *verbal preposition adjunction*, which adjoins the verbal preposition to the object NP,[15] a rule which must follow passive and object preposition deletion but precede both of the *wh*-rules. This ordering is consistent with other data, since obviously passive applies much earlier than both of the *wh*-rules and these latter must follow object preposition deletion [in order that movement under a *wh*-rule not falsely preserve an object preposition which would otherwise drop]. If verbal preposition adjunction can be placed in such a way as to predict automatically the fact that verbal prepositions like the *on* of *agree* do not drop under object preposition deletion, this analysis would not seem unattractive, despite its requirement of otherwise unneeded complex stem + preposition verbals.[16] The required ordering would have to be:

18.(86)   Preposition insertion
           Passive
           Subject preposition deletion
           Object preposition deletion
           Verbal preposition adjunction
           Wh-Q-movement, *Wh-Rel*-movement

This ordering seems consistent with all the data of which I am aware, so that the complex verbal analysis cannot be rejected on any known ordering grounds, and may well be right. I have not studied it in sufficient detail, however, to make a confident judgment.[17]

---

[15] One cannot formulate this rule as an operation which substitutes the verbal preposition for the normal object preposition. The reason is obvious. Such a substitution would have to precede object preposition deletion. But then the explanation for the nondeletion of the verbal prepositions by the latter rule would be totally lost.

[16] I say "unneeded" here because the alternative proposal to take prepositions like the *on* after *agree* as exceptions to object preposition deletion reduces their introduction to the ordinary process of preposition insertion, which adds such an element to every NP.

[17] One implication of this approach is that the break between *agree* and *on* is different in sequences like:

(i)   The committee agreed on the proposal.
(ii)   The proposal was agreed on by the committee.

That is, in (i) under the proposal in question *on + the proposal* is a constituent, while in (ii) *on* is grouped either with nothing or with the verb. This consequence does not seem radically at odds with intuitions about surface breaks, but it is hardly strongly supported either.

Another analysis of the problem posed by the prepositions following verbs like *agree* would seek to break both passive and *psych*-movement into two separate rules, one moving the subject NP to the right, the other the object NP to the left. It might then be possible to combine the right movement parts of these operations and the left movement parts, or possibly one or the other. Hence this proposal, already suggested by Chomsky (to appear) for passive on quite separate and distinct grounds, deserves consideration independently of the question of how verbal prepositions are to be treated.

If passive were so divided, it might become possible to state the left movement operation in such a way that the NP symbol in the rule could correspond to the "inner" NP of preposition + NP structures. This could be done, for example, if the rule were stated something like:

18.(87)   X, [[X_a, NP, Y_a,]   ] Y
 S VP VP S
 1 2 3 4 5
 Condition: 2 not contain NP

Hence the assumption is that the left movement part of rules like passive and *psych*-movement takes the leftmost NP in the predicate of a sentence without subject and makes a subject out of it. The subjectless condition required by 18.(87) is attributed to an ordering which would have the right movement part of the older rules precede the left movement part.[18] Observe, then, that given a tree like:

---

[18] Such an ordering would require amendement of Ross's suggestions for tree pruning. The present proposal is that any embedded S which does not directly dominate at least two constituents is pruned. This proposal would fail for any embedded passive structure since application of the right movement operation would destroy the S-node above the subject. This difficulty is obviously inherent in Chomsky's (to appear) analogous proposal. The natural suggestion is to restrict pruning to two cases: (a) where the dominated constituent is deleted; (b) where it is reordered *radically*, taking this to mean outside of the S whose pruning is in question. Notice that in the cases under discussion here, the subject stays under the S, if this remains, only not directly under it.

18.(88)

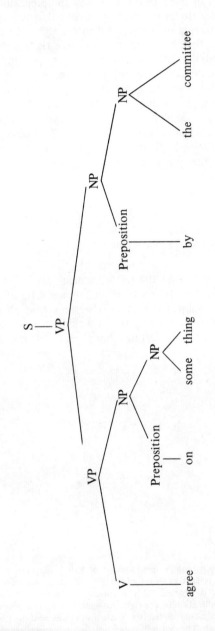

18.(87) can be applied in such a way that the rule refers either to *on something* or just to *some thing* alone. In other words, we now have the kind of alternatives which Pied Piping is partially suited to deal with. What needs to be said, then, is that in cases like 18.(88), which have unique, undroppable prepositions like *on*, Pied Piping for 18.(87) is blocked. For the *typical* case like:

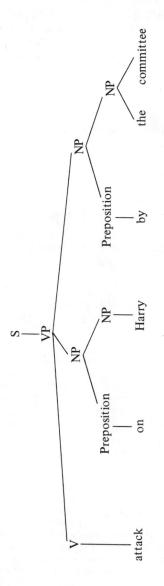

18.(89)

however, Pied Piping must be obligatory to yield:

18.(90) *a* Harry was attacked by the committee.
      b *Harry was attacked on by the committee.

In short, under this analysis, 18.(87) is seen as a left-moving rule for which Pied Piping is in general obligatory [supporting perhaps 18.(56) as against 18.(46)], with a set of constructions typified by the *on*+NP following *agree* marked somehow as not subject to this Pied Piping.[19] This leads to a curious correlation between those prepositions not subject to deletion by object preposition deletion and not subject to Pied Piping under 18.(87), a correlation not explained by anything known thus far. One could, however, search for some principle relating deletability to Pied Pipeability.[20]

I will not attempt to choose between the two analyses for *agree on*-type constructions just discussed. The key point is that under each there is good basis for assuming at least partial functioning of Pied Piping for constant movements independent[21] of complex-NP-shift and right-NP-drift. This then supports the idea of Section D that marking constant movements like right-NP-drift as subject to Pied Piping is not at all a desperate or *ad hoc* maneuver. There is reason to believe that Pied Piping functions far more generally in the domain of English constant movements.

F. EXTRAPOSITION OF PREPOSITIONAL PHRASE

At the end of Section D we referred to the existence of an additional rule which supported the Pied Piping analysis of right-NP-drift. This rule is illustrated by pairs of examples such as:

18.(91) *a* Evidence of gross negligence was discovered.

b Evidence was discovered of gross negligence.

---

[19] Observe most importantly that the kind of *ad hoc* restriction where a construction is marked as not subject to Pied Piping under a rule for which Pied Piping is applicable is not a unique phenomenon. We have seen the same thing already with respect to Pied Piping under the *wh*-rules. Ross (1967a:217–220) has observed that there is a class of cases in which Pied Piping under these rules is blocked. For instance:

(i) *a* What are you trying to get hold of?

b *Of what are you trying to get hold?

(ii) *a* Who couldn't he put up with?

b *With whom couldn't he put up?

[20] That is, one could try to define in linguistic theory some property, call it *vanishability*, which permits (blocks) both movement and deletion of an element. In view of the fact that prepositions like the *on* associated with *agree* can be reordered by Pied Piping under the *wh*-rules, this notion could not be an absolute for all transformational rules but would, evidently, have to refer at least to the difference between rules making essential use of variables and those that do not. This is not surprising really, since other constraints such as the possibility of lexical exceptions [see footnote 12], strength of crossing constraints, and so on are correlated with this distinction.

[21] Given our discussion of passive and *psych*-movement, and, in particular, the suggestion that these be broken down into separate left-reordering and right-reordering operations, one can rightly raise the possibility of combining the right-reordering parts of either or both passive and *psych*-movement with right-NP-drift. While this

18.(92) *a*   A contribution to the fund was made by Harry.
     b   A contribution was made to the fund by Harry.

18.(93) *a*   A criticism of that book has not yet appeared.
     b   A criticism has not yet appeared of that book.

Ross (1967a:301) refers to the relevant operation as *extraposition of preposi-tional phrase*. This rule rips a prepositional phrase which is the last constituent of an NP out of that NP and throws it to the right end of the next most inclusive S. The rule is thus a constant movement and supports Ross's generalization that rightward reorderings are always upward bounded:

18.(94) *a*   The fact that a criticism of that book has not yet appeared disgusts her.
     b   The fact that a criticism has not yet appeared of that book disgusts her.
     c   *The fact that a criticism has not yet appeared disgusts her of that book.

This rule involves many special and poorly understood constraints. It is, for instance, not at all clear what principle determines whether a prepositional phrase can undergo it:

18.(95) *a*   A friend of mine appeared.
     b   *A friend appeared of mine.

18.(96) *a*   Destruction of these resources must cease.
     b   *Destruction must cease of these resources.

Similarly, it is not clear whether this rule can be collapsed with right-NP-drift, with which it shares obvious properties: (a) movement of prepositional phrases; (b) reordering to the right. We assume in this section that they are distinct simply because they have not been recognized as one in the past and we cannot conclusively show their identity. But obviously one must investigate the desirable possibility of combining them.

---

possibility cannot be ruled out, it faces at least one fundamental difficulty. The right-reordering parts of passive and *psych*-movement must precede subject preposi-tion deletion, since they carry along the prepositions which the latter rule would delete with the reverse ordering. Subject preposition deletion must precede object preposition deletion for the most natural treatment of case marking. Consequently, the right-reordering parts of passive and *psych*-movement must precede object preposition deletion. However, objects without prepositions cannot undergo right-NP-drift, which is automatically accounted for by the preceding preposition condition of this rule. But the latter explanation depends on the fact that the prepositions of such NP have already been dropped by object preposition deletion. Consequently, identification of the right-movement part of passive with right-NP-drift yields an ordering anomaly, suggesting that despite their similarities these operations are distinct.

Although extraposition of prepositional phrase has not heretofore been discussed, it does involve crossing constraints:

18.(97) a   John gave a picture of my mother to me.
       b   John gave a picture to me of my mother.

18.(98) a   John mailed a picture of me to me.
       b   *John mailed a picture to me of $\begin{Bmatrix} \text{myself} \\ \text{me} \end{Bmatrix}$.

The crossing constraints are, moreover, exactly those predicted by Cross-Over VI for constant movements, since nonclause mates can be crossed:

18.(99) a   John mailed a picture of Mary's father$_i$ to the man who hated him$_i$.
       b   John mailed a picture to the man who hated him$_i$ of Mary's father$_i$.

Moreover, this rule provides some evidence for the correctness of the explanation proposed in Chapter 16, Sections B and C, for apparently anomalous crossings under Y-movement and *about*-movement. Recall that the explanation was that the cross-over principle only constrains the crossing of pronominal virgins. And we were able to show that coreferents crossed by these rules were not pronominal virgins at the point of application.

Observe, then, the analogous contrast for extraposition of prepositional phrase between 18.(98) and:

18.(100) a   I mailed a picture of myself to myself.
        b   I mailed a picture to myself of myself.

Under the assumption that reflexivization[22] precedes extraposition of prepositional phrase, an ordering consistent with all the known data, the contrast between 18.(98) and 18.(100) follows automatically from the hypothesis about pronominal virgins. That is, under this assumption, the movement rule will derive 18.(98) b and 18.(100) b by operating on, respectively, the schematic structures:

18.(101) a   John mailed a picture of me to me.
        b   I mailed a picture of myself to myself.

so that in the former pronominal virgins must be crossed, but not in the latter. Extraposition of prepositional phrase thus provides new evidence in favor of crucial aspects of our formulation of the cross-over principle, worked out in terms of other rules, particularly the pronominal virgin aspect, based up to now

---

[22] And the rule which reflexivizes elements inside of picture-noun nominalizations, if this is distinct from reflexivization.

only on *Y*-movement and *about*-movement. This rule thus seems to be a welcome addition to the class of rules supporting the cross-over principle.

However, just as we observed for *about*-movement at the beginning of Section A of this chapter, no version of the cross-over principle so far actually predicts the behavior of extraposition of prepositional phrase, and for exactly the same reasons. Again, the constituent actually moved by the rule, the prepositional phrase, is not that which enters into coreference relations, as the principle in effect requires. That is, as in previous cases, the "mention" condition seems to be violated.

The solution to be proposed is obvious. We also take extraposition of prepositional phrase to be a constant movement which is indicated as subject to Pied Piping. Hence we state the structure index of this rule roughly as

$$18.(102) \quad X, \quad \underset{NP}{\left[\quad Y, \text{Preposition}, NP, \quad \right]} \quad \underset{S}{Y_a \quad \right]}, \quad Z^{23}$$

$$ \quad 1 \qquad 2 \qquad 3 \qquad \underset{NP}{4} \qquad 5 \qquad 6$$

where Y_a is of course an abbreviatory variable. The rule will then say that the NP of term 4 is the one moved. However, since Pied Piping is applicable and obligatory [by 18.(46) or 18.(56)], this will automatically mean that the NP which dominates the preceding preposition plus the NP corresponding to term 4 will be the one moved. However, since the "small" NP in any relevant phrase marker will be the one both corresponding to term 4 and the one entering into coreference relations, the conditions of Cross-Over VI will be met. Hence again, the Pied Piping solution seems to preserve Cross-Over VI against apparently inconsistent data.[24] Once more we take this to show that both the cross-over principle and the notion of Pied Piping are essentially correct. It hardly needs stressing, incidentally, how much support these discussions provide for the assumption that the node dominating prepositional phrases is in fact NP. Without this, the Pied Piping explanation collapses. Put differently, the cross-over principle turns out to provide strong support for the NP character of prepositional phrases.

G. SUMMARY AND A NEW DIFFICULTY

To sum up the main line of argument of this chapter so far, it has been argued that two rules which are strongly supportive of most aspects of Cross-Over VI, namely, *about*-movement [now right-NP-drift] and extraposition of prepositional phrase, are seemingly inconsistent with its "mention" condition, known to be required independently. We have investigated two possible solutions to this

---

[23] The similarity of this rule with right-NP-drift is obvious. If they are truly identical, it would mean that the NP subscripted brackets in 18.(102) are redundant.

[24] There is a fundamental, hitherto undealt with, problem with the Pied Piping analysis of extraposition of prepositional phrase having to do with the notion of obligatory Pied Piping. This notion is quite imprecise in important ways. See Section H below.

inconsistency. One involved the possibility of reformulating *about*-movement in terms of rules moving non-NP. This had to be rejected since such rules were shown not to induce coreference crossing restrictions.

We then investigated an approach which took advantage of the similarity between the problems with *about*-movement and extraposition of prepositional phrase with the problems previously encountered with the *wh*-movement rules in Chapter 12. It was shown that the notion of Pied Piping could account for the facts, as in Chapter 12, if linguistic theory allows marking of constant movements with respect to whether Pied Piping is applicable to their operation. Support for this idea was derived from Ross's discovery about complex-NP-shift, namely, that it cannot strand a preposition. We argued that the Pied Piping approach to constant movements could handle this fact and thus do the work of Ross's condition about movement to the right [18.(48)]. We also argued that the obligatory character of Pied Piping in these cases was probably predicted by a principle [either 18.(46) or 18.(56)]. In section E, we attempted to show that possibly Pied Piping is even applicable in part to such constant movements as passive and *psych*-movement, which may have to be broken down into left-movement and right-movement components, possibly combinable.

Overall then, we conclude that the problems of this chapter, though real ones, are not true difficulties with the cross-over principle but only interesting and surprising evidences for Ross's notion of Pied Piping, which turns out to have a wider scope than that originally prescribed.

It must be observed, however, that a Pied Piping approach to constant movements raises a new, technical difficulty relating to the discussion of Chapter 17. Or rather, this difficulty is raised by the very idea of representing prepositional phrases as NP. For recall that the notions of Chapter 17, which distinguish nominally-complex NP from others, were not designed in such a way as to apply correctly when prepositional phrases are NP. By the definition in Chapter 17, for example, the circled NP in:

$$18.(103) \quad \text{By} \ \textcircled{me} \ \text{punch of} \ \textcircled{Jack}$$

are *not* peers if the prepositional phrases are regarded as NP. Hence Cross-Over VI would predict the crossability of such NP in cases of coreference, which is false. Just so, if it turns out to be correct that reflexivization involves a peer condition in English, as in Mohawk, we would also wrongly predict nonapplication of reflexivization in such cases.

Obviously, then, we must formally distinguish those NP-nodes which dominate preposition + NP sequences from those which dominate nominally-complex NP of the type discussed in Chapter 17. We must, in short, guarantee that prepositional phrases alone do not count as nominally complex NP. This seems to suggest a conception of grammar in which node markers like NP are not atomic, but rather complexes of properties. But this is no doubt required on many other grounds and has already been suggested independently by Chomsky (to appear), among others.

There are many ways in which the formal distinction could be drawn. It might be that NP-nodes added by transformation adjunctions, like preposition insertion, are formally distinguished automatically from NP-nodes with other ancestries and that this is the formal property involved in distinguishing prepositional phrase NP-nodes from true nominally-complex NP. On the other hand, it might be that the crucial property is the fact that, given a structure of the form:

18.(104)

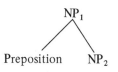

the reference of NP_1, if one can speak of such, is not distinct from that of NP_2, and formal markings of the coreference properties of NP, required if the cross-over principle is to be statable at all, must indicate this. On the contrary, all the truly nominally-complex NP of the type discussed in Chapter 17 were such that the reference of the dominating and dominated NP were distinct.[25] This is another property which might be relevant for the differentiation required.

Overall, then, while the problem must be solved in one way or another and we cannot pretend to know the right solution at the present, there is nothing in this technical difficulty which suggests any real inadequacy with the approach we have been following. Rather, it is only seen that our conception of grammatical structure must be further enriched in the direction of complex symbols for node labels, not a radical conclusion.

H. A FURTHER PIED PIPING PROBLEM

We have spoken in this chapter from Section D on of obligatory Pied Piping. We have not observed, however, that this usage is quite imprecise. It seemed relatively precise in context because in most cases we were dealing with

---

[25] Actually, this statement is not precise enough. It ought rather to be said that the dominating and dominated NP in cases like:

(i) a   Harry's critic
    b   His killer

and other truly nominally-complex NP are never bound. [For this notion, see Chapter 19.] That is, for example, (i) b is not interpretable as ambiguous, with one reading referring to a suicide. However, the reference of *his* is vague and there is nothing which states that it is necessarily distinct from that of *his killer*. Consequently, examples like:

(ii)   Harry's killer was Harry.

are not tautological but synthetic statements. This is, then, another point where one must distinguish between coreference in general and binding in particular. Such a distinction is unfortunately not made in the discussion of examples like (i) in Postal (1969). See Chapter 19.

relatively simple NP in which prepositional phrases were not dominated by higher NP. Under these conditions, speaking of obligatory Pied Piping has to mean movement of the NP-node over the whole prepositional phrase, since there is no other. However, Pied Piping in general permits NP which dominate an NP "mentioned" in a rule to be reordered in cases where the rule as such would only reorder the minimal NP. This permits any dominating NP meeting the conditions [no coordination and so forth] to be reordered. What, then, does it mean to say that Pied Piping is obligatory with respect to a fixed minimal NP when there are a number of higher NP dominating it, all meeting the general conditions for Pied Piping? Does it mean that any of the dominating NP can be reordered just as long as one bigger than the "mentioned" one always is? Does it mean some particular one of these?

That this is a very real problem can be seen from examples like the following:

18.(105)   An analysis of <u>the review of <u>Dixon's book</u></u> appeared recently.

Each of the structures underlined is an NP preceded by a preposition and inside of a still larger NP. What, then, does obligatory Pied Piping for extraposition of prepositional phrase mean? *Unrestricted* Pied Piping would predict that the rule could move any of the successively larger NP:

18.(106) *a*   Of Dixon's book
         b   The review of Dixon's book
         c   Of the review of Dixon's book
         d   An analysis of the review of Dixon's book

Actually, however, as pointed out to me by Ross, in cases like these only the *c* option is permitted:

18.(107) *a*   *An analysis of the review appeared recently of Dixon's book.
         b   *An analysis of appeared recently the review of Dixon's book.
         c   An analysis appeared recently of the review of Dixon's book.
         d   *Appeared recently an analysis of the review of Dixon's book.

Faced with such data, the first suggestion that comes to mind is that something must guarantee that only the "largest" Pied Piping analysis is permitted. The difficulty is that such a statement predicts that 18.(107) *d* should be the well-formed structure rather than 18.(107) *c*, since in the former the whole subject NP has moved, and this is the largest NP meeting general Pied Piping conditions in structures like 18.(105). However, I believe that the ill-formedness of examples like 18.(107)*d* is *not* a violation of any principle having to do with Pied Piping or the scope of its obligatory operation. Rather, I strongly suspect that the violation in such examples is a function of a general condition on English sentences whose precise formulation and formal nature are far from clear but whose validity seems supportable. This condition is a statement of the generalization that main clauses in English must have a subject in the surface structure.[26]

18.(108)   *The Surface Subject Constraint*
No English surface structure is well formed if its *highest* S lacks an *initial* subject, where an earlier stage of derivation had one, and the earlier subject NP was third person.

---

[26]One should study closely the relations between this condition and one discovered by Perlmutter (1968). He notes that it is a fact of English that no embedded clauses may lose their subjects in conditions which would yield subjectless S-nodes. Hence:

(i) *a* You claimed that someone was outside.
     b You claimed someone was outside.
(ii) *a* *Who did you claim that was outside?
     b Who did you claim was outside?

Perlmutter observes that the structure of the clause in (ii) *a* is:

(iii)

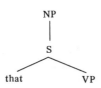

so that the present of the *that* blocks pruning of the clausal S above it. On the other hand, in (ii) *b* the *that* has been deleted, permitting this S to be pruned. Consequently (ii) *a* but not *b*, manifests a subjectless S, and this is blocked by the condition he proposes. Perlmutter notes that this condition is related to many other constraints on English with respect to the requirement that clauses contain subjects and he shows that there is a typology such that languages like French are like English in this regard, while others, like Spanish, are not. He relates these observations to such facts as the existence of a general pronominal deletion rule in Spanish, the absence of such a rule in English, and so on. Clearly, these observations of Perlmutter's must be closely linked to those underlying 18.(108) and ultimately they are probably a function of a single constraint, whose formulation I cannot at the moment, however, supply.

The only sentences in English which do not have initial subjects are imperatives, where the underlying subject was the third person,[27] and possibly various performative types like *screw you, hello, let's leave*, where the underlying subjects are first person, or combinations of first and second person.[28] 18.(108) explains why sentences with unspecified agents must always be passives:

18.(109) *a*   Mary was strangled.
      b   *Strangled Mary

why there is an asymmetry in psychological verbs:

18.(110) *a*   I was bored with her.
      b   I was bored.
      c   She was boring to me.
      d   *Was boring to me

---

[27]In the analysis suggested by Thorne (1966), second person elements are regarded as vocatives of third persons. If this is right, then the condition must be amended to refer to the property *vocative*. However, Thorne's discussion, based in large part on the possibility of *someone* in imperatives like:

    (i)   Stop him someone.
    (ii) Someone open the window.

seems to me far from fully compelling. I suspect that the *someone* in such forms and the *everyone* in such imperatives as:

    (iii) Everyone raise   {their} hands.
                         {your}

and the *nobody* in those like:

    (iv) Nobody move.

are derived from structures like   *some one of you* (plural)
                                     every one of you (plural)
so that a second person analysis of imperatives in a more direct sense can still stand.

[28]There are many real problems with this condition. One type concerns topicalized sentences like:

    (i)   Near him, Harry had a nice gorilla.

where I would wish to recognize a clause boundary at the point of the comma. This means that to meet the condition, *near him* must be the subject, which means an NP, and similarly for all topicalized elements. Naturally, this is a far from self-evident proposal although it is consistent with suggestions made earlier [see footnote 3]. Even more difficult are yes-no question clauses like:

    (ii) Did you eat raw hippopotamus liver?

which cause troubles for the condition of "initiality" in 18.(108). This does not seem to be a fundamental problem since it cannot be denied that such sentences as (ii) have subjects in their highest clause. They do show that the proper account of initiality is unclear though.

why there are English verbs which drop their objects (*eat*), but none which drop their subjects; why there are forms which drop their reflexive objects [*dress, wash*, many verbs of grooming, many verbs of masturbation] , but none which drop pronominal subjects and so forth.

Evidence of the correctness of some sort of constraint like 18.(108) and its relevance to the problem of 18.(107) *d* is provided by the fact that in those positions where a complex NP like the largest of 18.(105) is *not* in subject position, it *can* move under extraposition of prepositional phrase:[29]

> 18.(111) *a* I wrote an analysis of the review of Dixon's book for the *Times*.
>
> *b* *I wrote an analysis of the review for the *Times* of Dixon's book.
>
> *c* *I wrote an analysis of for the *Times* the review of Dixon's book.
>
> *d* I wrote an analysis for the *Times* of the review of Dixon's book.
>
> *e* I wrote for the *Times* an analysis of the review of Dixon's book.

I shall assume that the violation of 18.(107) *d* is independent of any questions of Pied Piping scope and is a function of some principle like 18.(108) which has to do with the obligatoriness of subjects. What this means is that the conditions on Pied Piping for extraposition of prepositional phrase permit both 18.(107) *c* and *d* just as they permit both 18.(110) *d* and *e*.

Looking at 18.(111), we see that obligatory Pied Piping here must be taken to mean that we find some NP—in this case, *the review of Dixon's book*—which meet the condition of the fourth term of the structure index of the rule, and then move *any*[30] NP "larger" than it. This entails that either the prepositional phrase or the whole NP can be moved. What is unexplained by this account of obligatoriness, however, is why in 18.(111) *a* the NP *Dixon's book* cannot be the one taken to correspond to the fourth term of the structure index of extraposition of prepositional phrase. This NP meets the conditions of the rule as well as *the review of Dixon's book* does. Why, then, cannot larger NP than it

---

[29] The weakness of the following argument is that it might be argued that the movement in 18.(111) *e* is not a function of extraposition of prepositional phrase with Pied Piping at all but rather of a fixed-up version of complex-NP-shift, with a modified account of the notion "complex" such that NP are complex without containing S-nodes. Such a modification is suggested already by Ross's attempt (1967a) to combine complex-NP-shift with other right reorderings of nominal elements. I simply assume in the text that this is wrong. If, however, movements like those in 18.(111) *e* are *not* due to extraposition of prepositional phrase, then the definition of obligatoriness given in the text below will have to be modified. See footnote 30.

[30] This definition assumes that complex-NP-shift is *not* at work in cases like 18.(111) *e*. If it *is*, then obligatory Pied Piping means not that *any* NP dominating the "mentioned" one is movable but rather that *only the next higher one is*.

be moved, including *of Dixon's book, the review of Dixon's book*? The fact that they cannot shows that the solution here must be broken into two parts.

18.(112) *a*   A principle which says that when a certain NP in a phrase marker is taken to correspond to a term of a rule like extraposition of prepositional phrase, obligatory Pied Piping for such a rule means the movement of any dominating NP meeting the general conditions for Pied Piping.

b   A principle to determine that in cases like 18.(111) *a* only the "large" NP can be taken to correspond to the fourth term of the rule.

What is interesting about 18.(112) *b* is that the principle required is a special case of that first suggested by Chomsky (1964) as a general solution to the whole question of constraints on reordering NP. Chomsky proposed a principle, since often referred to as the *A-over-A principle*. This requires in effect that in cases where a phrase marker is ambiguously analyzable with respect to a rule, and the distinct analyses differ in "size" as do those which would make either *Dixon's book* or *the review of Dixon's book* possible correspondents to the fourth term of extraposition of prepositional phrase in 18.(111), then the rule must always be applied in such a way that only the "largest" analysis is used. This restricts 18.(111) to undergoing extraposition of prepositional phrase in such a way that the NP *the review of Dixon's book* is taken to correspond to the fourth term of the rule. Consequently, the A-over-A principle, in conjunction with the definition of obligatory Pied Piping in 18.(112) *a*, will predict that 18.(111) *a* can be turned into either 18.(111) *d* or *e* but not 18.(111) *b* or *c*. 18.(111) *b* requires taking *Dixon's book* as the correspondent of the fourth term, a violation of the A-over-A principle, since there is a "bigger" analysis of 18.(111) *a* which can meet the conditions of extraposition of prepositional phrase. 18.(111) *c* involves no violation of the A-over-A principle. But it does involve a violation of the requirement of obligatory Pied Piping for the rule, since the NP moved is not larger than the NP "mentioned" in the rule but is that NP itself. On the other hand, an example like:

18.(113)   *I wrote an analysis of the review for the *Times* Dixon's book.

involves a violation of both principles, which seems consistent with its extremely deviant character.

Ross (1967a) has, I think, shown that the A-over-A principle is both false *in general* and not sufficient to explain what it was intended to explain. This demonstration does not, however, preclude the possibility that the A-over-A principle holds in some restricted domain of rules, possibly definable generally in linguistic theory, possibly requiring specification in individual grammars. It is clear for instance that extraposition of prepositional phrase must be subject to this condition. Possibly, this must be a function of an idiosyncratic marking of this English rule. However, a number of possible generalizations suggest themselves, including the following:

18.(114) *a*   Constant movements are subject to the A-over-A principle.[31]

       b   Constant movements reordering elements to the right are subject to the A-over-A principle.

       c   Constant movements subject to Pied Piping are subject to the A-over-A principle.

      d   Constant movements subject to obligatory Pied Piping are subject to the A-over-A principle.

Other alternatives can be reformulated. I have no basis for choosing among them at the moment. It follows that some rules must be subject to the A-over-A principle but that we do not at the moment have any real idea of how to specify the scope of this condition. We cannot rule out the possibility that it may be idiosyncratic but we also have no sound basis for doubting that its scope may be specifiable by principles of some generality.

    Summing up then, the problem noted with respect to the behavior of extraposition of prepositional phrase does not seem to throw doubt on the validity of the Pied Piping analysis for this rule. The facts seem to fall out, given the proper definition of obligatory Pied Piping, if it is recognized that the rule in question is subject to the A-over-A principle. Perhaps the stickiest problem is the requirement of a condition like the surface subject constraint, needed to explain the ill-formedness of 18.(107). But this seems to me to have considerable independent appeal.

---

[31] 18.(114) *a* is the strongest of these principles and thus the most interesting. It is, significantly enough, consistent with almost all of the data about constant movements known to me. And observe it would cover much of the work previously assigned to a principle on the conventions for applying end variables to phrase markers [footnote 2 of Chapter 11]. However, notice that 18.(114) would be violated by an NP reordering whose structure index did not mention the element preposition if this rule reordered NP out of prepositional phrases and was a constant movement. This means that, just as the data concerning the behavior of verbal prepositions like those in *agree on*, *decide on*, and such are crucial for questions of Pied Piping, they raise questions also about the A-over-A principle. If the rule which moves the object NP in such cases operates at a point where these prepositions together with the following NP form a complex NP, that is, if the structure at the point when this rule operates is the same as at the point when the *wh*-rules apply, then 18.(114) *a* is violated, and we can at best retreat to 18.(114) *b*, *c*, or *d*. It follows that the behavior of these verbal prepositions in English, traditionally treated as a minor irregularity, is fundamental to a number of theoretical questions about the form of grammar, and hence deserves intensive study.

19 CROSSING AND THE PROBLEM OF CONTRASTIVE STRESS

Perhaps the most fundamental untreated problem concerning the cross-over principle is that provided by examples with contrastive stress. It was observed at the very beginning of this study [Chapter 1, Section C], for example, that reflexive passives, which are ill formed when the reflexive word has ordinary stress, are well formed when contrastive stress occurs on this element.

> 19.(1) *a* *Harry was shaved by himself.
> *b* Harry was shaved by him*self*.

This same difference is also true of some, but not all, of the constructions we have discussed which involve constant movements other than passive:

> 19.(2) *a* *Harry is amusing to himself.
> *b* Harry is amusing to him*self*.

At first glance these facts seem incompatible with the constraints on the operation of constant movement transformations predicted by Cross-Over VI. These make no allowance for stress, emphasis, or anything of the sort. I believe, however, that rather than revealing any inadequacy in the cross-over principle, the fact that some contrastively-stressed examples are apparently not subject to the cross-over principle indicates that their grammatical structure is quite different from the analogous ordinary-stressed examples. By "quite different," I mean that the structure is by no means representable in terms of optional emphasis morphemes or the like.

Although the grammar of contrastively-stressed elements is incredibly intricate and little known, there are, I suggest, the beginnings of an analysis of contrastively-stressed NP which is not in conflict with the predictions of Cross-Over VI and which has independent virtues, if not the most overwhelming support. I propose that contrastively-stressed NP *are derived from predicate nominal constructions*.

Roughly, a form like:

19.(3) Charley cut himself.

is derived from a structure:

19.(4) Charley$_i$ cut Charley$_i$.

But a form like:

19.(5) Charley cut him*self*.

is, I propose, derived from a structure like:

19.(6) The one$_j$ [who$_j$ Charley$_i$ cut] was Charley$_i$ (himself).

This yields radically different structures for 19.(3) and 19.(5) and structures for each of these quite different from:

19.(7) *Charley* cut himself.

which in the terms being introduced would be:

19.(8) The one$_j$ who$_j$ cut himself$_j$ was Charley$_i$.

There is a fundamental and hitherto ignored point raised by structures like 19.(6) and 19.(8). Up to this juncture, we have spoken of coreferentiality between NP. We have not, however, observed that there are several different modes by which this relationship is represented in language. In fact, previously we have restricted discussion of coreference implicitly to the mode which I will henceforth refer to as *binding*. Binding is that mode of representing coreference which we have indicated notationally by repeated occurrences of the same lexical item with the same letter subscript [as in 19.(4)]. Binding then shows up in surface structures typically in that one of these subscripted occurrences remains as is with the appropriate lexical material, while all others are turned into pronominal forms by the operation of one or another of the rules of pronominalization. Certain pronominal forms may then be elided. As indicated in Chapter 1, we are taking no position in this work about *how* binding is represented formally in underlying structures. That is, we are not dealing in this study with the formalism (formalisms) that must underlie notations like those of 19.(4).

Once we begin to speak of predicate nominal constructions, however, one quickly sees that there is a quite different mode of representing coreference, a mode we can refer to as *predicational*. That is, in a sentence like:

19.(9)   *The killer* is *the one wearing a blue hat.*

the italicized nominals are coreferential. They designate the same entity. Yet clearly it would be wrong, and in fact impossible, to represent this coreference by use of notations like those of 19.(4) and all previous chapters. The central fact involved in all occurrences of binding, for which that notation was devised, is that coreferential entities are provided with only *a single description.*[1] In 19.(9), on the other hand, the entity is provided with two different descriptions. We can roughly characterize the difference between the binding and predicational modes of representing coreference as follows. Binding is a mode in which the coreference is indicated by the underlying syntactic structure of the NP themselves. In the predicational mode, these structures do not as such indicate coreference. There is nothing in the NP of 19.(9) themselves to indicate that they are coreferential. This information is provided by a predicate of identity of reference which links them.

Notationally, then, it would be misleading to represent 19.(9) with a structure like:

19.(10) The killer$_i$ is the one$_i$ wearing a blue hat.

Rather, we shall indicate the absence of binding in such structures by representations like:

19.(11) The killer$_i$ is the one$_j$ wearing a blue hat.

This is in fact the approach already presented in 19.(6) and 19.(8). Up to now we have stated crossing restrictions in terms of coreferentiality. But a little deeper consideration will quickly reveal that these restrictions, and, indeed, almost everything said about pronominalization and identity of reference in the literature on grammar over the last five years or so, really refers only to binding. This point is quite crucial for the study of contrastively stressed examples, as we shall see directly.

It has been suggested that contrastively-stressed NP are derived from predicate constructions. Such an analysis claims that contrastively-stressed and ordinary-stressed examples differ not just in "emphasis" but in cognitive meaning, that is, in aspects of meaning relevant to the determination of the truth

---

[1] This description takes the form of one or more restrictive relative clauses. To make this claim valid in complete generality it is necessary to assume that surface structure lexical nouns, *boy, car, rock*, and so on are derived from underlying restrictive relatives. There is a good deal of evidence for this. See Bach (1968).

of statements. This is in fact the case. Consider, for instance, the difference between:

19.(12) *a*   Only voiced consonants can occur in word final position.
　　　 b   Only voiced *consonants* can occur in word final position.

19.(12) *a* asserts that the only entities which can occur in word final position are voiced consonants. It is thus incompatible with the occurrence there of voiceless consonants, voiced vowels, and so on. 19.(12) *b* asserts that the only *voiced* elements which can occur word finally are consonants. It is not incompatible with the occurrence before word boundary of voiceless vowels. This difference correlates with the structures that these could be assigned, given the predicational origin of contrastive stress:

19.(13) *a*   The only ones which can occur in word final position are voiced consonants.
　　　 b   The only voiced ones which can occur in word final position are consonants.

The semantic fact that structures like 19.(13) explicate the meaning contrasts in those like 19.(12) is an argument in favor of the suggestion. Another is the fact that the predicate nominals in sentences like 19.(13) have the strong stress associated with contrastively-stressed NP in general. It is especially relevant to observe in this regard that the first person forms have a peculiarity. In my dialect at least, either of the following is acceptable:

19.(14) *a*   The only one who I will vote for is myself.
　　　 b   The only one who I will vote for is me.

This is not generally the case:

19.(15) *a*   The only one Harry will vote for is himself.
　　　 b   The only one Harry will vote for is him.

19.(15) *b* is not a variant of 19.(15) *a*. Observe, however, that exactly this difference shows up for contrastively-stressed NP:

19.(16) *a*   I like my*self*.
　　　 b   I like *me*.

19.(17) *a*   Harry likes him*self*.
　　　 b   Harry likes *him*.

Even if 19.(16) *b* is slightly less acceptable than the *a* form, there is no comparison with 19.(17) *b* which is totally unreadable as a variant of the *a* form. This peculiarity of contrastive NP in general will follow from the peculiarity in predicate position under our analysis.

As another piece of evidence supporting the predicational derivation, observe the relation between alternative answers to questions[2] and the derivation of contrastive stress. A question like:

19.(28)   Who did Charley insult?

with ordinary stress throughout *cannot* be answered with a sentence like:

19.(19)   Charley insulted his father.

with ordinary stress throughout. Rather, it must be answered by a sentence like:

19.(20)   Charley insulted his *father*.

with contrastive stress on that NP which "corresponds" to the "questioned" NP in the question sentence. This is quite general for "question" NP sentences. Their answers must have extra strong stress on the "corresponding" NP. However, crucially, it is also generally the case that such questions can be answered with predicate nominal constructions:

19.(21)   The one who Charley insulted was his *father*.

where the loud stress on the predicate nominal is obligatory. The natural suggestion is that, from a deep structure point of view, the structure like 19.(21) is the obligatory answer form and that answers like 19.(20) are derivatives from the predicational answers by way of a rule, let us call it *contrast movement*, which optionally deforms the predicate nominal construction into one whose surface structure is that of ordinary nonpredicational clauses.

An insistence on taking 19.(21)-like structures as the basic form of answers to *wh* questions brings out an important formal relation between *wh* question and answer. Namely, the *wh* question clause in the question must correspond to a relative clause in the answer. Thus:

19.(22) *a*   Who do you think won?
      b   The one who I think won is Charley.

19.(23) *a*   What did that show him about divine intervention?
      b   The thing that that showed him about divine intervention was that it is rare.

19.(24) *a*   Where did she assert that Charley left the road?
      b   The place where she asserted that Charley left the road is right here.

In other words, taking this point of view, an answer to a *wh* question incorporates the question clause as a relative phrase on the predicate nominal

---

[2] For introductory discussion of the question-answer relation, see Katz and Postal (1964).

subject. This reveals a much deeper correspondence between question and relative clause than their joint superficial use of largely the same apparatus of *wh* marking and *wh* NP movement. This relation is, however, only fractionally understood.

The rule of contrast movement required by the analysis we are trying to develop is highly structured and somewhat unique. It is the only rule of NP movement in English known to me which has the effect of moving an NP into *lower* clauses. That is, we have previously encountered three types of rules grouped into the classes of constant movements and variable movements:

19.(25) *a*   *Constant Movements*
   (i)   Intraclause rules (passive)
   (ii) Rules which insert NP into the next more inclusive clause (*tough*-movement, *it*-replacement)
   b   *Variable Movements*
   Rules which move NP across an unbounded number of *higher* clause boundaries

But the rule of contrast movement will be like none of these. It will have to take the predicate nominal NP and insert it inside of the relative clause on the subject. Hence, in contrast to a rule like *Wh-Q*-movement, which can rip NP out of lower clauses and raise them higher in the tree, contrast movement has the effect of placing an NP in a lower position. At the same time, this rule must make use of variables in an essential way since there is no bound on how far down the predicate NP may be placed. That is, it can be inserted in a clause embedded in another, embedded in another, without bound. This can be illustrated by such examples as:

19.(26) *a*   I saw *Bill*.
   b   I saw the man who said that Joan knew *Bill*.
   c   I saw the man who said Tony discovered that Joan knew *Bill*.

Hence we might roughly state the required rule as:

$$19.(27) \quad X, \; [\; \begin{bmatrix} NP \\ +Pro \end{bmatrix}, \; [\; Y, \; \begin{bmatrix} NP \\ +Pro \\ +wh \end{bmatrix}, \; W, \;] \;] \; be, \; NP, \; Z$$

$$\underset{1}{} \quad \underset{2}{} \quad \underset{3}{} \quad \underset{4}{} \quad \underset{5}{} \quad \underset{6}{} \; \underset{7}{} \; \underset{8}{} \Longrightarrow$$

$$1,\emptyset,3,7,5,\emptyset,\emptyset,8$$

That is, the rule replaces the fourth term by the contents of the seventh, deleting the second, sixth, and seventh.[3] The rule would thus, for example, operate on structures like:

---

[3] Deletion of the VP structure under sentence nodes like S_1 in 19.(28) must be taken to prune such nodes by way of a general convention like that suggested by Ross (1967c).

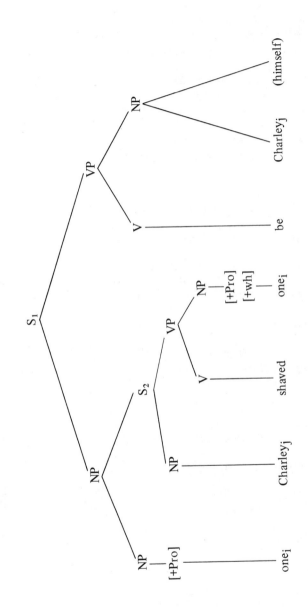

19.(28)

If *contrast movement* does not apply to such a structure, the result would be:

19.(29)   The one who Charley shaved was (*Charley*) (*himself*).

If it does apply, the result is any of the following:

19.(30) *a* Charley shaved *Charley.*
  b Charley shaved him*self.*
  c Charley shaved *Charley* him*self.*

Consider now the following facts:

19.(31) *a* Charley cut himself.
  b *Charley was cut by himself.
  c Charley cut him*self.*
  d *Charley* cut himself.
  e Charley was cut by him*self.*
  f **Charley* was cut by himself.

19.(31) *a* and *b* do not involve contrast movement, and their properties have already been discussed and explained. The remaining four are more interesting. According to our proposal, these derive, respectively, from strings like:

19.(32) *a* $[_{S_1}$ The one$_i$ $[_{S_2}$ Charley$_j$ cut one$_i$ $]_{S_2}$ was Charley$_j$ $]_{S_1}$
  b $[_{S_1}$ The one$_i$ $[_{S_2}$ one$_i$ cut one$_i$ $]_{S_2}$ was Charley$_j$ $]_{S_1}$
  c $[_{S_1}$ The one$_i$ $[_{S_2}$ one$_i$ cut Charley$_j$ $]_{S_2}$ was Charley$_j$ $]_{S_1}$
  d $[_{S_1}$ The one$_i$ $[_{S_2}$ one$_i$ cut one$_i$ $]_{S_2}$ was Charley$_j$ $]_{S_1}$

What happens in 19.(32) *a* and *b* has already been described. The predicate nominal, *Charley*$_j$, is substituted for the object NP of the relative clause in *a* and for the subject NP in *b*. This happens on the S_1 cycle. No relevant rules apply on the previous S_2. In *c* and *d*, the situation is more complex. passive is a cyclical rule [recall that it precedes reflexivization, which is cyclical] and hence must apply in the relative clause on the S_2 cycle. Contrast movement, on the other hand, cannot, because of the cyclical principle, apply until the next or S_1 cycle. In 19.(32) *c* passive applies, then, yielding:

19.(33) $[_{S_1}$ The one$_i$ $[_{S_2}$ Charley$_j$ cut by one$_i$ $]_{S_2}$ was Charley$_j$ (himself) $]_{S_1}$

And this is not blocked by Cross-Over VI since the NP crossed by passive are not related by binding. But in 19.(32) *d* the situation is quite different. Here, when passive applies on the S_2 cycle, it must cross two NP which are related by binding. But Cross-Over VI predicts this is impossible without violation. Hence, according to our assumptions, the structure underlying sentences like 19.(31) *f* involves a crossing violation, but this is not the case for sentences like 19.(31) *e*.

Observe that the contrast in sentences like 19.(31) *e* and *f*, which are really answers, is matched by the contrast in questions which correspond to them:

> 19.(34) *a*   Who was Charley cut by?
> *b*   *Who was cut by himself?

Thus far we have explained a good deal with this analysis, in fact more than we set out to. The original problem was only why reflexive passives are well formed when the reflexive word has contrastive stress, that is, why sentences like 19.(31) *e* are grammatical. But we have now developed not only a solution for this problem but also for why sentences like 19.(31) *f* are *not* grammatical, explaining the otherwise curious asymmetry. Thus far, however, the violations uncovered in contrastively stressed sentences have been explained as cross-over violations with respect to the rule passive. We have not shown contrast movement itself to induce any crossing restrictions. Consider, then, what happens if passive does not apply to 19.(32) *c*. We would then have the option of applying contrast movement on the final cycle to the subject of the relative. This should yield:

> 19.(35)   *Charley* (him*self*) cut Charley.

But this sentence is ill formed. However, in considering the derivation of this string, we can see that contrast movement would have to cross the predicate nominal over the object NP, with which it is related by binding.

Hence we see that contrast movement itself involves crossing restrictions. What is even more interesting is the fact that, according to Cross-Over VI, contrast movement is a variable movement rule, since its application path involves essential variables. This predicts that it should not be possible to cross coreferents of the binding type even when these are not clause mates. In fact, 19.(35) illustrates this, since the coreferent NP are not clause mates in the input. But even more interestingly we observe that contrast movement yields violations for such sentences as:

> 19.(36) *a*   *Charley* (him*self*) visited the man who hated Charley.
> *b*   *Charley* (him*self*) said that Tony knew that Barbara hated Charley.

That is, such sentences cannot be interpreted in such a way that the NP containing the word *Charley* represent the same individual. And here, unlike 19.(35), the coreferents which cannot cross are not only not clause mates in the input, they are also not clause mates in the output. Hence contrast movement seems to induce exactly the kind of crossing restrictions predicted for variable movement rules by Cross-Over VI.

The same point made just above about 19.(32) *c* can be made for 19.(32) *a*. Previously, we considered cases where contrast movement applied to this structure when the relative had not undergone passive. This permits contrast movement to apply without any crossing of bound NP, yielding the well formed 19.(31) c. Consider, however, what happens if passive is applied on the first cycle to 19.(32) a. This will yield:

19.(37)   [The one$_i$ [one$_i$ was cut by Charley$_j$]   was Charley$_j$]
             S_1 S_2 S_2 S_1

Now application of contrast movement must involve a crossing of bound coreferents. This predicts the ungrammaticality of the output, a prediction fully borne out:

19.(38)   *Charley (himself) was cut by Charley.

Here again we cannot interpret the occurrences of the word Charley to designate the same being.

In short, our analysis has not only explained the original facts we set out to deal with but has gone on to provide a basis for a strange and apparently mysterious fact about English. Nominals like "Charley (himself)" can co-occur with nominals like Charley [ordinary stress] in English sentences where a binding interpretation exists. But this is limited to those cases where the former type of nominal is on the right. And this follows from the contrast movement derivation of contrastively-stressed NP, together with Cross-Over VI.

20 THE CROSS-OVER PRINCIPLE AND RELATIVE CLAUSES

We have in previous chapters taken a class of restrictions with respect to the operation of *Wh-Rel*-movement to support the cross-over principle. The really fundamental importance of this principle to the correct description of relative constructions can, however, best be seen by considering in somewhat greater detail problems of coreference with respect to the formation of these clauses. Let us restrict the discussion initially to restrictives.

We shall assume, essentially irrelevantly, that at some stage of their derivation NP with restrictive relatives involve a structure like:

20.(1)

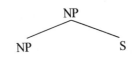

Hence for:

20.(2)   The one who Charley congratulated

we would have:

20.(3)

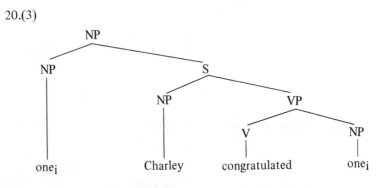

In these structures I ignore articles and such whose structure presents many problems and whose derivation is irrelevant to the points under discussion.

Given structures like 20.(1) there is a crucial condition that must be met if the restrictive relative clause specified is to be well formed. The S must contain an NP coreferential (bound) to the NP which is its sister constituent. This is a *necessary* condition, *not, however, a sufficient one*. With respect to the latter point, this NP must be in a position where it is movable by *Wh-Rel*-movement without violating any of the language-general or English-particular constraints on reordering of elements. 20.(4) and 20.(5) illustrate structures which fail this condition:

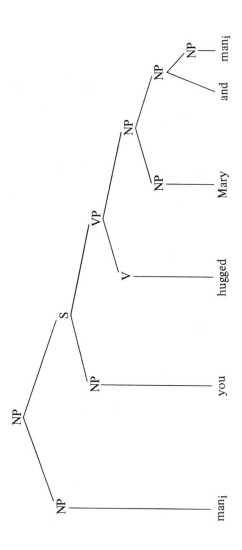

20.(4)

20.(5)

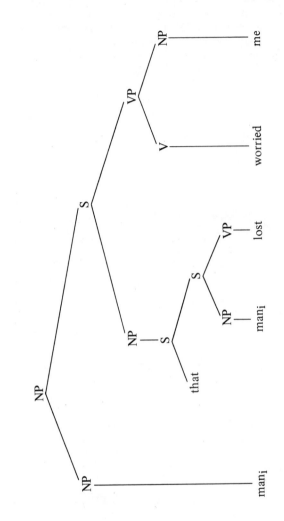

These meet the condition of having a coreferent NP but fail that of having it in a position from which it can be moved. Hence:

20.(6) a   *The man who you hugged Mary and
       b   *The man who that lost worried me

20.(4)–20.(6) a violate what Ross (1967a) refers to as the *coordinate structure constraint*; 20.(5)–20.(6) b violates what he calls the *sentential subject constraint*.

Consider again the condition that the relative S must contain an NP coreferential to its sister NP. Observe that this condition is met when this S contains not one but two, three, four, or more such coreferent NP. Moreover, no ban on this is possible because an infinite set of such relatives exist:

20.(7)   The man *who* said *he* didn't want me to think *he* hurt *himself*

Here the relative S contains four coreferent NP. This possibility of multiple coreferents raises a fundamental problem for the description of relatives. Observe that in general[1] only one of these must ultimately be converted to a *wh*-form and preposed to the front of the relative clause. The question immediately arises, therefore, as to what principles determine which of the multiple coreferents of the head NP are so converted and moved. That is, either the theory of grammar or any grammar of English must contain apparatus which specifies that:

20.(8)   Given a relative clause containing a set of n ($n > 2$) NP bound to the head of the relative, it is the _____ member of the set which is marked as a *wh* form.

Either grammatical theory or English grammar must contain principles which fill in the blank in 20.(8) correctly. Call this *the pickout problem*.

As far as I know, the pickout problem has not been independently dealt with. Two possible approaches to a solution have occurred to me:

20.(9)   cyclical pronominalization
20.(10)   the cross-over principle

We have in fact given evidence earlier which shows that 20.(10) is the only possible answer here. But this was implicit. Therefore I wish now to consider explicitly and in greater detail just why 20.(9) must fail and why 20.(10) succeeds in the cases where 20.(9) fails and is in fact, as far as I know, adequate for all cases.

Note that 20.(9) refers to grammatical rules of a certain type in general, not to particular rules. It refers to the general idea of having pronominalization rules apply cyclically. Consider, then, the basis for 20.(9) in terms of the operation of reflexivization, where there are, as we have seen, independent grounds for

---

[1] In certain coordinate structures, however, the requirement is that one NP be converted to *wh*-form *in each conjunct:*

   (i)   The man whose car was green and whose boat was blue
   (ii) *The man whose car was green and his boat was blue

How to build this constraint into a grammar precisely is quite obscure.

assuming cyclical application. Given this rule with this mode of application, a structure like:

20.(11)

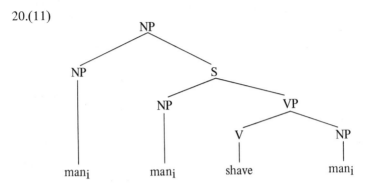

must be transformationally deformed in a definite sequence. Namely, reflexivization must apply on the embedded S before any rule can apply on the overall NP. Therefore, at the end of the first cycle, one and only one NP in the embedded S will be unpronominalized, that is, not marked [+Pro], [+Anaphoric], namely, that unaffected by reflexivization. Now in fact, it is exactly the NP which the normal operation of reflexivization leaves unaffected which must turn into the *wh*-form. This suggests a principle:

20.(12)   Given a relative clause structure of the form

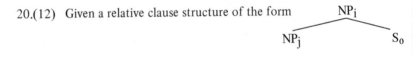

where S_0 contains from 1-n NP bound to NP_j, the coreferent which is *wh*-marked is that one left unpronominalized after the application of the last cyclical rule on S_0.

20.(12) is the natural solution to the *wh*-marking problem, given the assumption that rules of pronominalization are cyclical. The natural implementation for it would be to specify [+wh] as a feature assigned by pronominalization rules in a way analogous to the feature [+Reflexive]. The latter is assigned when the coreferent NP are clause mates. The former could be specified as being assigned when pronominalization takes place in a configuration like:

20.(13)

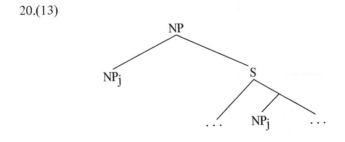

There are, however, two fundamental difficulties with 20.(12). First, it not only requires reflexivization to be cyclical, but also pronominalization, the latter because of examples like:

20.(14)

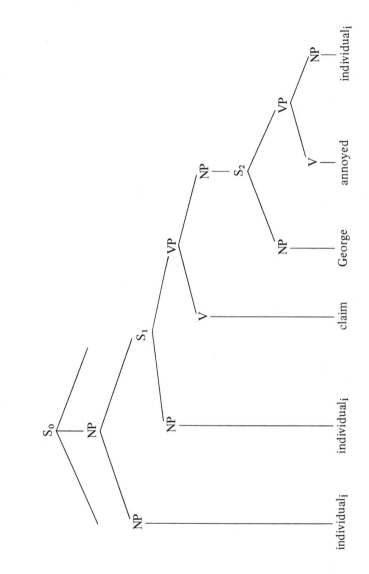

In this kind of structure, reflexivization is not applicable. Therefore, to preserve 20.(12), it is necessary that something indicate that pronominalization apply first to the object of *annoyed* and only then to the subject of *claim*. Just this would be predicted by having pronominalization cyclical. This requires application on S_1 before that on S_0. However, it was shown in Chapter 2 that pronominalization is not cyclical. Therefore, this explanation for why 20.(14) yields only:

20.(15)   The individual$_i$ who$_i$ claimed George annoyed him$_i$

and not:

20.(16)   *The individual$_i$ who$_i$ he$_i$ claimed George annoyed

fails.[2]

An equally serious difficulty with 20.(12) is provided by structures like the following:

20.(17)   [[The king$_i$]   [the fact that you struck king$_i$ startled
                                                  king$_i$]]
        NP NP   NP S   S NP

Consider just the embedded sentence alone, that is, in contexts where it is unembedded. This yields either of the sentences:

20.(18) *a*   The fact that you struck the king$_i$ startled him$_i$.
       b   The fact that you struck him$_i$ startled the king$_i$.

---

[2] It is possible to insure application of pronominalization on S_1 before it applies between any element of S_0 outside of S_1 and an NP inside of S_1 without the assumption of cyclical application. This can be done by restricting the application of pronominalization rules in cases of n $(n > 3)$ bound NP in terms of such principles as the following:

(i)   Pronominalization is *continuous*, that is, never applies between two coreferent NP if there is a third [unpronominalized] coreferent between them.

(ii)   Pronominalization is *inward oriented*, that is, it operates successively by finding that pair of coreferents hitherto unpronominalized which is closest to either the beginning or the end of the sentence.

(iii) Pronominalization is *right oriented* when operating left-to-right, that is, the operation described in (ii) begins at the end of the sentence and moves successively to the left. Analogously perhaps, pronominalization is *left oriented* when operating right-to-left.

Given such conditions, pronominalization must apply on 20.(14) between the subject of *claim* and the object of *annoy* and only then between the relative head NP and the subject of *claim*. The difficulty with (i)–(iii), which are not at all implausible, is that they are, as far as I know, otherwise unmotivated. Still, they must be borne in mind as possible conditions on pronominalization, none of which is known to be false. Any automaton which was going to actually apply rules would likely be subject to conditions like these.

That is, pronominalization may apply either forwards or backwards. This means that even assuming cyclical pronominalization, 20.(12) predicts that 20.(17) should yield two different relative clauses, one with the object of *struck* wh-marked, the other with the object of *startled*. Actually, both are impossible:

20.(19) *a*   *The king$_i$ who$_j$ the fact that you struck startled him$_i$
     b   *The king$_i$ who$_j$ the fact that you struck him$_i$ startled

20.(19) *a* is, however, explained by general movement constraints of the type studied by Ross (1967a), since no element may be moved out of such subject *fact*-clauses. However, this explanation is not available for 20.(19) *b*. The impossibility of interpreting the *him* in this clause as a coreferent of *king$_i$* is not given by 20.(12). The explanation for such cases is, of course, the cross-over principle.

The fact that 20.(12) cannot explain the ill-formedness of relatives like 20.(19) *b* shows that the constraints on coreference for relatives are not reducible to the requirement that the embedded S contain a bound coreferent of the head, nor to this plus 20.(12). There are still coreferent facts which require the cross-over principle. But given the cross-over principle, 20.(12) is completely redundant and unneeded. Every case that it covers *correctly* is explained fully by the cross-over principle, which in addition explains cases like 20.(19) *b*, for which 20.(12) provides no basis. Moreover, the cross-over principle covers the entire class of cases like 20.(14) without the impossible assumption that pronominalization is cyclical,[3] and without hitherto unneeded assumptions of the type referred to in footnote 2.

It follows that the correct solution to the pickout problem is provided by 20.(10) and not by 20.(9) and 20.(12). Put differently, the possibility of eliminating *ad hoc* [and, worse, ineffective] statements like 20.(12) is an important additional argument in favor of the cross-over principle. Summing up, in those cases where the embedded S of a relative clause structure contains $n > 2$ NP bound to the head, that one is wh-marked which can be moved by *Wh-Rel*-movement without violating the cross-over principle. In other words, the wh-marked NP is always the leftmost of the set of coreferents. No other principle of English grammar or of universal grammar is known which predicts this fact. The solution to the pickout problem is the cross-over principle.

---

[3]Given the cross-over principle, and in particular its conditions that only pronominal virgins are blocked from crossing, we can give a new argument that pronominalization is *not* cyclical. The left-right argument immediately shows that *Wh-Rel*-movement must precede pronominalization:

    (i) *a* Tom, whose description of the man who kissed her$_i$ Mary$_i$ hated with a passion.
       b Tom, whose description of the man who kissed Mary$_i$ she$_i$ hated with a passion.

We illustrated the above argument with restrictive relative clauses, but it is equally clear with appositives. A few examples:

20.(20) a Harry$_i$, who$_i$ killed himself$_i$
       b *Harry$_i$, who$_i$ himself$_i$ killed
       c *Harry$_i$, who$_i$ he$_i$ killed

20.(21) a Harry$_i$, who$_i$ said I hated him$_i$
       b *Harry$_i$, who$_i$ he$_i$ said I hated

Therefore, if pronominalization is cylical and not subject to conditions like (i)–(iii) of footnote 2, it will be able to apply in structures like:

(ii)

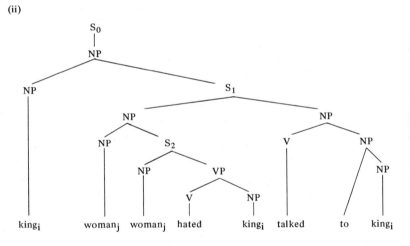

in such a way that the object of *hated* is pronominalized on the S$_1$ cycle. *Wh-Rel*-movement can, however, apply to the object of *talked* only on the S$_0$ cycle. But this means that at the point when *king$_i$* crosses its coreferent it is crossing a nonpronominal virgin. Hence we predict under these assumptions that the crossing is not a violation. But this is false:

(iii)   *The king$_i$ who$_i$ the woman who hated him$_i$ talked to

It follows that, given the cross-over principle, pronominalization cannot be cyclical and more generally cannot be such that NP like the object of *hated* in (ii) are capable of pronominalization before the application of *Wh-Rel*-movement.

21 AN ATTEMPTED PARTIAL ELIMINATION OF THE CROSS-OVER PRINCIPLE

From Chapter 13 on, each version of the cross-over principle we have considered has referred to a bifurcation of rules into constant movements and variable movements and associated partially distinct crossing restrictions with rules of these two classes. We have, however, only been able to uncover three relevant variable movements: *Wh-Q*-movement, *Wh-Rel*-movement, and *Y*-movement. It is most important, therefore, to consider any possible evidence or arguments which might suggest that facts concerning any of these three rules which we have taken to support the existence of the cross-over principle have a distinct explanation.

Just such a possible alternative explanation might seem to arise for the data about *Wh-Q*-movement, which has been so far taken as evidence for the cross-over principle. This alternative derives from the properties of nominals containing the special determiner form *some*, where I refer to the logical *some* of sentences like:

21.(1) *a* Some of my friends are nurds.
   b Some computer company has less than one hundred employees.
   c Some elephants have two trunks, one of which is invisible.

and not the "indefinite article" *some* of such sentences as:

21.(2) *a* There are some dwarf gorillas in my desk drawer.
   b John ate some batwings on toast.
   c Get me some fertilizer-merchant overalls.

There is a very good case to be made [see Katz and Postal (1964) for a *partial* justification] that the *wh*-forms of questions derive from *some*-forms. The evidence consists of the close distributional similarities between logical *some* nominals and *wh*-question nominals together with the fact that the semantic predictions made by such a derivation are justified by the interpretation of *wh*-questions.

Recall, now, the kind of evidence presented to show that *Wh-Q*-movement justifies the existence of a principle of grammar restricting the ability of reordering transformations to cross coreferential nominals. The evidence consisted of data like the following:

21.(3) *a*   Who$_i$ claimed Jack kissed her$_i$?
 b   *Who$_i$ did she$_i$ claim Jack kissed?

21.(4) *a*   Who$_i$ first recognized that God created him$_i$?
 b   *Who$_i$ did he$_i$ first recognize that God created?

Analyzing such examples, we observed that the banned cases of coreference were just those where *Wh-Q*-movement would have moved the *wh*-marked NP over its coreferent. And from this we went on to justify various versions of the cross-over principle.

It might be claimed, however,[1] that the very real restrictions illustrated by examples like 21.(3) *b* and 21.(4) *b* are a function of a quite different constraint having nothing whatever to do with any principle blocking the crossing of coreferent NP. It could be observed, for instance, that there are restrictions on coreference for nominals containing the logical *some*. In particular observe:

21.(5) *a*   Someone$_i$ claimed Jack kissed her$_i$.
 b   *She$_i$ claimed Jack kissed someone$_i$.
 c   *X$_i$ claimed Jack kissed someone$_i$.

21.(6) *a*   Someone$_i$ first recognized that God created him$_i$.
 b   *He$_i$ first recognized that God created someone$_i$.
 c   *X$_i$ first recognized that God created someone$_i$.

The *c* examples here are added to show that the form of the initial nominal is irrelevant. No nominal coreferential to the *some*-forms can occur in these positions.

Given this fact, together with the assumption that *wh*-marked question NP derive from *some*-forms, one might propose an explanation for the restrictions in sentences like 21.(3) and 21.(4) in terms of the properties of the underlying sources, which might be something like, respectively:

21.(7) *a*   Wh some one$_i$ claimed Jack kissed $\begin{Bmatrix} \text{some one}_i \\ X_i \end{Bmatrix}$.

 b $\begin{Bmatrix} \text{Some one}_i \\ X_i \end{Bmatrix}$ claimed Jack kissed wh some one$_i$.

---

[1] In oral comments at the Second Annual LaJolla Conference on English Syntax, January, 1968, R. Jackendoff argued against the need for a cross-over principle and, if memory does not fail, proposed in essence just the alternative explanation for cases under *Wh-Q*-movement which is discussed in the text.

21.(8) *a* Wh some one$_i$ first recognized that God created $\left\{ \begin{array}{c} \text{some one}_i \\ X_i \end{array} \right\}$.

b $\left\{ \begin{array}{c} \text{Some one}_i \\ X_i \end{array} \right\}$ first recognized that God created wh some one$_i$.

By the alternatives with the notation "X_i," I indicate that the exact form of the relevant NP is irrelevant to the present discussion. Given structures like these, it could then be claimed that the restrictions previously taken to be functions of the cross-over principle are actually simple reflections of the restrictions in sentences like 21.(5) and 21.(6), which obviously have nothing to do with crossing.

Although at first blush not without its seductions, this proposed alternative to the cross-over principle as a basis for the coreference restrictions of *wh*-question NP is impossible and rapidly collapses. To see this, one need only try to specify more closely the form of the restriction manifested in 21.(5) and 21.(6) which is supposed to explain the facts of sentences like 21.(3) and 21.(4). What is, for example, the difference between the well-formed 21.(5) *a* and the ill-formed 21.(5) *b*? The difference is just the position of *some*. In the former it is on the left of its coreferent, in the latter on the right. Considering the structures 21.(7) and 21.(8), where the *a* forms underlie well-formed questions, the *b* forms ill-formed examples, a somewhat more complex formulation of the restriction is required if it is to cover both surface *some*- and *wh*-forms.

One would have to specify it something along the following lines. Consider deep structures containing two coreferent NP, deep left and deep right, whose surface structure realizations are surface left and surface right [not necessarily respectively], where one of these latter is a *some*-form [including under this term the *wh*-forms] and the other an anaphoric pronominal [*it, he, her, them*, and so on]. The restriction would then be:

> 21.(9) Sentences resulting from such deep structures are ill formed where the surface structure realization of deep right is not an anaphoric pronominal.

Hence, in effect, 21.(9) prohibits an exchange of positions of the underlying NP by transformational rules.

Such a restriction is, however, totally at variance with the facts:

21.(10) *a* That Mary kissed $\left\{ \begin{array}{c} \text{some Greek}_i \\ X_i \end{array} \right\}$ was disturbing to $\left\{ \begin{array}{c} \text{some Greek}_i \\ X_i \end{array} \right\}$.

b (The fact) that Mary kissed some Greek$_i$ was disturbing to him$_i$.

c It was disturbing to some Greek$_i$ that Mary kissed him$_i$.

The structure 21.(10) a^2 yields either of the sentences *b* or *c*. But the latter is a violation of 21.(9), since the NP *some Greek$_i$*, which is here surface left, derives

---

[2] Here I have specified the deep structure in terms which ignore the fact that *psych*-movement applies in such sentences, which would reverse things. The point of the argument is unaffected, however.

from deep right, the switch being accomplished by application of the rule extraposition.

Returning now to 21.(5) and 21.(6), one can easily see that the violations they reveal are in fact nothing special about *some*-forms. That is, 21.(9) is a totally redundant artifact. 21.(5) *b* and similar examples simply violate the conditions for pronominalization. That is, to derive such sentences, this rule would have to have applied backwards in these contexts, which, because of the backwards condition, only permit forwards pronominalization. There is no difference between the restrictions in 21.(11) *a* and *b*:

> 21.(11) *a*   *She$_i$ claimed Jack kissed someone$_i$.
>   *b*   *She$_i$ claimed Jack kissed Mary$_i$.

The idea that the restrictions in examples like 21.(11) *a* can explain those in examples like:

> 21.(12)   *Who$_i$ did she$_i$ claim Jack kissed?

is thus totally mistaken. For this to be the case, the restrictions in examples like 21.(11) *a* would have to be statable at the level of deep structure or at least at a level of representation *prior* to the application of *Wh-Q*-movement. But in fact we see that the restriction in 21.(11) *a* is properly stated as part of the rule pronominalization, that is, it follows from the backwards condition. And we have shown [Chapter 2, Section B] that pronominalization *follows Wh-Q*-movement. Thus restrictions like those in 21.(11) *a* could explain those in examples like 21.(12) only if the latter could also be shown to follow from the ordering of *Wh-Q*-movement and pronominalization, the latter restricted by the backwards condition. But of course this is false. Just because *Wh-Q*-movement precedes pronominalization, this ordering provides no possible explanation of the restriction in examples like 21.(12). These examples meet the condition of pronominalization, and exhibit forwards pronominalization, which is not blocked in such contexts. Hence the restriction they manifest cannot be attributed to the same grounds as that in forms like 21.(11) *a*.

We thus conclude that there are in fact no known special restrictions on *some*-NP with respect to coreference relations of any relevance to the restrictions under study in this work.[3] The explanation for the restrictions in examples like 21.(5), 21.(6), and 21.(11) *a* has nothing in particular to do with *some*-forms but follows from the backwards condition constraint on pronominalization. This cannot explain the restrictions in examples like 21.(12) because

---

[3]There are restrictions of a coreferential nature on *some*-forms which are independent of any issues in this study, at least as far as I can see. For instance:

(i)   *Charley and someone played tennis.
(ii)   *I will bring a rifle and something.

Wh-Q-movement precedes pronominalization and such examples consequently manifest forwards and not backwards pronominalization, which is not in general blocked in such contexts. Hence, some explanation of restrictions in examples like 21.(12) is required which is independent of the constraints on pronominalization. Just such an independent explanation is provided by crossing restrictions. Examples of the type 21.(12) thus continue to stand as fundamental evidence for the existence of the cross-over principle.

Given the almost total parallelism between the behavior of coreferent NP under *Wh-Q*-movement and *Wh-Rel*-movement, the failure of the proposal examined in this chapter is hardly surprising. To be convincing at all, it would have to be shown that the identical restrictions for cases under *Wh-Rel*-movement could also be explained by the same kind of crossing-independent restrictions. This is hopeless because no such independent restrictions have been shown to exist for *some*-forms.[4] But even disregarding this fact, and assuming falsely that some special coreference constraints on *some*-forms were real, a general account of all the restrictions under the *wh*-rules would still be out of the question. First of all, a *some*-analysis of the *wh*-forms in *restrictive* relatives is far from obvious, even though I myself have experimented with it at times. But conclusively, such an analysis is totally out of the question for *appositive* relatives, which, however, involve exactly the same crossing restrictions under *Wh-Rel*-movement as do restrictive relatives:

21.(13) *a*   *John$_i$, who$_i$ he$_i$ claimed Mary kissed, is psychopathic.
       b   John$_i$, who$_i$ claimed Mary kissed him$_i$, is psychopathic.

That is, *some*-forms do not conjoin freely. One observes that the trouble here seems to rest on the fact that, in such coordinations, the reference of the *some*-form includes that of its conjunct. But in general coreferents cannot be conjoined:

(iii)   *John$_i$ and he$_i$ played solitaire.

Observe too that sentences like:

(iv)   Harriet and the ladies are in Chicago.
(v)   Harriet or the ladies can wash the floors.

are interpreted such that Harriet is not one of the ladies. A theory which can represent such restrictions precisely in terms of a single generalization about the coordination of coreferents does not seem to be on the horizon.

[4] As first observed, I believe, by S.Y. Kuroda (1969) [See also Langacker (1969)], there are restrictions on backwards pronominalization for "indefinite" NP; in fact, this process is blocked for such NP:

(i)   If he$_i$ comes in, talk to a man$_i$.

And this restriction includes *some*-forms:

(ii) *a*   If someone$_i$ calls, don't talk to him$_i$.
     b   *If he$_i$ calls, don't talk to $\begin{Bmatrix} \text{someone}_i \\ \text{anyone}_i \end{Bmatrix}$.

But these restrictions have no bearing on the argument of the present chapter.

The derivation of appositive *wh*-forms from *some* is impossible. Clearly, the embedded clause in 21.(13) *b* must have a form essentially like:

21.(14)   John$_i$ claimed Mary kissed John$_i$.

in which *some* has no place, either syntactically or semantically. Given these facts, the noncrossing explanation would leave the facts for *Wh-Q*-movement completely unrelated to the identical restrictions for *Wh-Rel*-movement, which is impossible to explain in terms of the behavior of *some*. The cross-over principle, on the other hand, provides a single general statement of the restrictions for both *Wh-Q*-movement and *Wh-Rel*-movement, and covers without special statement the operation of the latter in both restrictive and appositive clauses.

22 REASSIGNMENT OF *IT*-REPLACEMENT RESTRICTIONS

In Chapter 4, we considered a number of examples which appeared to illustrate that the rule posited by Rosenbaum (1967) and referred to here as *it*-replacement involves crossing restrictions. We took this to support the claim that the crossing restrictions first noted for passive were more general and in fact typical of rules moving NP. Although, historically, work on the cross-over principle developed in just this way, with *it*-replacement being taken as supporting evidence, further investigation has revealed that this rule is actually irrelevant for crossing constraints.

One difficulty with *it*-replacement was already met in Chapter 9. There it was observed that the crossing restrictions for all other constant movements are governed by the clause mate condition, that is, these rules are banned only from crossing pronominal virgin coreferents which are clause mates. But the NP which apparently are uncrossable by *it*-replacement do not meet this condition. No solution for this anomaly was offered.

Secondly, Lakoff (unpublished) has insightfully observed that Rosenbaum's analysis of constructions with *it*-replacement is incompatible with the cross-over principle in another significant respect. This has to do with the ordering of *it*-replacement, passive, and extraposition, and with the role of extraposition in the analysis of *it*-replacement constructions. I shall deal only with those parts of the argument that are most closely relevant to present concerns.

Recall the discussion of Chapter 16, Section F, in which raising was used as a basis for considering the question of cyclical application for reflexivization. Raising was defined in such a way as to cover *it*-replacement. We observed there that raising applies on a cycle *before* passive. Consequently we get derivations like:

$$22.(1)\,a \quad \text{Harriet believes} \underset{\text{NP}}{[} \text{ it } \underset{\text{S}}{[} \text{ Mary be insane }] \underset{\text{S NP}}{] } \overset{\textit{Raising}}{\Longrightarrow}$$

$$b \quad \text{Harriet believes Mary} \underset{\text{NP VP}}{[} \underset{}{[} \text{ be insane }] \underset{\text{VP NP}}{] } \overset{\textit{Passive}}{\Longrightarrow}$$

$$c \quad \text{Mary is believed by Harriet to be insane. (Mary is believed to}$$
$$\text{be insane by Harriet.)}$$

255

Given such derivations, together with the fact that passive precedes reflexivization, we correctly predict, as Lakoff observed, that passive application will be
blocked by the cross-over principle in cases where the raised NP is a coreferent
of the subject of the verb permitting raising from its complement, that is:

Raising

22.(2) *a*   Harriet$_i$ believes [it [Harriet$_i$ be insane]] $\Longrightarrow$
                          NP   S   S NP

Passive

b   Harriet$_i$ believes Harriet$_i$ [[be insane]] $\Longrightarrow$
                                NP VP   VP NP

Reflexivization

c   *Harriet$_i$ is believed to be insane by Harriet$_i$. $\Longrightarrow$
d   *Harriet is believed to be insane by herself.

In other words, 22.(2) *c* is blocked by the cross-over principle applying to
passive, since raising has made the two occurrences of *Harriet$_i$* clause mates
although this was not so in the input structure, 22.(2) *a*.

This class of facts is thus rather striking support both for the cross-over
principle and the raising analysis of such constructions. Lakoff notes, however,
that Rosenbaum's (1967) analysis was rather different in significant respects.
The latter's analysis involved an ordering of rules:

22.(3)   Passive
         Extraposition
         It-replacement
         Reflexivization

Under this approach, a sentence like:

22.(4)   Jack is believed by Harriet to be insane.

would have the following derivation:

Passive

22.(5) *a*   Harriet believes [it [Jack to be insane]] $\Longrightarrow$
                          NP   S   S NP

Extraposition

b   It for Jack to be insane is believed by Harriet $\Longrightarrow$

It-replacement

c   It is believed by Harriet for Jack to be insane $\Longrightarrow$
d   Jack is believed by Harriet for to be insane $\Longrightarrow$ (22.(4))

As a consequence of this mode of derivation, the application of passive on the
first step is not blocked even if the subject of the complement sentence is a
coreferent of the subject of *believe*. Consequently, the impossibility of examples
like:

22.(6)   *Jack is believed by himself to be insane. (*Jack is believed to
                                          be insane by himself.)

must be attributed to the operation of *it*-replacement in the third step. But here again we run into the fact that the coreferents crossed by *it*-replacement are not clause mates.

Consequently, using the analysis which places passive after raising, as in Chapter 16, Section F, and the beginning of this section, we eliminate one type of exception to the clause mate constraint for crossing under constant movements. In these *believe*-type cases, restrictions attributed previously to *it*-replacement are now rather attributed to passive, and in a way which subsumes them under the clause mate generalization.

Lakoff (unpublished) and Ross (1967a) observe that an important argument for the newer analysis [and much that it implies—which we are not going into here] is that Rosenbaum's approach requires *vacuous* extraposition operations, that is, cases where the rule changes the tree structure without affecting the string of terminal symbols. Rosenbaum requires this in order to turn trees like 22.(7) *a* into trees like 22.(7) *b* by way of extraposition:

22.(7) *a*

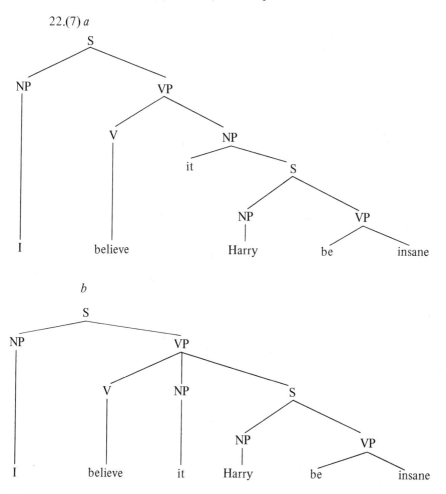

This is required in order to produce an environment defining the conditions for application of *it*-replacement. Lakoff (unpublished) and Ross (1967a) point out, however, that the possibility of vacuous application of extraposition has undesirable theoretical consequences and makes false predictions about English sentences.

The question arises, therefore, whether we can show that the original class of cases taken to indicate crossing restrictions for a Rosenbaum-type rule of *it*-replacement can be eliminated. These cases involved not constructions with passive like those discussed by Lakoff, but rather those involving verbs like *seem, appear*, and so on, which do not undergo passive:

22.(8) *a* It seems to me that I am insane.
    b *I seem insane to myself (me).

22.(9) *a* It appeared to Lucille_i that she_i knew Spanish well.
    b *Lucille_i appeared to her_i (herself_i) to know Spanish well.

If cases like these could be attributed to some other rule than *it*-replacement, the latter could be eliminated from the set of rules inducing crossing restrictions. And in fact the presence of the preposition *to* in such sentences, together with the distribution of the adverb *personally*:

22.(10) *a* It seems to me personally that you are wrong.
     b It appeared to me personally that he was being cruel to dogs.
     c Harry seems to me personally to be the best man for the job.
     d *Harry personally seems to me to be the best man for the job.

naturally suggest that these constructions undergo *psych*-movement so that the NP after the *to* is actually the former logical subject. Suppose, then, that the underlying structure of 22.(8) *b* is actually 22.(11) *a* and that derivations proceed as follows:

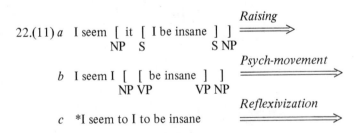

Then 22.(8) *b*-type sentences are blocked by the cross-over principle with respect to the rule *psych*-movement, independently known to govern such restrictions. More importantly, this rule in its application to 22.(11) *b* meets the clause mate condition for constant movements. That is, the previous application of raising has made the two occurrences of *I* clause mates in the main clause even though they were not clause mates in the original input structure 22.(11) *a*. The

point is that this reassignment of the crossing restrictions from *it*-replacement to *psych*-movement requires exactly the same ordering shift as the previous reassignment of such restrictions from *it*-replacement to passive. Namely, raising must precede *psych*-movement just as it precedes passive. This provides *psych*-movement and passive with essentially identical ordering properties, consistent with everything else known about them and with the possibility suggested in Chapter 18, Section E, that the NP reordering parts of these rules may be collapsible into one. Consequently, the newer analysis of raising constructions seems to have the utmost plausibility.

Moreover, this newer analysis of *seem-* and *appear*-type sentences as instances of *psych*-movement operation has several other supports. First, we have noted in several places that the logical subject of a *psych*-movement verb designates the individual who experiences whatever psychological matter the verbal element describes. But in *seem*-type sentences it is the object of the *to* phrase that meets this condition. Secondly, the newer version brings out the similarity of verbs like *seem* and *appear*, taken to undergo *it*-replacement in the old way, with those like *strike*, *impress*, and so on mentioned in Chapter 6 as illustrations of *psych*-movement without special comment. But the similarity of these is rather obvious.

I conclude, then, that the newer analysis is correct and that consequently the scope of *psych*-movement is even wider than previously suggested, including also all of the constructions similar to *seem* and *appear*. At the same time, there are no cases whatever known to me which indicate that *it*-replacement in any version induces any crossing restrictions. Consequently, this rule must be dropped from the class of rules upon which the cross-over principle is based. This course of action has both negative and positive aspects. It reduces the data base supporting the principle in an obvious way. However, in the other direction, it eliminates the inconsistency with respect to the clause mate condition for constant movements.

BIBLIOGRAPHY

Bach, E. (1968), "Nouns and Noun Phrases," in E. Bach and R. Harms (eds.), *Universals in Linguistic Theory*. New York: Holt, Rinehart and Winston.

Bouton, L. F. (1968), "Do-So Revisited." University of Illinois (unpublished).

Bullokar, W. (1586), *Pamphlet for Grammar*. London: Edmund Bollifant.

Chapin, P. B. (1967), *On the Syntax of Word Derivation in English*, Information System Language Studies No. 16. Bedford, Mass.: The Mitre Corporation.

Chomsky, N. (1961), "On the Notion 'Rule of Grammar,' " in *Structure of Language and Its Mathematical Aspects, Proceedings of the 12th Symposium in Applied Mathematics*. Providence: American Mathematical Society.

_____ (1964), *Current Issues in Linguistic Theory*. The Hague: Mouton & Co.

_____ (1965), *Aspects of the Theory of Syntax*. Cambridge, Mass.: M.I.T. Press.

_____ (to appear), "Remarks on Nominalization," in R. A. Jacobs and P. S. Rosenbaum (eds.), *Readings in English Transformational Grammar*. Boston: Blaisdell-Ginn.

Fillmore, C. J. (1965), *Indirect Object Constructions in English and the Ordering of Transformations*. The Hague: Mouton & Co.

_____ (1966), "A Proposal Concerning English Prepositions," in F. P. Dinneen, S. J. (ed.), *Monograph Series on Language and Linguistics No. 19*. Washington, D.C.: Georgetown University Press.

_____ (1968), "The Case for Case," in E. Bach and R. Harms (eds.), *Universals in Linguistic Theory*. New York: Holt, Rinehart and Winston.

Gleason, H. A. (1964), "The Organization of Language," in C. I. J. M. Stuart (ed.), *Monograph Series on Language and Linguistics No. 17*. Washington, D.C.: Georgetown University Press.

Gross, M. (1967), "On Grammatical Reference." Read at 3d International Congress for Logic, Methodology, and Philosophy of Science. Amsterdam, August 25–September 2, 1967.

Harris, Z. S. (1957), "Co-occurrence and Transformation in Linguistic Structure," *Language* XXXIII.

_____ (1968), *Mathematical Structures of Language*. New York: Interscience Publishers.

Hockett, C. F. (1966), "Language, Mathematics, and Linguistics," in T. A. Sebeok (ed.), *Current Trends in Linguistics*, Vol. III, *Theoretical Foundations*. The Hague: Mouton & Co.

Jackendoff, R. S. (1968), "An Interpretive Theory of Pronouns and Reflexives." Washington, D.C.: Center for Applied Linguistics, *PEGS Paper No. 27.*

Karttunen, L. (1967), *The Identity of Noun Phrases*. Santa Monica, Calif.: The Rand Corporation (unpublished).

Katz, J. (to appear), "The Logic of Questions."

———, and P. M. Postal (1964), *An Integrated Theory of Linguistic Descriptions.* Cambridge, Mass.: M.I.T. Press.

Kiparsky, P., and C. Kiparsky (to appear), "Fact," in M. Bierwisch and K. Heidolph (eds.), *Recent Advances in Linguistics*. The Hague: Mouton & Co.

Klima, E. S. (1964), "Negation in English," in J. A. Fodor and J. J. Katz (eds.), *The Structure of Language*. Englewood Cliffs, N.J.: Prentice-Hall, Inc.

Kuroda, S. Y. (1968), "English Relativization and Certain Related Problems," in *Language* XLIV.

Lakoff, G. (1967), *Deep and Surface Grammar*. Cambridge, Mass.: Harvard University (unpublished).

——— (1968), "Instrumental Adverbs and the Concept of Deep Structure," *Foundations of Language,* Vol. 4, No. 1 (February).

——— (1971), *Irregularity in Syntax*. New York: Holt, Rinehart and Winston.

——— (to appear), *Pronouns and Reference.*

———, and S. P. Peters (1966), "Phrasal Conjunction and Symmetric Predicates," in *Mathematical Linguistics and Automatic Translation*, Report NSF-17. Cambridge, Mass.: The Computation Laboratory, Harvard University.

Lamb, S. (1966), "Linguistic Structure and the Production and Decoding of Discourse," in V. E. Hall (ed.), *Speech, Language, and Communication,* UCLA Forum in Medical Science. Los Angeles: University of California Press.

Langacker, R. (1969), "On Pronominalization and the Chain of Command," in S. A. Schane and D. A. Reibel (eds.), *Modern Studies in English*. Englewood Cliffs, N.J.: Prentice-Hall, Inc.

Lees, R. B. (1960), *The Grammar of English Nominalizations*. The Hague: Mouton & Co.

———, and E. S. Klima (1963), "Rules for English Pronominalization," *Language* XXXIV, 17–29.

McCawley, J. (1967), "Meaning and the Description of Langauges," *Kotoba no uchu,* Vol. 2, Nos. 9 (10–18), 10 (38–48), and 11 (51–57).

——— (1968), "The Role of Semantics in Grammar," in E. Bach and R. Harms (eds.), *Universals in Linguistic Theory*. New York: Holt, Rinehart and Winston.

——— (to appear), "Where Do Noun Phrases Come From?" in R. A. Jacobs and P. S. Rosenbaum (eds.), *Readings in English Transformational Grammar*. Boston: Blaisdell-Ginn.

Pence, R. W., and D. W. Emery (1947), *A Grammar of Present-Day English.* New York: The Macmillan Company.

Perlmutter, D. (1968), *Deep and Surface Structure Constraints in Syntax*. Cambridge, Mass.: M.I.T. Doctoral Dissertation.

Postal, P. M. (1962), *Some Syntactic Rules in Mohawk*. New Haven, Conn.: Yale University Doctoral Dissertation.

_____(1964), "Mohawk Prefix Generation," in H. Lunt (ed.), *Proceedings of the IXth International Congress of Linguists*. The Hague: Mouton & Co.

_____(1966a), "On So-Called Pronouns in English," in F. P. Dinneen, S.J. (ed.), *Monograph Series on Language and Linguistics No. 19*. Washington, D.C.: Georgetown University Press.

_____(1966b), "A Note on 'Understood Transitively,' " *IJAL*, Vol. 32, 90-93.

_____(1966c), Review of R. Longacre, *Grammar Discovery Procedures, IJAL*, Vol. 32, 93-98.

_____(1969), Review of A. McIntosh and M. A. K. Halliday, *Papers in General, Descriptive and Applied Linguistics, Foundations of Language* 5.

_____(1971), "The Method of Universal Grammar," in P. Garvin (ed.), *The Place of Method in Linguistics*. Bloomington: Indiana University Press.

_____(to appear), "On Coreferential Complement Subject Deletion," in *Linguistic Inquiry*.

Rosenbaum, P. S. (1967), *The Grammar of English Predicate Complement Constructions*. Cambridge, Mass.: M.I.T. Press.

Ross, J. R. (1967a), *Constraints on Variables in Syntax*. Cambridge, Mass.: M.I.T. Doctoral Dissertation.

_____(1967b), "On the Cyclic Nature of English Pronominalization," in *To Honor Roman Jakobson*. The Hague: Mouton & Co.

_____(1967c), "A Proposed Rule of Tree-Pruning," in *Mathematical Linguistics and Automatic Translation*, Report NSF-17. Cambridge, Mass.: The Computation Laboratory, Harvard University.

Thorne, J. P. (1966), "English Imperative Sentences," *Journal of Linguistics*, Vol. 2, 69-79.

Warshawaky, F. (1965), "Reflexivization in Expressions like 'A Picture of Himself' " (mimeographed M.I.T. paper).